The Cafe (

and

The Mosquito Principle

Dr. Arno Burnier, D.C.

Disclaimer

The information presented is the author's opinion and does not constitute any health or medical advice. The content of this book is for informational purposes only and is not intended to diagnose, treat, cure, or prevent any condition or disease.

Table of Contents

Dedication

To my amazing wife Jane for her love, support, and wisdom; my best friend, love, and spiritual mate in this world.

To my beautiful children Boo and Tanya, without whom I would not be who I am today.

To my sister Florence for whom I have no words to express my admiration.

Acknowledgments

I wish to express my deepest gratitude for these special beings who influenced and impacted my life profoundly.

Dr. Jean Belaval; Dr. Thomas Gelardi, Founder and first President of Sherman College; Dr. Don Thomas, Dr. Guy Riekeman, President of Life University; Dr. Joe Flesia, Dr. Doug Gates, Dr. Reginald Gold, Irene Gold, Dr. Lyle W. Sherman, Dr. Earl Taylor, Dr. Milton Garfunkel, Dr. Pasquale Cerasoli, Dr. Donald Epstein, Dr. Sue Brown, Dr. Larry Webster, Dr. Lou Corleto, Dr. Amy Burke, Dr. Jay Komarek, Dr. David Serio, Dr. Jason Deitch, Dr. Michael Sarnoff, Dr. Wade Port, Dr. Boo Burnier, and Dr. Gilles Lamarche. Surely, I omitted some, yet you know who you are. So deeply grateful to be on the same Life Train.

A huge thank you to Liza Cherubini, D.C., for her tireless energy, focus, and clarity in the final edit.

My heartfelt thanks, gratitude, and appreciation to all the MLS and MPTC staff for their support, commitment, service, and dedication over so many years; you are too numerous to list. Without you, we could not have made a difference in countless lives.

Very special recognition for Gurumayi Chidvilasananda from the Siddha Yoga Path.

About the Author

Born in Paris, France, Dr. Arno jumped the pond following his heart and Soul's calling. His extraordinary life journey facing health challenges, remarkable healings, and a *state* of enlightenment led him to become a renowned national and international public speaker sharing his message of health, healing, wellbeing, and spirituality to thousands worldwide while practicing his beloved vocation for forty years. His influence and impact continue to transform countless lives.

Father of two adopted children, and husband to his wife Jane of forty-plus years, he splits his time between Colorado and Baja, Mexico. Life and Nature are his teachers.

"If you think you are too small to make a difference, try sleeping with a mosquito!"

Dalai Lama

"Life is my religion, nature is my church, trust is my faith, love is my sword, and surrender is my mantra."

Arno Burnier, D.C.

Chapter 1: Welcome to the Cafe of Life

Since early in my life, I have felt a deep pull to contribute by making a difference in the world. I don't think I am unique in that inner calling; I believe such aspiration lives in most of us.

I may have been born with a humanitarian gene, or maybe such a gene resides in all of us. In my case, it was activated by circumstances and personal experiences. Who knows? The bottom line is I care deeply about humanity.

For many years, I avoided stepping into leadership, frightened by the responsibility and the magnitude of the task. Making a difference appeared overwhelming. Why? Because humanity is so large and the world so huge, how can I possibly have an influence? Yet history shows that one single individual can galvanize humankind to greater heights or bring the world to the brink of extinction.

No one is too small to contribute and make a difference toward a better tomorrow for all. That's *The Mosquito Principle.* However, a self-sabotage mechanism held me back early on, the doubting monkey voice sitting on my shoulder. Sounds familiar? Am I too small to have an impact? Can I single-handedly drop a rock in the lake of human consciousness to make a difference toward the betterment of humankind?

As small and insignificant as I felt in the cosmic realm, at twenty-seven, I chose to make a difference. That is when my voice, personal power, inner drive, commitment, and dedication were born. For the last 44 years, I have made a life-altering impact in the lives of tens of thousands of people, and by ripple effects, in countless others.

What is it in me that has influenced others so profoundly? Has it been my passion for my chosen profession or, rather, my vocation? Was it the knowledge and personal experiences I shared on public speaking platforms? Was it my way of being in the world? After searching long and hard, I believe that it is my unwavering commitment to my health and to live and lead by example. My top personal values are spirituality, health, integrity, contribution, fitness, nature, adventure, openness, and love. I am convinced that living by them has made an impact.

Sharing in this book my journey and experiences through life, I hope to make a difference in your life. I seek to inspire you to commit to your health and healing. I trust it will cause you to question many of your beliefs and lead to a transformation toward better health, vitality, self-awareness, and personal empowerment. Writing has yet to be my forte, as English is my second language, learned strictly on the street. Over the years, I have preferred and loved direct contact with audiences. Many people told me over and over that my presence, energy, and public speaking delivery were impactful and memorable. Audiences got the message, the knowledge, by transmission beyond words.

This book is another pebble I am throwing into the waters of life. What will come out of it is unknown to me. However, I am open to whatever might show up.

In my early twenties, I was fortunate to stumble by accident, or rather by grace, into a vitalistic worldview about life, health, healing, the human body, wellness, and wellbeing; a perspective that embraces both the physical and the metaphysical. It opened my eyes and expanded my mind. It transformed me, my wife, my family, and countless others on so many unforeseen levels. It changed my relationship with my body and health and transformed my views on symptoms, sickness, disease, birth, and death. It gave me a direct connection with spirituality. I acquired a deep understanding of the nature of healing and its many layers. My values about education were altered. It caused me to question and rethink social, religious, and culturally established beliefs. It gave me a GPS with which to live life.

A profound metamorphosis took place; an inner transformation came about.

I desire that the pages that follow will have a similar impact. I hope it will lead you to make new decisions and choices about how you live life and handle your health and healing.

Transformation is possible. All we need to do is choose, decide, and act; knowing that it starts with us and that we are powerful. The choice is to consciously select trust over fear, gratitude over complaints, and acceptance over drama at every moment. Decide to turn inward and cut out the media's negative and fear-driven programming. The critical step, I believe, is to make health, happiness, and contentment our true wealth. If we think about it, what else is there?

The moment we focus on our health, contentment, and vitality, something happens inside. We become aware, conscious, and connected. We are in a state of awakening. The action is to stay on the new path long enough to acquire a way of being that embraces health as a daily priority. Trust, gratitude, and acceptance, guided by our inner wisdom, will follow organically. Dismantling our unconsciously acquired beliefs is the key. Rewiring your brain through neuroplasticity is indeed possible. Old patterns may die hard, but they succumb over time to our relentless willingness to transform and become healthy on all levels. Understanding the many facets of health is necessary for this pursuit.

What is shared in this book is simple. It is about life and health. It is mostly common sense. In today's world, common sense is a rare commodity. B. J. Palmer, D.C., wrote in the early 1900s, "Common sense is very uncommon." Little did he know how true this epigram would become as we progressed in time. Today, it appears that common sense has bitten the dust. The simplicity of the message may make it challenging for some to take in. "How can it be that simple!" might be the skeptic's motto, but ultimately, the truth is simple.

For everyone who transforms, like the hundredth-monkey phenomenon and the butterfly effect, the entire world's health and consciousness evolve. It all begins with us. It is amazing how the world changes when we change. Gandhi stated, "Be the change you want to see in the world." My friend Dr. Donald Epstein, D.C., often said during conferences, "Oh my, how you have changed since I changed!" How true!

If we desire a more conscious, healthier world, we must first become healthy and more conscious ourselves. We first need to wake up. It is said there are three kinds of human beings; those who are asleep, those who are sitting up in bed, and those who are fully awake. I hope that the words of this book may cause the one asleep to sit up or even awaken fully and those sitting up to shine brightly with a contagious vitality. For all those who are already fully awake, it might provide validation, reinforcement, encouragement, and support. Indeed inner awakening, with health as our number one priority, is a simple step toward a powerful outcome.

My vision is to elevate human consciousness in matters of Life, Health, Healing, Wellness, and Wellbeing. It could be summarized as, "Let's make humanity conscious, aware, and healthy." My experience is that focusing daily on one's health requires being conscious and aware from moment to moment. My mission is to seed a new paradigm for living from the inside-out. It is to bring forth proactive, positive health care and healing, wellness, and wellbeing for humanity.

Why? Because many disciplines, such as chiropractic, acupuncture, massage, bodywork, meditation, life coaching, energy work, and Reiki, to name but a few, provide services that are positive for human physiology and our being as a whole.

Could genuine health care, in contrast to the existing health care system, which is, in reality, sickness and disease care, be a gateway to our awakening? Why should we wait to be sick, to have a symptom, a problem, or an illness to take care of ourselves? Why not water the garden of our body regularly rather than wait until it is depleted and dried out to take care of it? How about being an active participant in our own health rather than surrendering our power passively to someone else to handle?

What is preventing us from benefiting from regular life and health-enhancing care? Such care can be used proactively in Salutogenic care, the type of care that supports health, healing, wellbeing, and the expression of our potential. It is a broad vision. It lives within me in every awakened moment. I carry this vision at the forefront of my mind at all times. It does not matter whether I am with like-minded friends, strangers, or on a motorcycle ride through the majestic West of the United States with rowdy beer-drinking bikers; I share my vision at appropriate times at every opportunity.

Of course, I had to engage myself on the very path I envisioned, or all that was to follow would be empty words. I believe that our actions and our beings speak louder than our words. I have done so since 1973 with unwavering intensity and discipline. Living from the inside-out, being proactive about health and fitness, and engaging in natural healing when faced with trauma, injuries, symptoms, or illness has been my dominant mode of operation. Has it been easy? No. Has it been worth it? You bet. At first, I had to shift the levers of my mind, beliefs, patterns, and operating systems from outside-in to inside-out. In the early going, it was demanding, requiring sacrifice and self-discipline, but in the end, it was nothing but sweetness.

As we focus on our health and life from the inside-out, the connection to spiritual life and inner laws deepens, and the collective field of consciousness rises. The body of humanity becomes healthier. Individual human beings blossom by expressing greater vitality and health, thus releasing their full potential.

Many of us have been domesticated, indoctrinated, and, yes, I dare say, brainwashed by so many educational, social, medical, religious, and cultural upbringings that it can be a challenge to turn inward for guidance. If you are in your forties, education, society, the church, and the media have more likely programmed you for most of those years. It would only be fair to ask you to invest the same number of years in bathing yourself in an inside-out paradigm by tuning to the inner broadcasting station. Actually, this would only wipe the slate clean; you would have had equal exposure to each paradigm.

The good news is that such an investment of time may not be necessary. As much as the wisdom of life has made every attempt to protect us from the outside-in programming during all those years of indoctrination, it will support us and accelerate our transformation from the inside-out once we turn inward. All we have to do is open up, trust in life, tune in to the heart's voice, and listen to our Soul. Soon the shift begins, healthy choices become clear, and we are on our way. Once aware and awakened, there is no turning back.

Chapter 2: Cocktail Hours

The impetus to write a book, which I resisted for years, came from the demands of audiences worldwide who attended my talks, lectures, seminars, and trainings. If it had been my choice, I would have refused. Yet life has been knocking at my door for years, so I finally decided to surrender and answer the call. Thanks to those who have repeatedly asked me to write about my experiences and life. You are making my life miserable!

No, just kidding. Yet, life is short and the little time left seems to be eaten at a fast pace sitting at a computer, typing away. In retrospect, as I am spending hours writing, something very soothing and rewarding is emerging. A sense of a deeper meaning to my life and a sentiment of serving those who would read these words have arisen. A feeling of contribution emerges; leaving a legacy is comforting in some ways. So, I am grateful to all those whose paths I have crossed and who had the courage to persistently ask me to put my words, thoughts, and experiences on paper.

I read long ago that One who proves things by experience increases knowledge. Much of this book is based on personal experiences, observations, and/or witnessed happenings.

It is about life, health, healing, wellness, wellbeing, personal growth, and enlightenment. It combines a vitalistic philosophy of life and principles with sharing actual experiences.

It has been said that between the bird and the book, one is better off following the bird. I have never been big on theories and so-called scientific studies. My experience with them is that, in no time, a new scientific study invalidates the previous one. Science is fantastic and yet always a work in progress. In reality, many scientific studies are flawed because they are pre-designed to validate the desired outcome of vested interests. Richard Horton, the editor of *The Lancet,* recently wrote, "Much of the scientific literature, perhaps half, may simply be untrue." The *New England Journal of Medicine* recognized that only about 10% of all scientific medical studies have any scientific validity. Peter Russell, the author of *Waking Up in Time,* wrote, "One of the constants in science is that its theories will change over time."

This is not to deny the value of many scientific studies. They can be stepping stones to build upon and move scientific development upwards. Yet it is crucial to put things in perspective and not to give them the final word.

Most of what has been uncovered by science already existed in nature and/or had been written eons ago in spiritual texts the world over. In other words, there are other ways of knowing, experiences being one of them. B.J. Palmer, the developer of chiropractic, stated, "The facts of yesterday are displaced by the facts of today; they, in turn, will be displaced by the facts of tomorrow." Information is just that, in-formation. Indeed science evolves one funeral at a time. Grounding ourselves in knowledge and wisdom rather than giving data, scientific studies, and information, the last word might be worthwhile. Norman Cousins, the author of *Healing Heart,* wrote, "Where is the knowledge lost in information, and where is the wisdom lost in knowledge?" How pertinent is this in the age of information? In my life, I have followed the bird. A knowing emerges out of personal experiences. It has served me well to follow the bird.

As much as scientific studies can help in some cases on the journey of learning, in writing this book, there will be none quoted. However what is shared is the knowledge and wisdom gained by observations. No one can deny another human being's experiences. They have been lived and, as such, stand. Those experiences have the potential to inspire others and bring knowledge and wisdom to the foreground.

For some, what I write about may sometimes challenge the limits of what is credible; for others, it might confirm what they already know, have experienced, or felt intuitively possible.

Being a hyper-perceptive and sensitive human being, I am like a canary in a coal mine. I feel and perceive intensely. I have a keen sense of what is coming next. I am a spark plug and a candle. People may say I am a bit of a visionary with a keen intuition. Intuition arises from a realm higher than the intellect. It cannot be accessed by or from the intellect. However, intuition can be downloaded into the intellect. Some of the content within this book is downloaded. Many will ask, "Where did you read about this or that? Where can I find out more about it?" The answer is that intuition downloads frequently have no precedent.

In these pages, I have attempted to be as exact, authentic, and real in describing what I have witnessed or experienced. Because of the passage of time, the accuracy of dates and times may not be exactly as I recall them. That is the leeway I am allowing myself, as I did not keep a journal, to my dismay.

For readers needing proof and scientific validation, I ask only that you stay open-minded, reflecting on the reality that life cannot be recreated as a scientific experiment. It happens in time and space. It happens once. It occurs in the now moment. Attempting to duplicate that moment becomes impossible because we are in the next now moment. The countless, innumerable variables and components that were at work in the previous now moment have already changed by the next now moment. In other words, life is not replicable. Simply stated, one cannot step into the same river of life twice.

The mechanical approach to life may fall apart when dealing with life, health, healing, transformation, and enlightenment, which are vitalistic, dynamic processes. Objectivity is being displaced by subjectivity. The observed and the observer, the observer and the observed, become a blurry mix. The vitalistic model of life cannot be validated with a mechanical yardstick. Contemporary science is not scientific enough to duplicate real-life situations. It cannot bring back all of the countless variables involved. Could science today reproduce all the events, timings, variables, and circumstances that lead someone to fall in love, have spontaneous remission, or experience enlightenment? I think not.

My sole intention is to share the knowledge and principles that my experiences and witnessing brought forth. My desire is to infuse the pages with my love for life and my vision for a better and healthier humanity. I know that within every human resides a liquid crystal oscillator that moves when the truth is spoken, heard, written, or read. By the same token, we all have a bullshit meter. In some, both of these internal devices may be buried under layers of beliefs, indoctrination, and socialization. Smothered under what Don Miguel Ruiz, author of *The Four Agreements,* refers to as domestication. It is my hope you will be deeply moved. That something within will oscillate and resonate with perennial truths and principles. Then your time and mine are well spent.

I have written the book in a menu style. You can take it in as a full, healthy gourmet meal, with multiple courses and pairing wines, or just a la carte, selecting a dish you wish. Some courses may have repetitive and common ingredients present in prior dishes. That's because butter, salt, and spices might be used over and over in culinary feats. What's not to like if it impacts the palate at a deeper level? So, enjoy the journey with an open heart and mind. Know that when you transform, you assist the rest of humanity in that transformation. As small and insignificant as a mosquito is, it can make a huge difference. With it, a night can be hell; without it, it can be a delight. In other words, your health, healing, and your transformation matter.

Universal Intelligence

16

Chapter 3: Snacks

The Wounded Healer

Most who enter the healing arts, especially in the so-called alternative holistic field, have deep core wounds that need healing. Many might not be aware of this until later in their careers as they grow, mature, and evolve on their journey, the journey of the wounded healer. *"Physician heal thyself,"* words written in Luke 4:23, are indeed pertinent.

In short, we seek to heal others to heal ourselves. Yet this wounding, in need of healing, belongs to all mortals. It lives in all of us. It is built in life's design for us to attend. Unbeknownst to me at the time, my journey into health, healing, and wellness started early in my childhood. I can now see the various events of my life as a preparation for what was to become my vocation, calling, and purpose in life.

I was born in Paris, France, in 1951, six years after World War II. My inborn gifts, identified over time, were keen perception, sensitivity, passion, intuition, compassion, kindness, and vitality. As a child, I was a bundle of joy, feelings, and energy, soon to be suffocated under the blankets of my childhood. Being raised in an upper-middle-class bourgeois family that pretended to be more blue blood than its wealth could permit, I quickly sensed the incongruence.

It was marked by a visceral unease permeating the gut of our family. It soon became a knot that turned my insides into a pretzel. Digestive issues plagued me early on, manifested by chronic flatulence. In other words, I was releasing a lot of hot air, which might have been necessary to vent the incongruences I felt in my world but could not mentally process at a young age. In truth, my eating French bread along with cheeses at every meal did not help the matter much.

My mother was my father's second wife but was not his last. She was, however, the one to whom he stayed married the longest, in spite of having mistresses in nearly every town of France, Belgium, and Switzerland. This did not make for a happy marriage or a joyful family. My mother had lost her father from suicide the day the Germans marched triumphantly into Paris. He hung himself, shamed by the French defeat and capitulation. She also lost her first love to the Gestapo's firing squad. After fleeing Paris on the crowded roads, harassed by machine gun fire from the Messerschmitts of the German Luftwaffe, she became a nurse in the French Resistance. She had fallen in love with a member of the underground; her boyfriend was arrested in a reprisal round-up of civilians and shot in front of her very eyes.

Those two events damaged her emotionally; she was hypersensitive by nature, so her heart closed off. Tragedies became the comfortable and familiar background of her life. My mother was stunningly beautiful. She was bright, talented, intelligent, resourceful, courageous, creative, and overly sensitive. Domineering and controlling, she became an extremely difficult woman, incapable of showing her love. She was emotionally fragile and became increasingly so as a result of the numerous tribulations that she was to live through. She found refuge in her sharp and keen intellect while keeping her feelings at bay. She lived in her head with a shut-down heart epitomized by her mantra, "I don't have to ever tell you I love you; you know I do."

My father was a handsome man of extraordinary charisma and great vital force, combined with a tremendous sexual appetite. A woman magnet and a womanizer, he was emotionally immature. He had lost his mother at the tender age of twelve and lived with great independence from then on. This gave him the gift of living in the now moment and the drive to enjoy life as if every day were to be his last. Self-absorbed and self-centered, he left a trail of damage and devastation in the wake of his countless relationships. He was a man of great courage, perseverance, determination, willpower, and strength. He had an insatiable thirst for justice. He fought each and every injustice that crossed his path to its rightful resolution. An adventurer at heart, he traveled the world extensively. This drive made him an absentee father who would return to deliver punishments, via belt or horsewhip, to his children for their unruly behavior.

World War II tarnished my parent's youth. My mother was a member of the French Resistance, and my father was a Captain in the Swiss Army. He was in charge of refugees. He organized frequent trips from Switzerland to Paris to deliver milk and food convoys contracted by the Germans. On his way back, he reloaded his trucks and emptied milk vats with Jewish children and Jews in hiding. It was through the underground that my parents met. His heroism in helping Jews reach the safety of Switzerland won him a black belt of the heart. Until the day he died, he was able to travel the world, welcomed by Jewish friends and connections made during the war.

By the time I was born, we had a stern family with three children and little time for laughter. Being proper, polite, disciplined, and well-mannered was more important than expressing personal feelings. I was the youngest and the last child my parents had together. I acquired a half-brother in my early twenties. He disappeared from my life when his mother was killed in a car crash eighteen months after he came into the world. Her Corsican family took him away from my aging father, leaving no traces. By then, my father was in his mid-sixties and in a deep depression. He lost the will or desire to fight for his son and go after the Corsican mafia. In truth, he felt that his deceased wife's family would provide a better environment to raise the baby. After all, he had been a nearly absent father to my siblings and me, except for giving us the belt upon his return from various escapades. So how good a father and single parent could he have become?

Trauma is not Drama

My sister Florence became the most central, influential, and important figure in my life. Stunningly gorgeous with deep brown eyes, voluptuous lips, and a ten physique with a flowing golden mane down to her lower back, she was sexually abused, molested, and raped in a chronic and repetitive manner from the time she was three until she became a teenager. My step-grandfather was the culprit. He was a white Russian, a former Cossack officer of the Tsar, who fought the Red Army and escaped the communist revolution through China. He found safe passage to Japan and then Europe by hiding in the belly of merchant marine vessels. He gained political asylum in France by joining the Foreign Legion. He fought at Monte Cassino in one of the hardest-fought battles of World War II during the Italian campaign.

Not to make excuses for his behavior, but I am sure he returned to civilian life a damaged human being with marked traumas and what is now called PTSD. He sexually tortured my sister's body and Soul in sick, demented, and unspeakable ways for nearly ten years, sometimes daily during our summer vacation at my grandparent's house in the Loire Valley. The abuse took place, I found out later in life, when my brother and I would have our afternoon naps. Strangely, my step-grandfather was also kind, loving, and caring, full of amazing magic tricks. All these great memories and experiences with him allowed me as a teenager to forgive him and emotionally care for him to the end of his life. My family and grandmother had permanently cast him out once the cat was out of the bag. As a young child, I visited him numerous times in the nursing home, where he was confined until his passing.

My sister emerged from this nightmare a destroyed human being. Wild, rebellious, angry, and marginal, she went out of control in society, running amok and committing petty crimes. Her rage turned to outrageous behaviors to the degree that the French legal system emancipated her by the time she was fifteen. She could now be tried as an adult. Psychologists and psychiatrists concluded that a year of sedated sleep would produce amnesia and erase her disturbing memories. They were dead wrong!

She came out of a year of artificially induced sleep outraged and infuriated, committed numerous suicide attempts, and dove into drugs and prostitution with a vengeance. Sex was the only way she knew how to relate; it was familiar to her and gave her a sense of control. She spiraled downward into years of misery until she found stability in a husband who fathered a child, only to die in a car crash by the time their daughter was three. This further devastated my sister. She resumed a nomadic life of drugs and prostitution with her daughter by her side.

She had two more children by unknown men. She found temporary refuge in the Friedrichshof Commune, run by Otto Muehl, a well-known Austrian artist and philosopher. She lived there outside Vienna for years, secluded from society, in apparent peace. But, once entirely cut off from the world and completely dependent on the commune, the subterfuge unfolded, and the Trojan horse unloaded its cargo. Muehl, the revered savior and guru, showed his true face - a sexual pervert. He enforced and controlled sexual relationships for every member of the Friedrichshof commune with the demented twist that all children had to lose their virginity to the guru and/or his wife. This ultimate deception touched my sister at her most sensitive chord and nearly finished her off. After escaping from the compound, she settled for a marginal life of poverty, searching for meaning and a resemblance of stability. She exposed the crimes perpetrated at the Commune of Friedrichshof in Austria to the authorities. Arrests were made. The scandal hit the national press in Austria and Germany.

Remarkably, in the winter of 1996, she confided to me that if she had to do her life over, she would not change a thing. She was coming into acceptance of her life. In the late spring of 2000, during a heated conversation and argument, I shared with her that inner peace and healing could only come through full forgiveness of, and ultimately gratitude for, all those who had wounded and damaged her. At the time, she could not accept this thought or take that step. She shunned me as being insensitive to her plight and suffering. Five months later, by the time she was 52, the thought of forgiveness and gratitude had journeyed into her consciousness. She did forgive fully, not only the perpetrator but also herself. Of course, it was not her fault. Yet the guilt, rage, anger, and shame carried by countless victims of sexual abuse also festered within her. It kept on impacting her life. Forgiveness was one giant step, but extending gratitude was not yet reachable.

My sister found transient islands of peace in her life. Yet her self-image, which she had coined The Mop, was so low, dirty, or nonexistent that receiving love was nearly impossible. The duty of The Mop was to sweep away human waste that oozed out of every pore of her being, she confided to me in 2019. To date, the demons of her past resurface at times when her buttons are pushed. Her being is still raw and covered with wounds. Her journey into core healing is ongoing. To my astonishment, her path through the darkness has led her to compassion and love. She knows the deep recesses of her dark side, more so than most humans who are so often clueless and unaware of that aspect of themselves.

It is said that all paths lead to Rome. I am so amazed that her trials took her, in many ways, to gain a similar understanding and healing as mine. Her heart, courage, tenacity, and perseverance in life inspire me to this date. She is my heroine, my mentor, and the strongest person I know. Her life reminds me constantly to do my best not to judge, a task I find tremendously challenging. We do not know the background, so how can we judge others for their actions, words, or behaviors? I often think of all the debased looks and the venomous words hurled at her by well-meaning people holding a moral high ground; when indeed, they knew nothing of her heart, her journey, her courage, her keen, bright intellect, and her resilience. She had been a prostitute and drug addict for part of her life. I can only imagine the wretched looks, nasty thoughts, and insulting words she must have endured from men and women alike. How easily can we judge when we know nothing about each other? Yet I know her. I know her heart. I know her qualities, love, passion, and courage. I know who she is beyond what she may have appeared to be.

I know that few could ever return from what she had endured and that she displayed astonishing inner strength. I also know how many men she comforted, giving them tenderness and pleasure. She has been and will always be my mentor. Who would have known that a street prostitute could be a mentor? How quickly most cast the stone!

My brother, being the oldest, took the load of our broken family. He attempted suicide by slitting his wrist one evening when I was ten. I was awakened by the noise and commotion of his fallen body to find him and the bathroom floor covered with blood. Emotionally wounded, he struggled through life in search of love while conforming to society. He became conservative, rigid, entrenched in his world, and controlling beyond measure. Alcohol became his daily companion. This led to violent and irrational rages. Any attempt to assist him failed. He remained a secluded, unhappy man. My mother's passing dealt a greatly needed-blow to his ivory tower, creating a small crack in his armor. Subsequent health problems tenderized the openings, leading to some healing.

My parents divorced when I was twelve. My brother was living alone by then, and my sister was already history. So I was left with my mother and became her surrogate husband on many levels, but not sexually.

Awakening the Healing Touch

This was the background of my early life. I had witnessed and felt the pain of those around me. I was the link and the hub among all of them.

I took on the soothing, healing role early on. It was the only place where I felt some kind of control over our family's chaos. My wounded heart followed my sister in most of her moves, always connecting with her, feeling her plight and pain. Her tragic life taught me compassion. I wanted to ease her suffering and, later on, my mother's pain. I remember instinctively placing my hands over my sister's belly when she complained of severe abdominal pain, likely caused by pelvic inflammation. Soon, her pain was soothed.

I recall her chronic migraines splitting her head and body in half, not literally, but figuratively.

I now understand this plague as her body's attempt to dissociate her from the nightmare that was her life. At times I would ease her pain by making her laugh. But what I recall most was my deep desire to eliminate the suffering I was witnessing all around me. Having no tools to do it effectively, I resorted to touch, humor, laughter, peacemaking, and my tender heart. As an adult, I now comprehend the power of the pure love a young, innocent child could use to heal. Unbeknownst to me, at that age, I was being primed by life to become a facilitator of healing.

I believe that this family turmoil, combined with strong sensitivity and keen perception, prepared me for my life as a chiropractor. I found, later in life, that our deepest wounds could be our greatest blessings and gifts. They can become the gifts that fuel our inner journey toward self-improvement, growth, personal transformation, and core healing if we so decide. Our family history, if painful, tragic, or negative, need not be a heavy burden. It can be turned into blessings to be transmuted into gifts with which to shower others.

The Bright Side

Now I do not want to portray that my childhood was without bright, carefree, and fun moments. I had plenty of those, mostly outside the family context. I had my animals. I would not call them pets because they were so unusual; turtles, mice, guinea pigs, cats, dogs, a lamb, birds, doves, and a rooster were part of my menagerie. That is sometimes what you get as a kid when your parents feel guilty for being either absent or checked out.

Yes, I had all of those at one time or another in our sixth-floor apartment in a wealthy district of Paris. They had to be cared for and transported nearly every weekend in the rear of the station wagon to our country home in the Valley of Chevreuse, west of Paris. I found refuge in caring for my furry friends. Through the special bounds established with them, I nurtured the power of touch. Frequently, I brought wounded animals back to health. At other times my attempts to save them failed. I sobbed, watching them die, feeling helpless and disheartened. Unknown to me, my heart was awakening.

The Boy Scouts were my true introduction to nature, self-discipline, focus, endurance, hardship, and leadership. Post-World War II Boy Scout troops in France were like children's paramilitary organizations. We all wore U.S.

army surplus gear and behaved like toy soldiers. I loved the challenges, the forests, the survival trips, the summer camps with their makeshift wars, the rigor and hardship of long marches loaded with heavy backpacks, and the school of life the Boy Scouts provided. My love and respect for nature and understanding of it were born during those years of scouting. There, I first learned about ecology and respect for life and the environment. I quickly understood that respect for nature started with respect for oneself. Inner and outer ecology were intimately tied together. I was fascinated by the skills needed to set up camp for three weeks at a time with my patrol and leave the grounds as if we had never been there. Later on, the U.S. National Forest slogan pack it in, pack it out was a constant reminder of those formative years.

The Good and The Bad

The Catholic Church brought me two opposite experiences. One was of solemn, mystical nature during the time of my first communion, and the other was more sobering as I was sexually molested, along with my brother, by two different priests. It took years for me to understand that I must differentiate the message from the messenger, something that, to this day, I aspire to heal.

As a burgeoning teenager, I was again sexually abused for a few years by a pedophile who was my boss and, in many ways, a father figure. I was also sexually molested by our family physician, who had become a family friend. Later on in life, I came to find out that sexual abuse is by far not solely committed to women. Men and young boys are also frequently sexually molested. This disturbing fact remains a taboo subject for men and society in general. I hope the Me Too movement will open the door for a male version of it in the near future. Much healing is needed for men in this world.

Martial arts, which I started when I was eight and pursued into my late forties, also provided me with many teachings. It gave me a sense of focus, concentration, respect, self-control, discipline, and the channeling of inner energies of self-repressed anger.

Being a rebellious teenager during the French cultural revolution of the '60s, I experimented with drugs, diving heavily into hashish, marijuana, LSD, and mescaline. This was my means of escape by numbing myself out and exploring alternate realities. To this day, I credit those experiences for opening up my mind. Indeed, there was more to reality than what meets the eye.

As I matured, my love for nature and animals was suddenly transferred into love and admiration for women. As a teenager, my first love was totally platonic and lasted a few years. When it ended, I was so devastated I ran off to Germany. I spent a year in a military college to let the emotional pain subside. I could not stand to remain in Paris and walk her street, which happens to be the one I also lived on, and have so many triggers pour acid on my wounded heart. Any place where we had been together brought memories too painful for my heart. The greatness and purity of my love for her were damaged when we broke off. I was disillusioned. I believe that my heart began to close for the first time. I was now careful and emotionally guarded, always wanting and needing to be safe and in control, keeping the upper hand in romantic relationships so as not to be hurt again. I had entered my own ivory tower, solidly guarded by my emotional armoring.

Revolt of Youth

In 1968 I found an outlet for my idealism, my repressed anger, and the expression of my sense of freedom. The student revolution and uprising of May 1968 was the stage. France, which has long been the bedrock of political movements and ideals, was ripe for such an explosion. Certainly, I was not a communist, nor even interested in politics. Being able to roam free on the streets of Paris, vent my anger, and express the rebellion of my youth by joining in with the crowd during demonstrations, was exhilarating.

Somehow destroying properties at my high school felt good because, symbolically, it was destroying the establishment and the system that had so repressed personal expression in my generation.

The French educational system in the '50s and '60s was stern, disciplinarian, repressive, and physically abusive, if not brutal, yet provided a strong academic education. Corporal punishment was considered normal back then. Many times I experienced the pain of square metal rulers being smacked on my hands. I was frequently humiliated, having to stand in the corner of the classroom with the dreaded Donkey Hat on my head because I did not know the answer to a particular question. I had my front teeth broken for having bubble gum in my mouth. The gum was first smeared by my teacher in my hair; then, while I was asked to rinse my mouth, I was kicked in the rear end and thus crashed my teeth into the copper faucet.

As a child, I developed internal rage for my teachers and disgust for school. This rage was further fueled by the divorce of my parents and the discovery of my sister's plight. I became a violent bully, picking fights with kids during recess. I can hardly recall a day in high school that did not involve street fights.

Now I was in my late teens, and individualization was taking place. I bought a motorcycle, hung out at sidewalk cafes with my friends, and took off on weekends to various country homes outside Paris to engage in the sexual revolution. Soon, a motorcycle gang formed. Stealing became a way of life for us. I became a small-time thief, running scams and living a lie. I was carrying a gun, stealing motorcycles at night so we would have spare parts for our amateur motorcycle racing passion. I had lost respect for myself, my health, my being, or anyone else. I indulged in drugs, alcohol, coffee, and cigarettes, abusing my body in wretched ways.

All of this took place in my last few years of high school and later while attending The Rene Descartes Medical University in Paris. After two years of hard medical studies, my girlfriend became pregnant. Given the circumstances, conjecture, and culture of the time, abortion was our only plausible solution.

The Belly of The Beast

I quit the University and started working at the Amboise Paree Hospital to earn money to pay for the abortion. I worked in the Ear, Nose, Throat, and Stomatology department, specializing in advanced experimental cancer therapy. I befriended a young prominent M.D. who took me under his wing. He allowed me to attend many surgeries, perform simple procedures under his supervision, and open hospital doors that otherwise would have been closed to me. It was during that year that my life began to take a turn due to pivotal moments and numerous insights:

- I witnessed how out-of-touch the doctors were with their patients. If it were not for the nurses bringing them up to speed at the door of the gallbladder in room 106, most doctors would have had little to no idea who the patients were, what was done to them, or the medications they were on.

- It became apparent to me that caring and healing came mostly from the nurses, nurses' aides, and sometimes the cleaning crew, who knew more about the patient's condition and state of being than the doctors. However, they had to keep their mouths shut or get in trouble with the resident intern or the chief of service.

- I observed that power, ego, control, money, and hospital policies were the driving forces in patient care, above and beyond the interest of the sick.

- There was no doubt for me that the medical establishment was knowledgeable about symptoms, sickness, disease, and pathology. But, it came up short when it came to health, healing, and wellness.

- I was amused by the fact that dietitians were attempting to provide proper nutrition to hospital patients. Hospital food would, over time, make a healthy person sick, so it certainly couldn't make a sick person healthy.

- I learned years later that the best diagnosticians in the world, the Mayo Clinic, have a 35% rate of accurate diagnosis; this on patients who are already so pathological that being correct with a diagnosis is less of a challenge because what ails them is, by then, quite obvious. This meant that at least 65% of patients were treated for conditions they did not have. On December 15, 2022, The U.S. Department of Health and Human Services, analyzing nearly 300 reports published between January 2000 and September 2001, revealed that 7.4 million misdiagnosis errors are made every year in Emergency Rooms, with 2.6 million people receiving harm and 370.000 permanently disabled or dead. The leading conditions misdiagnosed were stroke, myocardial infarction, aortic aneurysm, spinal cord compression injury, and venous thromboembolism. Diagnosis or Di-agnosis, after all, means two not to know; the doctor and the patient. This is why a second or third opinion is frequently sought. Yet many sick people did heal, recover, and leave the hospital. They got well, in many instances, not because of the treatment but in spite of it.

- I concluded that there had to be other factors involved, such as enrolling the three great physicians: Time, Patience, and Nature. There is a force, and intelligence, know-how within that does the healing beyond the surgeries or medications. Our body has an innate ability to heal that is beyond our wildest imagination, especially if we can drop the barriers of negative expectations and embrace the seemingly impossible.

- It became obvious to me that rest, sleep, and the supine position de-stress the neuro-spinal system, freeing vital energy and allowing healing. From a sympathetic, fight-flight, stressed-out defense physiology, patients could let go, sleep, relax, be taken care of, and move into a parasympathetic state. The very state where healing, growth, and transformation can occur. Additionally, letting go of daily life's concerns and worries might also contribute to healing.

- I remember watching in horror a man who had had his cancerous larynx, pharynx, and jaw removed smoke a cigarette through his tracheotomy. He sucked on the deadly stick while contorting his body into a grotesque posture to inhale the smoke. We had done extensive reconstructive surgery, including skin grafts, to give him a resemblance of looking human again. This incident taught me that something was drastically wrong and incongruent with the Healthcare medical system, which I recognized later on as being a Symptom, Sickness, and Disease-Care System. One needs to know back then, in France, smoking was allowed everywhere, including hospitals.

- I observed with disgust the brutality and blood of tonsillectomies that were portrayed as minor surgeries. The violence and lack of care for the anesthetized patient during surgeries shocked me.

Those three years in medicine caused me to question the medical approach to health and healing. As much as the path I had taken led me to dive into medicine as an outlet for my desire to help and heal others, life had something else in store for me.

Unexpected Blessing

Speed was in my blood. I was racing motorcycles. Fast two-stroke 125 cc crotch rockets all souped-up. This truly was to be a gift in my life. It was the fall of 1972; the second elimination heat of a motorcycle road race was on. After taking third place in the first heat, I was excited as I waited at the start of the next qualifying round. On the second lap, I entered the 90-degree right turn at the end of the straightaway. I hit an oil patch and crashed down. A few days later, I experienced powerful migraine headaches and loss of sensation and strength on the right side of my body.

The motorcycle accident, or rather "on purpose," as I believe there are no accidents in the Universe, would prove to be a gift. In forty years of practice, when I asked patients who came in as a result of car crashes, the circumstances of their lives always did match the mode of the collision. Head on, they were going way too fast, having too many ventures going on, and being ahead of themselves. Rear-ended, they were stuck, undecided, doubting themselves, and needing to move forward. T-boned, they had deviated from the beam of life, being out of integrity with themselves or others, having affairs, or being lost in life. For me, the motorcycle crash opened an unimaginable life. It was a blessing in disguise. Within a month, I landed in Dr. Jean Belaval, D.C.'s office. He was a chiropractor and a specialist from the United States. I was told he was trained in nerve systems and spinal trauma. At the time, in 1973, there were about 90 doctors of chiropractic in France, for a population of 55 million. I had never heard the words chiropractic or chiropractor; I did not know anything about it. Back then, the practice of chiropractic in France was neither legal nor illegal. There was no legislation or legal status about it.

Consequently, doctors of chiropractic practiced in a gray area and had to be somewhat secretive. Jean Belaval's chiropractic office was located at 76 rue Bonaparte, in the lavish and expensive 6th district of Paris. His patients had to ring an intercom on the street level and announce themselves before the main door to the building could be opened. Then they had to take the elevator to the 5th floor and ring another bell at the door of his office. At that point, the receptionist would look through a peephole to see that the person was indeed who they expected and who they said they were. There was a level of protection to avoid annoying intrusions by the authorities. In spite of these barriers and the fact that no chiropractors could promote themselves publicly, Jean Belaval was seeing 100-120 patients a day, five days a week, practicing long hours.

First Encounter

I recall entering his office for the first time. The place was elegant and lavish, with exquisite works of art. A stunningly stylish, radiant, and beautiful woman secretary greeted me. She led me into a packed waiting room. When it emptied, I was ushered into Dr. Belaval's private office. He introduced himself, shook my hand, and guided me to be seated. Then he asked, "Tell me what is going on with you." I remember sitting in front of Dr. Jean Belaval and dispensing my medical history along with my various symptoms.

I was trying to impress him with my medical knowledge by using elaborate medical terminology. I was young and full of myself from my year in the hospital under the wing of the chief of oncological service. During my entire deliberation, he remained perfectly silent, listening intently. He did not speak a word aside from occasional acknowledgments and nods. When I was done, he let a long silence stand while he looked straight into my eyes, into my Soul, and said, "There is nothing I can do about what is wrong *with* you; what I can do, however, is address what is right *in* you." Silence filled the room. Then he stated: *"You cannot fight darkness; you must turn on the light."* Another silent space, then: *"You cannot fight disease; you must turn on life."* He had spoken with clarity, conviction, commitment, and personal power, all infused with passion. The impact and simplicity of these three sentences penetrated my entire being.

In 1973, such discourse was a radical departure from the world of symptoms, sickness, and disease in which I had lived. It represented a new paradigm, approach, and consciousness about health and healing. Even today, it is still avant-garde. At that very moment, after hearing those words,

I was transformed. A light bulb went off in my brain. This man was talking about life; about turning on the light, which is life in our being. He had spoken with utmost simplicity.

I had spent the past three years studying symptoms, sickness, disease, and pathologies, seeing patients arrive at the end of the road to undergo drastic medical procedures. Ample technological, professional, and financial resources were spent on patients with one foot in the human junkyard — or graveyard. I knew intuitively that something was wrong with that approach and system, yet I had no other avenue to enter at the time. I did not know any alternative. How could society spend so much money, time, energy, and human resources attempting to reverse disease and so little promoting health, healing, and wellbeing?

So, when Dr. Jean Belaval offered a fresh, innovative, and different approach to life, health, and healing, I was ripe and ready for it.

Going Deeper

In later interactions, he proposed to support life on an ongoing basis in the body rather than attack symptoms to suppress them. Why should one wait until malfunction and pathology take hold to care for one's health? He shared his commitment to promoting health and healing rather than fighting disease. He was convinced that the resistance of the host, through keeping a strong immune system, was more crucial than worrying about germs, bacteria, and viruses. He already knew about the symbiotic relationship of the microbiome with the human body as long as proper function and balance were maintained.

He viewed illnesses as islands of discomfort in an ocean of wellness. He infused in me the powerful capacity of the human body to adapt, heal, and self-organize. Our own bewildering complexity was the proof of astonishing biological organization. He encouraged total trust in the inborn, innate ability of the body to heal and remain healthy. He made every effort to eradicate in his patients the fear of disease and symptoms injected into society's psyche by the medical system, our culture, and the media. To him, being proactive about one's life, health, and wellbeing made more sense than reacting to symptomatic crises. He explained that most symptoms are the natural intelligent language of the body sending us messages about how we live.

This was a viewpoint I was not taught in medicine. Those symptoms were mostly warning signals, enticing us to make life changes and letting us know that something was off or wrong in our way of thinking, being, and living. He presented the revolutionary idea of freeing the huge positive internal potential for health and healing rather than focusing on silencing symptomatology. He was passionate about addressing the well, the spring, and the cause of life and health in human beings. He considered himself to be a member of the Cousteau Society of the internal environment of humanity. It was fascinating to spend time with him.

I was always eager for more, impatiently waiting for our next encounter.

Dr. Belaval reveres the sanctity of the human body and the temple it is. He would share his belief that to the degree we had polluted the oceans, seas, rivers, and lakes of the earth, we had polluted the body's internal fluids. To the degree that we had harmed the forests, we had damaged the breathing apparatus of our being. To the degree that we had released radioactivity in the atmosphere, we had altered our own genetic material. For him, everything was interconnected and interrelated. This concept was foreign to most in medicine and society, except for native cultures and their shamans.

He shared living principles pertinent to our body and its physiology. Having studied the natural laws of life, he applied them to human beings in health and healing. His words still resonate today in my mind, the way he spoke them with such passion. All this made complete sense to me; it inspired me. He was dispensing a philosophy of life, a new compass to direct my life. That day, on my first visit, I found my life's purpose, the reason for my existence, my vocation, and my Soul's calling.

Surrendering to Life

From that day on, I can say that my life ceased to be mine. I realize, looking back, that it was from that encounter forward that I became a servant of life, answering whatever was demanded of me. I unknowingly surrendered my life to a greater purpose at that moment. My life became Life's way; I had merged with the flow of the River of Life. I began to follow my gut and bliss to serve a higher purpose. I did not plan my future, did not push the River of Life, did not buy nor bully my way into places or situations. I surrendered to what was inevitable and the feelings and drive I had in my heart. I stopped living from my head and the impending collapse of my rational mind and began to follow my intuition and the tugging of the strings of my heart. I quit making lists of the pros and cons of life's decisions. I no longer evaluated the pluses and minuses at life's bifurcation points. If it felt right in my heart, I went for it blindly without question or delays, in total trust.

I accepted with full surrender what life presented me. Total trust became the enzyme of my healing. In time, over the years, I was to emerge from the challenges and trauma of my early life victorious, more whole, and empowered. I know now that core healing is always possible. It is an individual choice from moment to moment. We all can benefit from the journey of core healing. The inherent basic wounds of humiliation, abandonment, betrayal, injustice, and rejection have touched humanity. Should we take a moment to remember, we will know the truth and reality of it. It is in life's design for humans. Indeed, we all need healing at a deep level. Our wounds are invitations to core healing and transformation.

As a result of this surrender to my inner calling, I discovered flow, a rhythm to life that came with ease. I stumbled into synchronicity, serendipity, providence, and grace. Or rather, I tapped into those elusive life properties; they were and are, after all, always there in the field, waiting for us to align ourselves with the invisible blueprint and design of life. I started receiving care from Dr. Jean Belaval and healed quickly. Yet, it was not the physical healing that impacted me most; the philosophy of life and the vitalistic health paradigm Dr. Belaval dispensed inspired me deeply. I developed a strong friendship with him.

He invited me to observe and witness what was going on in his office. I saw hundreds of people streaming through his office every day, praising him and the results they had experienced through the adjustments. Most of them had come to him desperately as a last result, having tried everything that conventional medicine had to offer them. I realized the level of service he was providing with daily extended hours. I witnessed his joy and passion, his dedication and commitment. The love he was pouring out to his patients was clearly returned to him. They loved him abundantly, with respect and deep gratitude. It was all so inspiring. Dr. Jean Belaval became a father figure and a professional role model to me.

I aspired to be like him, have a successful practice, help countless people, and live the passion I felt inside. Retrospectively, I realized that it was in that first interaction that I decided I would do whatever that man was doing. During that first visit, I chose to become a chiropractor, no matter what it would take.

Being Tested

But life tested my resolve. I was called to military service, a requirement in France for all able young men. I was summoned to Fort Vincennes in the late spring of 1973 for a physical examination. Having made my decision to attend Chiropractic College in the fall of that year, I was determined to be exempt from military service. But how? I was in good health, fit, had no physical defects, and had a sound intellect and acute eyesight. So I decided to stay up for a week, drink coffee in excess, chain-smoke cigarettes, and ride my motorcycle throughout Paris to stay awake, hoping to look so ragged and strung out that the military would reject me.

Sometimes specific situations require drastic measures. So the morning of the exam, I found myself standing at the counter of a typical Parisian cafe across from Fort Vincennes, ordering yet another cup of coffee. A young man at the counter suddenly asked, "Are you here as a recruit?"

"Yep! And I have every intention of not making it," I replied.

He said, "Me too. You want to drop acid with me?"

Providence had blessed me. He handed me a tab of Purple Haze acid and took one himself. We finished our coffee and walked across the street to the recruitment center. By the time I faced my first interview, I was foaming at the mouth, and the officer's face was melting in multi colors in front of my eyes. Needless to say, I was delighted when I saw a large red X placed over my file. I had just been discharged. I was free to go study chiropractic without delay.

I was elated!

I rode my motorcycle from Fort Vincennes all the way across Paris back to my house Rue Mirabeau, high on LSD. It was a full east-to-west trip across the bustling city with car brake lights and traffic signals appearing as dancing flames. Car horns and exhaust noises felt like supersonic jets passing by my ears. Somehow I made it home unscathed. Truly a miracle. I slept for five straight days, with only bathroom breaks.

It was now June, the beginning of summer vacation for all of France. I was due in the U.S.A. to start school in October. So I took off on my motorcycle for the French Riviera with the charming town of Cannes as my destination. This is where Dr. Belaval had his second practice, to which he commuted on his private plane. I spent the summer between his office and meeting other chiropractors, such as Michel Marmier, Jean Jacques Chaterouse, Jean Jacques Lob, and others. They all had such fire and passion that it validated my decision to go to chiropractic college in a big way.

Soon Jean Belaval invited some of my friends and me onto his yacht. It became obvious that he was highly successful and wealthy. Yet that observation did not enter my mind in deciding to become a chiropractor. My sole motivation was the deep inspiration to be part of a humanitarian and revolutionary profession, which seemed increasingly more like a vocation.

Indeed, on that fateful day during my first visit, I found my life, mission, and bliss. From that point on, it never left me. Still today, forty-plus years later, I contribute with as much enthusiasm and passion as I had then.

I can honestly state that from that day forward, I began what I call An Endless Vacation. Why An Endless Vacation? Because I no longer worked, practicing every day became a joyful process I always looked forward to. Chiropractic became my hobby. Did I have responsibilities, commitments, stringent schedules, and energy output? Yes. But work, no. From that moment forward, I engaged in the journey of living life from the inside-out, guided by my heart, inner voice, and intuition. The life and health principles passed on to me by Dr. Belaval became my daily roadmap.

I felt fortunate to have touched my Soul's calling and to follow it blindly in full trust and surrender. I wish all human beings could have the opportunity, courage, and willingness to embrace their calling. I believe that this alone would lead to a better humanity. What a difference it would potentially make.

Taking Flight

Having found my life's path, I left France against the advice of my friends, and peers, the skepticism of my parents, and the voices of reason and logic. I flew from Paris to New York's JFK airport, transferred to La Guardia airport via my first helicopter ride, and on to Spartanburg, S.C. America, here I come! What a dream as a young European to land in the U.S. of A. The land of freedom and possibilities. My first encounter was a strong culture shock. I had dreamed for months about South Carolina and the United States. Just the French words for South Carolina, Caroline du Sud, sounded so soft, sensitive, beautiful, and romantic. The first name, Caroline, a woman of the South, seemed to melt my heart.

I was in for a rude awakening. I faced a cultural blow of considerable magnitude. In 1973, Spartanburg, S.C., was not exactly the City of Light I had just left. Far from it. It was a quiet town with a deserted downtown and empty sidewalks. It was still the Deep South with all that it entailed. The best movies in town were *Chainsaw Massacre* and *Last Motel Out Of Town.* You get the picture of what I stumbled into. I was used to a bustling pedestrian city. The void of crowds on the street had an eerie feeling, almost scary. I had to accept and surrender to where life had brought me.

Yet my life became magical. Everything fell into place with astonishing ease. Life works. Life is supportive when we move in total trust following our hearts. It is said that the power of total trust is one of the most powerful forces in the world. The Bible spoke of how faith can move mountains, mountains of problems, challenges, and obstacles. A metaphor not to be taken literally, yet a reality when we trust life.

It soon occurred to me that I was not creating my life but rather riding a life that unfolded in front of me and for me. There is an unseen blueprint, a grid, and a flow that can be found when life within and life without is lived with trust. There is a Universal Intelligence, an organizing principle that underlines all things. We can merge with it, and when we do, life unfolds perfectly with ups of ease and downs of lessons, which are opportunities for personal growth. Of course, we do not create life; we are born into life. Dropped on the moving sidewalk of life. Life will continue long after we have fallen off its conveyer belt. When we embrace life with total trust, life becomes simple. Simple is not always easy to accept, yet simple is beautiful.

We just have to be aware enough to read the signs on the highway of life and answer the calls. We can become servants to something greater than ourselves, our Soul's greater purpose. I believe it is our Soul and spirit that hold, in the energy field, a pre-designed life that we can choose to surrender to and live for. Of course, we can turn away from it, but it appears that flow, providence, grace, serendipity, and synchronicity might be partially turned off, if not totally cut off.

Decades later, I am still grateful for Dr. Jean Belaval, who spoke his truth and did not hide behind the walls of society's acceptable expectations. He stood firmly for what he believed and knew deep inside. He was fearless of possible rejection. Certainly, his inside-out perspective and approach to life, health, and healing were far from mainstream in 1973. It was radical, revolutionary, and evolutionary, counter to the outside-in mainstream health paradigm. It opened up a new understanding of the human body, symptoms, sickness, disease, birth, death, health, healing, spirituality, education, ecology, and life. It was and has been transformative in taking care of myself and raising a family. It has been empowering to regain the authority of my own being by turning inward and listening to the inborn wisdom and intelligence for answers.

A vitalistic health discipline such as chiropractic was mostly unknown in Europe. It was regarded as fringe quackery in the United States due to the defamation campaign launched by the American Medical Association and the medical profession. It is gaining respect and support as time passes, while conventional medicine is being looked upon with increased skepticism and suspicion. Today, vitalistic approaches are becoming the norm of the emerging wellbeing model in health and healing. The existing sickness and disease care model is slowly but surely, bankrupting many individuals and small businesses while inherently flawed and unsustainable. In 2020 the U.S. healthcare spending grew by 9.7 percent, reaching 4.1 trillion or \$12,530 per person, while ranked 35th in the world in overall health. It has failed to deliver its promised outcome. Obviously, there is something drastically wrong with it. Being proactive, doing something positive for our being, our health, and our physiology regularly, is, I believe, the emerging and upcoming wellbeing model for humanity. It can make a significant difference in humanity's health when embraced individually and collectively.

Innate Intelligence

Chapter 4: Hors d'oeuvres

Our Body is a Gift

Like most, I had taken my body for granted for years, not giving it much thought or attention, oblivious to its importance. Then in 1973, the symptoms I experienced following a motorcycle crash led me to a visionary chiropractor who woke me up. His words and approach jolted me out of my slumber; my life was forever transformed. A new paradigm of health and healing emerged, like a sunrise. For the first time in my life, I saw my body for what it truly is: a most special precious gift.

Until we love, respect, and honor the bio vehicle we were given, we are still in a daze. By awakening to the gift the body is, we take a great step upward in consciousness. The human body is a gift from God, the Universe, and Life. A gift with no strings attached. We may do whatever we want with it. Yet, where on earth will we live if we do not take care of it? Our body is the only one we have. There is no replacement. It is a one-time deal. So how should we treat it?

Our body is the vehicle through which we experience and express life. Do we want to ride life in a superbly well-tuned, fueled, and oiled performance vehicle or in a beat-up, rusted, heavy clunker? As Jim Rohm, entrepreneur, author, and motivational speaker stated, "Do you treat your body like a barn or like a temple?" Deep within, we all know the answer. Sadly, due to a lack of awareness, most humans treat their bodies like a barn, not like the temple that it is. Most take it for granted until it fails. Then they stumble out of their stupor if, and when, their body breaks down or if they are fortunate enough to encounter a health professional who awakens them.

The Bible talks about the body being the temple of the Lord. Indeed, it is the temple of the spirit within. There is an immaterial component to it. The human body is much more than it appears. Could knowing what we are truly made of motivate us to care, honor, treat, and respect our life pod? At first, the body appears to be strictly physical, a pile of systems, organs, tissues, cells, molecules, and atoms. As with all matter, it seems to be solid. Science tells us it is actually energy containing information in motion. From a scientific point of view, managing the flow of energy, the potential genetic programs available within our D.N.A., and the information we feed our being with can be paramount in life and health.

Understanding the human body as a bio-energetic information whirlpool made of physical, mental, emotional, and spiritual components, all interrelated and interacting within a social and cultural context laden with belief systems, creates the need for a new approach to our health and healing. In its totality, our body operates as a multi-dimensional open, dynamic system within the biosphere and the cosmic environment. Indeed, like all living biological entities, it is extremely complex. An infinite amount of input and information constantly bombards us. From barometric pressure to changes in temperature, humidity level, sounds, light, ideas, emotions, thoughts, beliefs, words, and movements, the beat goes on ad infinitum. Our body is porous. There is a constant in-and-out flow of energy and information. In light of its bewildering complexity, the sole fact that it can maintain a stable dynamic homeostasis is a miracle in and of itself—a tribute to its divine ingenuity and design.

Much has been said about the mind-body connection. Yet mind and body are not even a reality without the spirit or life force that animates matter. Sadly, life force has been forgotten as the one essential component. It is possibly the most misunderstood force on earth. Without life force, we are nothing but a corpse. Indeed when the light goes out, we are a goner. The spirit is not only animating the body. The body is actually engulfed by the bio-energetic field of spirit.

We are spiritual beings experiencing a physical body. The life energy of the spirit cocoons us.

High-sensitivity devices have shown this biofield as almost butterfly-like, labeled a torus. The human torus is a micro version of the earth's torus, a micro version of the torus of our solar system and galaxy, which is, in turn, a micro version of the torus of the Universe. Consequently, when we are in tune, attuned, connected, and aligned with our spirit, we are in sync with the Universe or Uni-verse.

In spite of how it might appear, our body is dynamic and in constant motion. We are truly living clay. We are malleable and ever-changing. Cells die constantly and are replaced by new ones. Even our genetic sequencing of nucleotides within our D.N.A. is turned on or off depending on our environment and behavior as revealed by the field of Epigenetics. In many respects, the body we had in 2014 has little to do with the 2023 model. If we are married for more than 20 years, we may actually be on our third spouse, as the body is recreated anew every seven years. Maybe there is no need for divorce after all! We are not frozen sculptures or rocks; our bodies can transform. A long-distance runner can turn into a bodybuilder by changing training. Over time, the muscles will respond according to the law of demand and supply. The reverse is also true. Indeed dynamic metamorphosis is possible.

Reflect on the glow and transformation of women's bodies in and out of pregnancy. What about the astonishing transfiguration of our facial features and radiance when in love versus when depressed? We are truly fluid, energetic beings. There is hope and possibilities for everyone to obtain a healthy, fit human vehicle.

Now the stranger-than-fiction thing about the human body is that people with multiple personalities display different physical characteristics. Eye color changes and disease such as diabetes in one personality is gone in another; even scars may be present in John but not in Marc. Incredibly, the same D.N.A. resides in all those personalities. As strangely as it appears, various gene sequences are activated depending on each personality's energy field and life-force flow. Could our energy body be the cause of our physical attributes and not so much our D.N.A. as previously thought? Everything is pointing in that direction. Matter transforms its shape according to the vibratory frequency of the energy/information that flows through matter.

The Chladni plate, a drum loaded with sand connected to a vibratory device, clearly shows the patterns of sand changing multiple times, depending on the frequency of vibrations flowing through the plate. Nikola Tesla wrote, "If you want to find the secret of the universe, think in terms of energy, frequency, and vibration." Energy healing, vibrational medicine, healing with touch, sound, light, love, and freeing energy flow within the pipeline of life force are all scientifically sound approaches to health. In countless ways, we are far more energy in vibration than actual physical solid matter.

Our body is affected by context, thoughts, beliefs, behavior, energy flow, and environment, amongst countless other factors. Change any of these components, and the body morphs. Elderly people, who were asked to listen daily to music from their youth, have been found to get physiologically younger, as shown by the improvement in vital signs, monitored blood factors, and overall function.

The human body is 70-80% water by weight. It doesn't say 70-80% soda. It says water. That is about the same ratio as the earth has between land and water. Do you think drinking water might be an asset over downing soft drinks loaded with sugar and chemicals? What we know about water from the work of Dr. Masaru Emoto, author of *The Hidden Messages in Water,* is that words, sounds, music, and consciousness affect the crystalline properties of water. As we express love, joy, gratitude, and compassion, our body's water manifests new properties. H2O is not just the molecules of hydrogen and oxygen anymore. It is also the information it carries. Words, thoughts, and emotions are powerful agents. Could the awareness of our speech, emotional state, and mindset have a strong influence on 70-80% of our bodies? Hmm, our brain is 77% water; could this be an untapped potential that can be reprogrammed energetically with new input and information? If so, this idea is very empowering. We have control. We are accountable and responsible for much of our health. This is where the power of love, particularly self-love, to activate new sequences of our D.N.A. comes into play, as Gregg Braden brilliantly explained in the book *The Science of Compassion*.

From a metaphysical viewpoint, there is a hierarchy of order in how we are created. We emerge from the great void of nothingness where all things exist in potentiality. We were created from universal and spiritual dimensions, from intangible to tangible, invisible to visible, and from immaterial to material.

All creative processes follow this hierarchy- universal to spiritual to mental to emotional to physical. First, there is inspiration, a thought flash. Then the mind thinks about the creative input, formulating a plan. In turn, emotional enthusiasm and excitement emerge. Finally, the inspiration is manifested into physical reality. Everything is always created from universal through the spiritual, trickling down in steps to the mental, emotional, and physical realms. In this hierarchy of order, can the mind control the physical? Yes. Some yogis can override the physical by mentally controlling various body functions. Biofeedback and hypnosis are well-known examples of mental control over the physical and emotional. There is a controller behind the mind who decides what the thinking is. That is the empowerment available to all of us, as *I* has the power to choose. Our mental dialogue, and our beliefs, have a definite clear impact on the physical. We are and can be in charge after all, if we so decide.

Currently, Dr. Joe Dispenza, D.C., is leading the field of quantum healing, having risen to worldwide notoriety. He has demonstrated and proven that changes in thinking patterns, behavior, and personality, achieved through specific meditation methods, lead to profound healing.

When confronted in 2017 with bone cancer in my left humerus, my mind ran amok for a month. All potential negative scenarios were constantly showing up. Dark, depressing circular thoughts were running in a continuous loop. Then I caught myself, stepped out of the dread, and chose new healing thoughts of vitality, vibrancy, and living. Right away, cancer was no longer getting a hold on me. I could discuss my situation with friends as if it were not mine. It was now something no longer attached to my being. It became an outside foreign entity. Within a year, it had vanished. Changing my thoughts changed my physical. The *I* within me, the observer of my thoughts, took charge. Who knows if this was the sole factor in the reversal of the pathology? Certainly, it was clear that the change in mental focus made a profound difference in my inner state. Of course, I had also created my own natural healing protocol to shock my physiology out of the existing pattern.

Since the mind can dominate the physical, we must be careful not to speak against our body, as in my damn shoulder hurts or my stupid foot is busted. With growing awareness, we can be caring and loving with our words, never speaking against ourselves. White light meditation, directed mentally to infuse every part of our body with healing light, has a powerful effect.

I implemented this practice daily in my healing protocol. In my 40 years of practice, I observed over and over a shift in people who attended health educational programs. Their bodies and health became a priority. They were made aware, conscious, accountable, and responsible for their thoughts and health decisions. An awakening took place. Unconsciously acquired beliefs vanished. Their inner healing journey began.

Can you envision every child educated as to the responsibility of treating their body with utmost care and respect? The song *Teach The Children Well* by Crosby, Stills, Nash, and Young comes to mind. The support, encouragement, and reinforcement of parents, who live by example, can be a great asset. A new humanity would manifest should all educational institutions promote the human body as a sanctuary. As part of the world community, caring for our body could be transformational for humankind.

All in all, our human vehicle is truly our most precious possession. There is no greater investment than in ourselves. Any amount spent, in a proactive way, to mine and mind the riches of our body pays huge dividends. In the end, we all have a social, moral, financial, and spiritual responsibility to take care of it. For health practitioners, congruence is especially critical. It demands that we live by example to inspire our clientele and patients to follow suit. For every individual honoring their body as a gift, treating it with utmost care and respect, the body of humanity is impacted. In that single step, we make a difference.

Awakening to America's Drug Culture

In 1973, when I left France for the United States, I did not speak English. My total command of the language was words learned from the music of the Beatles and the Rolling Stones; All you need is love, Michelle ma belle sont des mots qui vont très bien ensemble; Yellow Submarine; and Strawberry Fields. None of these were very helpful, except that my girlfriend's first name was actually Michele. She ended up coming with me to the U.S.A. As the lyrics state, she was indeed beautiful. For some strange reason, I also knew the following words: The sky is blue and a big pig. The latter might have gotten me in trouble with the police if spoken out loud. Since my command of the English language was nearly nonexistent, I plucked myself down in front of the television as much as I could as my self-prescribed English crash course.

I was quickly astonished at the number of drug commercials bombarding my brain. On top of the constant drug advertisements, every other show on prime-time T.V. was a medical show: *The Hospital, Saint Elsewhere, The Doctors, the Nurses, Doctor Marcus Welby, M.D., Doctor Trapper John, medical examiner*, etc. I became aware of the relentless, not-so-subtle brainwashing the American public received. Of course, if one is raised in front of the T.V., like most in America, one cannot see the forest from the trees; thus, nothing appears wrong with this persistent and consistent programming of the human psyche unless one wakes up.

When I explored the town of Spartanburg, S.C, I began to see something that, coming from another culture, was unusual and bizarre; Drugstores, Drug Emporiums, Thrift Drug, aisles of medications in supermarkets, gas stations, and convenience stores. Drugs were readily available everywhere. This was and still is today a drug-laden, drug-ridden, pill-popping culture and society. This was not at all what was taking place in Europe. Actually, it is not what is taking place in most of the rest of the world.

I came from a society in France in 1973 where if you wanted an aspirin, you had to get a full medical examination, get a doctor's prescription, and go to a pharmacy. After placing your prescription slip on a swiveling tray, you would get a tube of aspirin. Here in the United States, drugs were readily available and pushed on society through a well-orchestrated marketing campaign. I was shocked.

Soon, in the late '80s, the slogan *Say No To Drugs* became popular as Nancy Reagan promoted a war on drug campaign. Yet the pharmaceutical drug manufacturers kept assaulting human brains. What a confusing message. It basically stated that over-the-counter drugs are not drugs, yet they are. A very large percentage of the American public is consuming large amounts of medications, creating dangerous cocktails of drug interactions, leading to abnormal physiology and latent pathologies. Then came the amphetamine craze, first prescribed by physicians for weight loss, only to be written indiscriminately to anyone and everyone wanting a stimulating buzz. The pharmaceutical industry and medical profession, the actual drug dealers, generated this epidemic. Right in its wake followed the opioid epidemic, again generated by the medical profession. Oxycodone was prescribed at an alarming rate. Overnight, countless greedy and unscrupulous physicians opened prescription shacks near the on-off ramps of major highways, delivering an endless supply of the addictive drug.

My early awakening to America being a drug-ridden society came from my self-taught English course, confirmed by these subsequent epidemics. It strengthened my resolve to educate the public about health principles and a natural, drugless approach to health and healing.

Clearly, many medications have life-saving values. Of course, there is a time and place for medications. To deny this is to be fanatical and dogmatic. Yet to pop pills for every symptom, ache, pain, or discomfort is engaging in a dangerous game of drug interactions, side effects, and toxicity with dire long-term consequences. Is the general public being lied to, or is it mostly blind and gullible, totally bypassing the due-diligence process? I feel both apply in this situation.

Today, drugs are paraded on nearly every other page of popular magazines. Medical shows on television have repositioned themselves toward what medicine excels at; emergency repairs from injuries and trauma care. Television's drug commercials are as numerous and pervasive as ever, accounting for 75% of their total ad spending, pushing over-the-counter drugs and medications on an unsuspecting, naive public. Most Americans are caught in a vicious cycle. Pharmaceutical marketing companies have designed countless syndromes with acronyms for which you can ask your doctor about, along with medications that might be the answer. Indeed it is a well-orchestrated strategy to push drugs to the vulnerable public. The Food and Drug Administration (F.D.A.) spells it out perfectly. Approve junk food and foods laden with chemicals, which over time lead to diseases, then offer drugs to cover symptoms, and you have a deadly effect on human health, yet a booming economy. For all those who have not awakened yet, awareness of the insidious drug culture may lead to radical changes in how health and healing are approached.

The Casual War

Countless individual medical practitioners have great intentions, caring deeply about the patients they are treating and doing their very best. There is a time and place for medicine. However, medicine is greatly abused, misused, and overused. This occurs at a tremendous cost and causes needless suffering to society and individuals. We have been at war for the last 100 years or more as a society. It is a Casual War. It is a hidden and insidious conflict, with yearly mass civilian casualties, injuries, and permanent disabilities. Every year in the U.S.A., so-called health professionals are perpetuating, mostly outside their conscious awareness, involuntary mass murder, and no one wants to talk about it. This silent war is being waged on the human body by the pharmaceutical-medical complex and its complicit prescribers.

Gary Null, Ph.D., in his book *Death by Medicine*, the award-winning journalist and *New York Times* best-selling author reports the number of people who die every day in the U.S. from medical errors, iatrogenic illnesses, and medications' adverse effects is equivalent to six jumbo jets falling out of the sky every day. No doubt this would cause public outrage and demand the immediate grounding of all airlines and a congressional investigation, should this be reported daily by the media. However, the same media is tight-lipped about the mass murder committed in the name of medicines because it is heavily financed by pharmaceutical companies that are the fourth-largest spender of T.V. ads in the U.S. More Americans are dying yearly at the hands of medicine than all the American casualties in WWI and the Civil War combined.

The perpetrators, the pharmaceutical corporations that have infiltrated the hospitals, medical schools, governmental boards of directors, insurance companies, and medical practices, have become so bold that they advertise and market their wares on television, in magazines, and on social media around the clock.

The public has become dull by years of programming. It is so brainwashed that the drug industry can make it clear in their commercials that this or that drug may cause liver damage, renal failure, dizziness, loss of coordination, cardiac arrest, and even death — and people are still willing to take it. Regularly, placing an acronym on a few bundled-up symptoms is creating new syndromes. Sure to follow suit are drugs and medications as a might fix solution for that syndrome. Drug sales representatives influence medical doctors, and the perks offered to them are being complicit in prescribing willingly.

Greed, corruption, and profit, entangled with economic imperatives, are at the root of this devastating war. This is a war with no end in sight, as we keep going on search-and-destroy missions, doing batteries of tests, attacking sickness, waging war on disease, bombarding tumors, eradicating bacteria, wiping out viruses, and silencing symptoms. The linguistics of war is so insidious; society has become blind and deaf to it. The warmongers are at work, and the casualties are mounting. Yet it is clear this war cannot and will never be won. The current approach to human health has failed and continues to fail. The law of energy placement dictates that whatever we put energy into will grow larger. Give energy to sickness and disease, and it will only grow. In contrast, give energy to health, healing, and wellbeing, and it will grow.

There are more illnesses today than ever before. Actually, there are more sick people than there are people. According to *The Giant Book of Health Facts* by Terri Schlichenmeyer, countless deal with more than one disease at a time; cancer, diabetes, degenerative arthritis, and ulcerative gastritis all wrapped up in one person.

The deep irony is that civilians, who are the main casualties of this war, are voluntarily financing the war. Donations are pouring in at grocery stores' checkout counters, hardware stores' cash registers, walk-a-thon, phone-a-thon, dance-a-thon, bike-a-thon, concerts, bake sales, and other multitudes of disease fundraising events. The latest trend is to ask everyone at checkout counters, Would you like to round your bill to the next dollar and give the change to a disease foundation?

Over the last 30 years, much has been done by many anti-war activists to raise public awareness to no avail. Marylyn Fergusson, Harris L. Coulter, Deepak Chopra M.D., Jeremy Rifkin, Robert Mendelsohn M.D., Gary Null, and Bernie Siegel M.D., among many others, have been sounding the alarm. Chiropractic and naturopathic professionals, along with other holistic health practitioners, have been seeking an end to this war while also providing an alternate path to peace. Today, with the information highway, things could come to a head, and it might be time to say no more. No more Vietnam War on the human body.

Of course, much good has come from medical care and procedures. Medical care does save lives in many situations. There will always be a time and place for medicine, surgery, and emergency care. Yet the overutilization of medicine, the focus on treating disease rather than promoting health and vitality, and the constant marketing of medical procedures, pharmaceutical drugs, and over-the-counter pills to suppress symptoms have become rampant and dangerous.

Awareness of the harmful impact of the pharmaceutical-medical cartel on human health is necessary to bring back medical care and utilization into a safer place. Should you want to know the extent to which the pharmaceutical industry is entrenched in greed, watch the movie *The Constant Gardener.* Do not fail to stay on to the end and to read the credits and postscripts. This line will appear: "This movie is like a vacation postcard compared to reality." Truly evil.

In light of all this, what action steps shall we take? First, stop giving to disease foundations, stop fueling the war, and the pharmaceutical-medical complex killing civilians by the hundredths of thousands yearly. Whenever I receive a phone call asking for donations to a disease foundation, I respond with, "Thank you for calling, but I only give to health, healing, and wellbeing professions." This usually is followed by a long silence from the caller, maybe a moment of reflection. Start giving to organizations, educational institutions, and professions with a positive, life-enhancing, health-supportive, physiologically positive service. Professions such as chiropractic, naturopathy, osteopathy, acupuncture, shamanism, craniosacral and massage therapy, bodywork, herbalist, and life coaching. We all vote with our dollars; we are powerful in effecting transformation.

This is an invitation to join the revolution and evolution of the healthcare system. Get on social media channels and become a proactive health and wellbeing activist by sharing your new awareness. Sounds like a radical statement, yet we can no longer keep on the same course if our own wellbeing and that of nations and humanity are our focus and priority. The train we are on has not delivered the promised results. It has actually produced the opposite outcome. We have more diseases and sick people than ever, and there are more mass casualties than ever.

One might argue that preventative medicine is a valuable health service. Yet, under deeper examination, preventative medicine does little to nothing to enhance human health. It might detect early pathologies so that early treatment by drugs, surgery, radiation, or chemotherapy can be applied in the hope of a better prognosis or outcome. Preventative medicine might have some value in individual cases; it could save lives, but it does not produce the desired outcome as a whole. It still focuses all of its resources on what we don't want — sickness and disease — rather than what we desire, health and vitality.

We all have heard of people dropping dead of a heart attack, a stroke, or internal bleeding days after being given a clean bill of health during a preventative medical checkup. In many situations, a full medical workup will detect normal pathologies at an early stage, pathologies that the body is entirely capable of reversing on its own. Yet, the patient is frequently injected with a dose of fear along with interventions and their inherent risks of iatrogenic effects. Some tests such as mammograms and procedures such as colonoscopies used in preventive medical check-ups present potential risks, have questionable value, and can damage the human body. Fear alone, generated from the news of a diagnosis, creates a negative physiology, biochemistry, immune response, and outcome.

When I was in practice and clients would ask me what was wrong with them, I would let a pensive silence pose stand, then reply with a concerned look on my face: "I think you might have a very serious pathology of the spine." Immediately their overall body language would express fear, anxiety, and a depressed state. Then I would say, "No, I am just kidding… how is that serving you for me to tell you what is wrong with you; many other doctors have done that before. I am only interested in releasing what is right in you. You have tremendous potential available for health and healing within you." Again their demeanor would perk up with relief and hope.

Today, the present healthcare system is placing a heavy financial burden on individuals, families, small businesses, and corporations. Between 2000 and 2010, the U.S. spent $16 trillion on healthcare with little to show for it. As reported by The Commonwealth Fund, America is one of the sickest countries in the industrialized world, ranking last in overall health.

The revolution and evolution needed have become an inescapable reality. It is a must and part of the evolution out of the darkness into the light. It is clear that such upheaval, reform, and reorganization will not come from the top down, the institutions in power, or the corporations with vested interests. They will not stop the Casual War from which they all profit. The belittling labeling by the medical profession of people who have taken steps toward taking care of themselves health-wise as health nuts shows how entrenched the medical establishment is in keeping things as they are. Drug companies have launched slanderous media campaigns discrediting the value of healthy lifestyles, as pointed out by

Gary Null, Ph.D., in his book *Death by Medicine*. So it must come from a grassroots movement.

Martin Luther King, Jr. once said, "Freedom is never given freely to the oppressed by the oppressor." The oppressed have to rage out of their condition to gain freedom. It must start with us, with you and each individual. It must start by creating a demand at the grass-root level for a new approach to life, human health, and wellbeing.

We are moving from the age of darkness into the age of enlightenment. Every voice counts. Your voice counts. Everyone can make a difference. Every true health practitioner is responsible for taking a stand by informing and educating the public. Silence is complicity. As we limit the use of the pharmaceutical-medical system to repair injuries, emergencies, and life-threatening conditions, we are bound to hit the tipping point.

However, success is rarely granted when society is *against* anything; it is usually achieved when it is *for* something. Choosing to be *for* life, *for* health, *for* healing, and *for* wellbeing while engaging in proactive, life and health-enhancing care is becoming imperative. This step demands awareness, self-responsibility, and self-accountability in most decisions and actions of daily life.

This is how the new paradigm for life and health will gain ground, take hold and bring the Casual War to an end.

Being *for* vitality and health brings an inner inquiry: What am I thinking right now? What am I choosing to put into my body, mind, and Soul? What am I watching on T.V. or Netflix? Better, what is causing me to want to watch T.V.? Is there much, if anything, on T.V. that is elevating my being, or am I getting dumbed down? What am I doing for myself today to support my body in health and fitness? What action am I taking to enhance my wellbeing? What daily habits have I established to vitalize, energize, and honor my being? Am I living by example as an instrument of change and transformation?

New habits and patterns may not come easily at first. We all remember the constant battle our parents had to fight to get us to brush our teeth. They were *for* dental hygiene. In time we grew the daily habit. It paid big dividends. A single trip to third- or fourth-world countries is enough to imprint on us the value of dental hygiene. Most of the populations of those countries have rotten teeth or missing teeth because dental hygiene has not yet become a daily habit. I recall breaking the ice with a joke at the start of a public talk at a Tri-City, Tennessee auditorium; the audience laughed, exposing many with dental gaps, the result of poor dental care.

I knew I was in for a tough climb toward a new awareness of health during my presentation. It may take time to end the Casual War. Every individual making the shift, taking a stand, bringing awareness to others, engaging in new health-enhancing behaviors, and making their voices heard on social media contributes to peace. Each and every one of us can make a difference.

The Power of Blind Trust

When I arrived in Spartanburg, S.C., I realized I only had the phone number of the president of the college, but I was armed with a strong sense of purpose; a fire was burning inside. I knew I had followed my heart's calling. On arrival at the Greenville-Spartanburg Airport around 10:00 pm, I found no one waiting for me. The small airport emptied quickly of all the disembarking passengers. I tried unsuccessfully to dial the Sherman College president's number. Finally, with the help of a stranger waiting behind me to use the wall telephone, the call was placed. He communicated with the voice on the other end and then hung up. My helper gestured to me, in the universal language of hand signals, to sit down and wait. I did so for what seemed to be an eternity. The place was now deserted. I became anxious, alone with my suitcase in a strange land, knowing no one, and incapable of speaking the language.

At last, a tall gentleman walked straight toward me. His name was Dr. Reginald Gold, D.C., my future philosophy teacher and a world-renowned chiropractor and public speaker. With a big smile, he welcomed me, and we walked together to the curb with a bounce in our steps. I was pumped. I was safe. I had a friendly connection. Reggie, as everyone would call him, drove a Citroen-Maserati, an exotic fast French car, which he skidded throughout the turn as we sped around the entrance ramp of Interstate 85 North. Instantly I knew I was in good company and in the right place: fast car, speed, and an eccentric man with big sideburns. Life had undoubtedly taken me where I needed to be.

Dr. Gold dropped me at the Travelodge in downtown Spartanburg. The next morning, I woke up early, stepped out onto the balcony with no one in sight, and was in a quandary as to what to do. Suddenly, it dawned on me that I had no address for the college, had never seen a brochure from it, nor had filled out an application to attend. All I had taken with me across the ocean was the phone number of the president of the school. I operated on total blind faith and trust by embracing the words and recommendations of Dr. Jean Belaval.

I had followed the tugging of the strings of my heart with passion burning brightly within me.

Within days it became clear there was no college. There was only an idea, a vision of a college. There was, however, a vacant Southern Bell Telephone building on Main Street to be rented. Prospective students from all over the United States and a few other countries began to gather throughout the area. I had flown from France to America after being told I would attend the best chiropractic college in the world, and there was none. For some inexplicable reason, I did not panic or burst out in anger and frustration. I did not seek another college and did not consider a lawsuit or any kind of restitution. I surrendered to life, supported by the passion within. There was an aura of rightness about it all. The enthusiasm and the fire burning in everyone involved, from future administrators to faculty and prospective students, was intoxicating. Within weeks the vacant Bell Telephone building was rented. Volunteer students began to build the classrooms. Soon thereafter, classes started. I could only think of how many great, highly successful ventures started from scratch in a garage. Honda, Apple, and Microsoft, among others, all had humble beginnings.

The gift of trusting life paid off big time; I ended up receiving the very best education possible in my field at the time, and I believe ever since. I had exceptional, dedicated, and passionate teachers. Their work was their vocation, and they were highly successful in their field. Why would I state that I received the best chiropractic education available? Simply because we were taught unadulterated pure chiropractic in great depth. We were given rock-solid foundations. This would prove to be of extreme value once in practice when facing a world that had been indoctrinated into a totally different paradigm about health, sickness, disease, healing, and how to take care of one's body.

A great validation of the teachings was the presence of many successful Doctors of Chiropractic in Spartanburg and surrounding areas who practiced exactly the model we were taught. Didactic theoretical learning was confirmed by actual observations in practice and real experiences. Dr. Earl Taylor, D.C., Dr. Don Thomas, D.C., Dr. Thom Gelardi, D.C., Dr. Leslie Wise, D.C., Doug Gates, D.C., Guy Riekeman, D.C., and many others were living examples of what we were being taught in classes. Since there was nearly nothing to do culturally in Spartanburg, S.C., at the time, except being in nature, we immersed ourselves in our studies 24-7-365 for four years. Every moment of our day was involved in chiropractic. Our weekends were spent with the president, faculty, and college administrators during social gatherings. We ate, breathed, and drank the inside-out life and vitalistic health paradigm around the clock. This proved to be a blessing, as it takes total immersion in the vitalistic inside-out health and life model to counterbalance all the years of social programming in the mechanistic outside-in sickness and disease medical model. Within four years, I had transformed and tapped into a source of knowledge within. I now had an inner G.P.S. to live life with.

Message from the Pioneers

At school assemblies, we were exposed to the chiropractic pioneers, chiropractors who went to jail for the principle they served. This was enormously inspiring. Those pioneers were not fanatical; they were committed to a principle, to a calling and vocation. Fanaticism is being willing to jail or kill others for a belief or ideology. Commitment is being willing to be jailed or die for a principle. These doctors had courage, foresight, fortitude, commitment, and dedication. They were driven by a powerful vision.

With time I realized the depth of the principle to which they were committed: a Life Principle, the like of Human Rights, Non-Violence, Anti-Apartheid, Equal Rights, Love,

Justice, and Freedom, all intangible principles that could elevate the quality of human life. All the great beings throughout history, which ended up ahead of their time in bringing forth principles, were either ridiculed, jailed, persecuted, or killed. They were committed to intangible and invisible principles that could better human life worldwide and were willing to go to jail for it. It took centuries for some of those principles to find their way into human life. It might take years for the chiropractic paradigm to transform human behaviors in regard to health and healing, yet it is, I believe, an inevitable future.

These pioneers did not go to jail because they believed they had a better mousetrap. Nor did they go to jail believing they had a natural treatment for various illnesses or symptoms. They certainly did not go to jail because they thought they had a treatment for back pain. They went to jail, away from their families, because they knew a vital principle that could improve the quality of life and contribute to the evolution of humanity toward better life expression and health.

As reported in *The Spinal Column,* the Palmer College student newspaper, "Go to jail for chiropractic!" became a popular slogan among the chiropractic community in the early days of the profession.

This chiropractic martyrdom captured the hearts of the press and the public at large. Crowds of up to 1,200 people were said to have gathered to voice their outrage at the senselessness of these arrests and jail sentences. More than 100,000 pieces of mail poured into one prison regarding the arrest of a husband and wife chiropractic team who were forced to say good-bye to their twin 3-year-old girls at the jail's door for their 100-day sentence. Thirty-three hundred chiropractors were sent to prison, and 12,000 were arrested 15,000 times, meaning many stuck to their guns and did not back off.

I know of no other health professions having such a historical past. To me, it is a tribute to the conviction, perseverance, and commitment of chiropractors and to the defining principles and philosophy of chiropractic to serve their fellow human beings. As a student, it was deeply inspiring.

Today, some 125 years later, the Life Principles I was taught are insidiously permeating many realms of society, particularly in the holistic health disciplines. Even traditional western medicine is beginning to embrace many of the understanding and health principles of chiropractic. Books written by Deepak Chopra, M.D., Bernie Siegel, M.D., Larry Dossey, M.D., and Andrew Weill, M.D., amongst countless others, invoke, without giving it credit, the very principles so eloquently formulated by the founder and developer of chiropractic.

The Shift from Old to New

Coming from France and landing in the Deep South in 1973 was a challenge and a cultural shock. Racism, prejudice, segregation, and bigotry were prevalent then. Not exactly the cosmopolitan Parisian mindset I knew. Like many of my classmates, I adapted by immersing myself in my studies. The intense focus on studying a new approach to life, health, and healing was necessary and critical.

To shed the programming and socialization we have all insidiously received in the fear-based, symptom suppression, war on sicknesses and diseases, crisis-oriented, outside-in, mechanistic medical model of life takes time and fortitude. Becoming well-versed in an inside-out, proactive, health, healing, and wellness vitalistic paradigm of life demands significant introspection, reflection, and letting go. It is a process that has to counter years of mechanistic inductive thinking with years of vitalistic deductive reasoning. In the process, we have to let go of the belief that true health comes from the outside-in. That it comes from a potion, a lotion, a drug, surgery, or medication. We have to forfeit adherence to the prevailing wisdom endorsed by nearly everyone. We need to withstand the opposition and sometimes ridicule thrown at our new thinking from family, friends, and society at large. We have to question everything we have assumed or been taught and socialized about:

- Is there an inborn intelligence within all creation, including the human body?
- Is the human intellect a match for our innate intelligence?
- Does the human body display evidence of astonishing organization and design?
- Do germs cause diseases, or does a weak immune system and overall poor health make germs pathogenic?
- Do flies bring garbage, or does the rubbish attract them?
- Could it be that it is a sick, malfunctioning, and run-down body that allows diseases to take hold in the first place?
- Could early trauma be the primary cause of disconnection from our true Self and, consequently, a leading cause of disease?
- Does all the intelligence and wisdom of the universe create us to be sick or to express radiant health?
- Isn't health the dominant expression of life in all living creation?

- Could health be our universal God-given birthright?
- Aren't bacteria and viruses an essential part of our internal ecology, our human microbiome?
- Why do some people get sick when exposed to pathogens and others do not?
- What causes people living, working, and breathing in the same environment to be sick and others not; is the cause internal or external?
- Is how we *feel* a true reflection of how we *function*?
- Is the absence of symptoms a valuable gauge to determine our state of health?
- Could symptoms be, in most instances, an intelligent and normal expression of health, messages to get our attention, asking for changes in how we live, actually warning signals?
- Why do identical twins with the same D.N.A., living in the same household, eating the same food, and breathing the same air, have significantly different health outcomes?
- Does feeling good necessarily equate to being healthy?
- Does having symptoms necessarily equate to being unhealthy?

- Could there be such a thing as cleansing, healing, and adapting symptoms?

- What controls organic function in the body?

- Are the brain, nerve system, and genetic makeup the master controllers of all cells, tissues, organs, and systems, as we are told?

- Does not a corpse possess a brain, nerve system, and genetic makeup, along with all its parts, organs, systems, and cells?

- What is the difference between living, breathing, walking, and talking human beings and corpses?

- What actually controls body functions if it is not the brain, nerve system, and D.N.A.?

- What constitutes organic life?

- Could interference with the nerve system be caused by chemical, mental, emotional, or physical stressors?

- Could clearing the nerve system of blockages lead to better function and health, regardless of the deck of genetic cards we were all dealt at birth?

- Could sickness be a necessary part of the health picture, a necessary evil to challenge and upgrade our immune system?

- Is it actually possible to have health without the challenge of illness?

- Is there a difference between illness, sickness, and disease?

- Is the birth process a natural female body function, or is it a condition requiring medical intervention?

- What is the actual ratio of errors in the perfection of nature in relationship to gestation and birth?

- Are there interconnectedness, interrelationship, and interdependence in all tissues, organs, and systems in the body?

- When we step on a dog's tail, at which end does it bark?

- Could a symptom or pathology in one place be caused by a malfunction in another location?

- Can we actually separate mind, body, spirit, environment, cultural socialization, and belief systems, or should it all be viewed as a whole?

- Is the human body a closed mechanical system with limited variables or a dynamic, open system with infinite inputs, outputs, and variables?

- Since the observer's mind affects the observed, could diagnosis collapse the field of all possibilities in healing?

- What could the placebo and nocebo effects teach us about the capacity of the body to heal or not heal?

- Since there are no diseases that people have not recovered from and spontaneous remission is a clinical fact, what does that imply as far as our healing capacities?

- Should a common sense, non-invasive, non-toxic approach to supporting the body back to health be the first step, preceding other medical interventions?

- Why are we seeing people healing from cancer as heroes, but giving lip service to others staying healthy and vibrant throughout life?

- Doesn't taking care of ourselves on a regular basis with proactive, positive care make more sense than abusing ourselves and seeking reactive palliative symptomatic relief care?

- Why place nearly all our resources on fighting disease and nearly none on promoting health?

- Could scientifically studying health provide greater understanding and better outcomes than studying disease?

- Would giving health days make more sense than giving sick days, thus reinforcing positive behavior?

- What are the key essential components necessary to have a life?

- Since death is unavoidable, could it be approached as a normal, natural body function rather than an event to be avoided at all costs?

- Could interference with the flow of life energy be a primary factor affecting one's health?

- Does lack of evidence mean evidence of lack?

- Is there more to the human body than what we actually see?

- How often do we traumatize our internal organs versus the frequency of trauma sustained by our body frame and skeletal system?

- Since back problems are the oldest and most frequent affliction of the human body, could taking care of the neuro-spinal system be a key to human health?

Endless questions to ponder and many more to arise.

With deductive reasoning, starting from the premise that the Universe is intelligent, one comes to new perspectives. Quite a process and gymnastic of the mind. We must forfeit acceptance and stand up for a new viewpoint while risking social rejection. Basically, it means swimming upstream against the constant river of mass beliefs and the prevailing narrative. Old beliefs die hard, while new ones struggle to emerge and take root in the consciousness of humanity. Not too long ago, the earth was flat, the center of the Universe. Pythagoras single-handedly challenged the established belief of his time. Thereafter Copernicus confronted the Christian belief that the earth was the center of the universe. Bloodletting, exorcisms of evil spirits, and preventative routine removal of tonsils, appendixes, and breasts, amongst many other medical procedures, were believed to be scientific only to be proven ineffective or harmful.

In shifting beliefs, at first, it is one against countless. Over time it becomes many against the masses. Then the new perspective gains ground. In the end, the new understanding, knowledge, and consciousness win the day. We have seen it over and over throughout human history. Over time the new consciousness prevails. The radical thinkers of today become the ethics of tomorrow.

It is said that for every new idea, there are 100,000 soldiers guarding it. To shift from an outside-in to an inside-out paradigm takes courage and perseverance. However, once we pass through many layers of programming, we begin to access a sense of knowing, an intuitive feeling that the direction we are taking is true and truth. A recognition of an inner knowing takes place.

At some point in the process, we touched home base. We realized we had not been taught anything we did not already know. We only had layers and blinders peeled away so that we could see clearly. A veil was lifted. A remembering or *re-membering* takes place. There is a great feeling of empowerment to be set free. Now we have a template, a touchstone within, to bounce any situation, question, or doubt against. Then, wait in stillness and let the answer or solution come forth. Indeed, inside-out living is coming home to oneself, the great inner universal wisdom. Freedom, at last, is ours. That inner knowing that something within that speaks is now the authority, dwarfing outside authorities as to the final say. The practices of silence and solitude or Soul-I-tune are worthwhile paths to make the connection within. Soon we are empowered with an internal homing device. A deep trust in our deeper self emerges. Every human being living in that place makes a difference in the world because when we transform, the world transforms.

Psychogenic Experiment

While on Hilton Head Island, I experimented with Psilocybin mushrooms in the way that American Indian medicine men have. I had read about the sacred healing and hallucinogenic power of plants. It stated that one must fast the day prior to the full moon and then take the magic mushrooms in sets of seven. Mushrooms on Hilton Head Island were readily available in cow pastures right after a big rain. Collecting them fresh in large garbage bags was an easy task. Once home, the mushrooms were blended with juice, and the magic potion was ready to deliver its potent effects.

These shamanistic journeys made me realize that, indeed, there is an underlying field of intelligence permeating and connecting all life. I encountered the reality of the Life Force and the mystical world of spirit. I recalled witnessing the Life Force pulsating in all living things, from trees to plants, to animals and human beings, as a vibrant red streak at the center. In trees, it emanated from the very center of the trunk. In plants, it was present within the stem of every leaf. In animals and humans, it courses within their spinal column, better named their neuro-spinal system. In all, it radiated outward as a brilliant yet more subtle energy field from the inner core.

Years later, Alex Grey's *Sacred Mirrors'* artistic renderings reminded me of what I had experienced. Indeed the human body is vibrating energy interconnected to the world around it. The nerve system creates an energetic-information distribution network that permeates the entire body, linking it to the outside web of life. Such observation has validated the vital importance of the nerve system as the medium to deliver life force to all parts of the human body.

I witnessed that all things are made of the same stuff; a contiguous substance that varies in density and tone with atoms and molecules vibrating at high frequencies. Science tells us that 99% of reality is not perceived by the senses. Psilocybin opened a new level of perception, penetrating deeper into a reality not available in normal daily perception.

The physical and mental effects were astonishing. I could dive into a pool, swim the length of it repetitively without using my arms, just wiggling my body like a fish, and come up on the other side with enough momentum to sit on the edge in one shot. So much energy was being delivered to my body by the plant. Apparently, this amount of power and energy can be available to us in a normal state. Elderly grandmothers have been seen lifting a car to free a trapped child.

Thereafter, in the bathroom, I could enter the showerhead with my mind and go through the wall. Some of the feats described in the book series called *The Life and Teachings of the Masters of the Far East* by Baird T. Spalding were temporarily available to me. Physical reality had morphed into a more fluid, permeable energetic medium.

On one psychogenic journey, I ingested what was said to be the magic number- 112 mushrooms. I lived that night and into the next day a full, intense mystical experience.

My experiments with psychedelic mushrooms while on Hilton Head Island have been an essential catalyst to open my mind to understanding the nature of parallel realities. Through those psychedelic experiences, I realized matter's energetic and vibratory properties in all living systems. We, humans, are energetic beings. I witnessed what quantum physics and, long ago, mysticism, spirituality, and perennial philosophies have enunciated; that everything is made of the same stuff, that everything is one, and that matter is energy in vibration.

I had limited my use of psychogenic substances to natural compounds. I used them, with respect and reverence, following the teachings of native cultures. I had experiences that profoundly affected my life. These shamanic journeys validated the truth of the natural laws and life principles I had studied in chiropractic.

It transformed definitions of Universal Intelligence, Innate Intelligence, Life Force, and the Triune of Life into a perceived reality. There has to be a valuable reason why shamans and traditional healers worldwide used psychogenic plants to open up the perception of higher realms of reality and consciousness.

The cumulative harvesting of all my experiences has contributed to a new perspective. I no longer see human beings as static, mechanical machines made of solid matter. I approach them, especially in practice, as dynamic, ever-changing, malleable, bio-energetic systems. Indeed Susan might still be Susan a week later by name, yet no longer in body, mind, and spirit. This shift was born from these encounters with parallel realities opened by the magic mushrooms.

Recently the Netflix documentary titled *Fantastic Fungi* gave me solace and comfort that Psilocybin had increased neural connections within my brain rather than killing brain cells. As stated in Stalking The Wild Pendulum by Itzhak Bentov, "Spiritual does not mean that it has anything to do with religion. It has to do only with the development and refinement of the nervous system and the accompanying rise in the level of consciousness."

The magic mushroom had increased nerve synapse connectivity, thus allowing for a new level of consciousness and perception of reality.

The Reckoning

By the fall of that year, my body was exhausted; practice, beach time, waiting tables, and psychogenic trips had taken their toll. What came up must come down. I was now facing the other side of the coin, the yin and yang of life. I was still young and immature. I also tested my first wife's love with a one-night stand, got separated from her, and divorced soon after. I had been married for a year. My heart was broken, just like I had broken hers. Now with a wide-open heart, I could clearly see my stuff, my baggage. How unconscious I had been. Blind to my behavior and selfishness. The sudden separation triggered my pre-verbal wound of abandonment. I felt destabilized, disoriented, off balance, and panicked. I had deep inner work and healing to face.

It was now the end of the tourist season. Hilton Head Island settled into the quiet of late fall and early winter. Restaurant businesses went into a low, soon-to-close mode. My chiropractic client base declined markedly. I was now under mounting financial strain.

I collapsed into a nervous breakdown and a deep depression, which took me to places I had never explored. Within a few weeks, I became catatonic, agoraphobic, and non-verbal. Any physical possessions became too much of a responsibility. I let go and threw away everything but a few articles of clothing. I threw into a large Dumpster the entire photographic early history of Sherman College, which I had taken with a Nikon, and put into a collection of printed negative strips. All of my precious Green Books, a collection of the writings of B.J. Palmer, the luminary genius of our profession, was disposed of. My large collection of animal vertebrae vanished in the trash. Everything went, except my car, which I drove to the safety of Atlanta, where I had a few friends.

I was now reaping what I had sowed. I practiced without a license in the hope of getting arrested and exposing the South Carolina State Board of Chiropractic for their dubious non-recognition of the College from which I had graduated. Yet, to be honest, my deeper motivation for practicing illegally was rebellion, anger, and ego. Yes, I was ready to go to jail for practicing without a license, but there was still an ego component to my intent. So, life threw me on the mat to teach me a lesson. One cannot come from ego and anger when serving a principle. Intention and motivation must be pure — or a significant price may be paid. As an anti-nuclear activist, Joanna Macy puts it, "Reality is so organized that it requires we live in a certain way, or else we suffer terribly."

My nervous breakdown/depression proved to be a cleansing, clearing, and healing process, a shedding of layers of ego, a lightening up of baggage, a thinning of my armor, and an introduction to the wisdom of vulnerability. I now believe it to be a natural built-in process for transformation. It seems to have a nine-month cycle when un-interfered with drugs or medications, allocated enough time for the gestation and birth of a new being. Since that experience, I invite those going through a nervous breakdown/depression to let it evolve naturally, with a support system around them, until it comes to a resolution organically.

This might appear to be an irresponsible offering to many. However, my personal experience led me to stand firm in the knowledge that such a breakdown is built into life's design for us to grow and transform. Over time it bears fruit. The life-long work of Dr. Gabor Mate, M.D., epitomized in the film *The Wisdom of Trauma,* gives credence to my stand on nervous breakdown/depression.

I was very fortunate to have the foundations of a solid vitalistic philosophy of life that kept me hanging in the process. I was also blessed by the full support of an African-American friend who looked after me in Atlanta. He literally fed, washed, bathed, and, best of all, accepted me and my state of being with unconditional love. To this day, Knox is the recipient of my nightly gratitude.

Eckhart Tolle, in his book *The Power of Now*, shared his experience with depression, sitting on a park bench for months. It was his dark night of the Soul that led him to his present stage of enlightened consciousness. As Donald Epstein, D.C., founder of Network Spinal Analysis, stated, "Depression happens when you make it all about you." In retrospect, how true that was for me. I had to peel away layers of ego, self-importance, and egocentrism. The stone had to be sharpened; huge blocks had to be chipped away for a clearer form to emerge.

B.J. Palmer talks about becoming a hollow bone in order to become an instrument of healing. Since my own experience, I have witnessed and supported many friends who were going through a similar process. Invariably they emerged empowered, lighter, and brighter. Most became amazing facilitators of healing and transformation in their chiropractic practices. It appears that the Universe tests, slams to the mat, and crucifies those who are called to serve a higher purpose, particularly in the field of natural healing.

Having bathed in the human potential and personal growth movement, I found nervous breakdowns and depression to be efficient and cost-effective paths to self-improvement. Of course, proper life support must be available, as one cannot handle their most basic human needs. The love, acceptance, and caring of my friend, Knox, in Atlanta, brought me back to a level where I could fly back to France. Yet the very prospect of such a trip felt overwhelming and daunting.

A few weeks before my departure back to Europe, I got rear-ended in my 1968 Pontiac Firebird on Peachtree Street in Atlanta, GA. What a great metaphor life was giving me, "Time to get off your butt and move forward by giving me a kick in the rear end." I very much needed that push to make the trip. In such a crisis and state of being, returning to the parental home, to the larger womb, seems to be the best way to completely let go so that the process of a nervous breakdown and depression can unfold naturally. As long as I remained with my friend Knox, there was still a layer of holding-on left inside that I could not release fully. With this restraint, I could not birth my new Self. I was stuck in limbo inside a figurative birth canal.

At that moment, I realized that life is an ongoing process of letting go. We let go of our mother's womb at birth, of the breast when weaning becomes a must; thereafter, we abandon our pacifier, the comfort of the crib, and the warmth of diapers. In time we surrender the safety of our parent's hand in street crossings. Soon we take flight away from the security of our home. Graduating from high school, college, or university leads to relinquishing relationships we cherish so deeply. As life progresses, we face some broken romantic ventures, often divorce, and countless losses of all kinds. With growth and maturity, we let go of who we thought we were to uncover a more authentic Self. In the final moment of life, we exit our mortal shells. Indeed life is all about surrendering and letting go, especially of fears. The quicker we forfeit holding on, the better off we are.

Back in Paris, at my mother's apartment, I spent months in deep depression, contemplating suicide. The thought of handling a single daily task was overwhelming. The accomplishment of one simple chore was exhausting. Emerging from sleep demanded an enormous effort. All I wanted was to stay in bed, hidden under the covers. Any awakened moment triggered a cyclic mental loop of frightening, destructive thoughts. I was totally decomposing my prior self. My perpetual internal dialogue, running like a continuous tape, was that I was worthless, nothing, a piece of human nothingness with not a single thing to offer. I was spiraling downward toward the bottom. My sense of self-worth was down to zero. I know that anyone who has come through the darkness and hell of a full nervous breakdown/depression can thoroughly relate. It was the dark night of the Soul, so often referred to in spiritual books. I had finally hit bottom with no place to go but up. A point of light appeared at the end of the tunnel I had been in.

By the spring of that year, I traveled through France to the town of Arles, where my sister lived. I worked, almost mute, as a dishwasher in exchange for room and board at a restaurant called Poisson Banane. This was a valuable and humbling experience. Silence was my constant companion. Self-examination was chronic through observation. I was making snail-pace progress in my healing. The thoughts of suicide had receded.

Months later, I traveled to my father's house in the back of the French Riviera and worked the land on his property. Gardening, plowing, weeding, and harvesting olives proved to be restorative. Back to nature, connecting with the land and Provence's tender, soft light was healing. Slowly I was coming back up. I was healing organically. It was a departure from recovering. I did not want to recover or *re-cover* my old self, which was the very self that had gotten me into that painful situation. I wanted to heal at my core and uncover a new self.

Thinking that a short vacation could speed up the healing process, I was taken by my father and his latest girlfriend to the Canary Islands, off the coast of Africa. There, we had a bitter fight about his numerous affairs while married to my mother. He threw me out of the hotel room with an overnight bag and my return ticket to France. I had five U.S. dollars in my pocket. I landed at the Nice Airport with the obvious choice of going back to the security of my mother's apartment in Paris or throwing myself into life and the unknown.

The Crucible, Choice Point, and Life's Providence

I was at a bifurcation point, a crucible. It was a decisive moment of inner choice common to the human experience. I pondered my choices for hours, frozen in fear when looking at the unknown, drowning in despair and mediocrity when thinking of a return to the security of my mother's home. It became clear to me that a secured life was a dead life. Life begins by facing fear and causing it to back down. I had to take a risk. It is said that life begins at the end of our comfort zone; how true it was for me at that moment.

The philosophy of life I studied for four years is a philosophy of life in trust, the study of natural laws, universal laws, and the unseen matrix and intelligence of life — a philosophy of life with all its mystery and magic. Now was the time to put it into action. Innately, I knew my life was waiting for me at the end of my comfort zone. My life was to be retrieved at the edge of the unknown. I had to face my fears head-on. I had to lean over the edge. I needed to trust life. The French poet Guillaume Apollinaire wrote, "Come to the edge. No, we will fall. Come to the edge. No, we will fall. He pushed them, and they flew."

So between the known and the unknown, risk or security, I chose the unknown and the risk. I had to extract myself from the bench I had been sitting on for what seemed like an eternity. I threw myself into the trust of life. I stepped out of the airport to the curb and stuck my thumb out, hoping for a ride to *anywhere*. Within minutes, a car pulled over. The driver asked, "Where are you going?"

I replied, "Wherever you are going, that's where I am going."

I ended up being dropped off in Monaco near the stunningly beautiful Monte Carlo Casino. I still had my five U.S. dollars in my pocket. As I looked around to orient myself, a sign caught my eye, American Bar.

Having just spent years in the United States, I was naturally drawn to it. I walked into the establishment, which I later found was the only American bar in Monte Carlo. I sat at the counter without ordering and asked if they could give me a job. A few minutes later, the bartender placed a hamburger, French fries, and a drink in front of me. Amazed, I understood the gesture and devoured the food. Later on, the owner told me I had an appointment scheduled the next day for a job interview at the majestic Loewe Hotel on the promenade by the sea. "The tab is on me," he stated before shaking my hand. Providence had graced me.

I left the premise with great appreciation. I hiked to Villefranche, the nearby village overlooking the sea. I found a small pension on the hills above Monaco. Naturally, as I asked for a room, the man at the front desk inquired about the length of my stay.

I replied with confidence, "A week or two." He handed me my room key without asking for a credit card or a cash deposit, which of course, I could not have produced. Providence was showing up again.

I started working the next day at the luxurious Loews Hotel on the Monaco promenade, still depressed but encouraged by the security of a job, food, and lodging. I was grateful for the providence that had graced my life the last few days. Having no money, I ate at the hotel when on shifts. On days off, I gathered food by rummaging through the leftovers of street markets. The written words of B.J. Palmer, D.C., about his humble beginnings resonated in my head. He had been sleeping in dark alleys on wooden crates. At least I had a bed. Dr. Palmer founded Palmer College in Davenport, Iowa. He became a world-renowned celebrity, an inventor, a world traveler meeting nearly every head of state, a writer, a philosopher, and a scientist. He was a visionary. He befriended all the luminaries of his time. He saved at age 19 the city of Davenport, Iowa, from bankruptcy. Maybe there was hope for me of a better future.

Over the next few weeks, I befriended other waiters and their friends. Once in a while, I splurged for an ice cream on the promenade. Months later, one afternoon while at work, a phone call came in for me. I was astonished. Who could it possibly be? To my surprise, it was a young woman named Bunny. I had met her briefly while eating ice cream a few days earlier. She was inviting me to a party after work at her apartment. I had been alone for months, and the prospect of someone being interested in me was both uplifting and terrifying. In the throes of depression, my sense of self and personal value was extremely low. I accepted the invitation, went to the party, fell asleep on her living room couch, and woke up in her bed. I do not recall how I got there or who lifted me into it.

This young woman was an adopted child. Her mother had committed suicide years earlier by throwing herself out of her New York apartment window. Her adoptive Dutch father had just passed away a few months earlier. Depression had met depression. We had something in common. Our energies were symbiotic. We were in vibrational resonance.

Our relationship served us both. We were able to heal through mutual support.

One afternoon, I remember walking along the sea on my way to work at the Loews Hotel; silently, I heard a voice in my head, "You have been depressed, nearly non-verbal, totally introverted, and empty for nine months. It does not mean it will always be that way." I had reached a turning point. I was empty, and in that emptiness, something magical was to appear.

During my nervous breakdown, my eyesight had become a tunneled vision with a boxed-in narrow focus. Life had appeared in shades of gray, not in Technicolor. But within seconds of hearing the voice in my head, my eyesight shifted into an open focus and clear, full-color vision. I saw the next ten years of my life clearly and vividly unfold in front of me. My entire vision came to pass in the years that followed.

Now I had a burning desire to return to the United States to open a practice. But I had no money to fuel the trip and the start-up. I talked with my girlfriend about my project. My plan was to leave Monaco at summer's end, go to a ski resort in Switzerland and work the winter season in restaurants to save enough money for my return to the U.S. One morning, I found 10,000 U.S. dollars stacked up on the bed. Bunny gave me that money to return to America and live my dream. I was astonished; providence and grace had shown up again. Suddenly, it dawned on me that I had been totally blind to my surroundings. She was a multimillionaire living in Monaco's large, luxurious, and very expensive apartment. Her father had been a rubber industry baron. Priceless works of art, antique furniture, Faberge Egg collections, and authentic paintings from great masters surrounded me. I had been oblivious to it. To the defense of my blindness, not once had she paid for a coffee, an ice cream, or a meal when we had gone out. I accepted the money under the condition that I could pay her back with interest. This I did within a few years.

The synchronicity of events, the serendipity of time and place, the providence and grace of it all, and the natural flow of actions turned a philosophical understanding of Universal Intelligence into a knowledge grounded in the reality of my experience. I was back in the flow of the River of my Life, its perfection, signs, and messages. Surrender and trust were paying off. When we trust the flow of life implicitly, miracles happen. I know now that all things are interlaced, interconnected, and interdependent. I also knew trust and surrender were prerequisites for merging with the Universal Design. I had to empty myself in order to connect with my SELF. How could all this unfold so perfectly? There was no accident or coincidence, just the amazing play of the Universe. I had found my place in life's mosaic as a player and participant. My take-home lesson was; to face the fear head-on, trust life, and surrender fully.

From Vision to Reality

In the fall of 1978, I flew back to the United States. The only connection I had left was with Michael Frigiola, a D.C. and former classmate and friend. He lived in Langhorne, PA. He had just started practicing with his wife, Cathy. We had known each other from our time together on Hilton Head Island. They knew my past until just before my nervous breakdown. Kindly, they gave me hospitality and a landing place.

Needing transportation, I quickly bought a cheap van. As I drove around Bucks County, PA, going through Main Street Yardley, a sign came to my attention, Dr. Claude Lessard, D.C. I had known Claude from my time at Sherman College. He had been a few classes behind me. He was a jovial, good-hearted, intelligent bear of a man. He had just started his practice.

We got together and quickly decided we would join in practice — another amazing synchronicity of events. So began our journey of building a Point of Light practice in conservative Bucks County. Our business card stated,

Chiropractic — an Evolutionary, Revolutionary Approach to Life and Health.

Within a year or so, we parted over his newfound born-again Christian religion. As a born-again Christian, he could not entertain working with the devil, a friend, and a partner who had not embraced his faith. He announced this unexpectedly in a letter left on my desk, dissolving our partnership. He was going to buy me out. I was stunned.

Yet again, I fully accepted what life was offering. He was taking the religious path. I had chosen the spiritual path. He saw the devil everywhere and in most people. I wanted to see the best and good in everyone, in spite of my constant fight to stop judging others, which I failed to win too frequently. I am still at it today, gaining some ground in avoiding judgment of others. I surrendered fully and left for the Poconos Mountains to ski for a week. I needed time out as a reset. Upon my return, Claude changed his mind and decided I should buy him out. He had chosen to join another chiropractor in his booming practice in Levittown, PA., who was also a born-again Christian, so Claude's new decision and reversal made sense.

Again I surrendered to what life was offering. I could see that opening myself up and surrendering to life brought out the best for me. It was a lesson I kept close to my mind and heart. Surrender, surrender, surrender to what life presents. Indeed it was a present, a gift. Yet I did not know what life had in store for me. What would happen now? Would the practice crash? Would I be able to be thriving and successful without the synergy we had together? Would the new financial commitment of the buyout strain and drain me?

The Yardley Chiropractic Center became a beacon of light, not only for the public in Yardley but also for countless chiropractors and chiropractic students on the East Coast. In the end, it all turned out perfectly. As my friend Abby Kramer, D.C., would say, "Good, bad, perfect... Life works!"

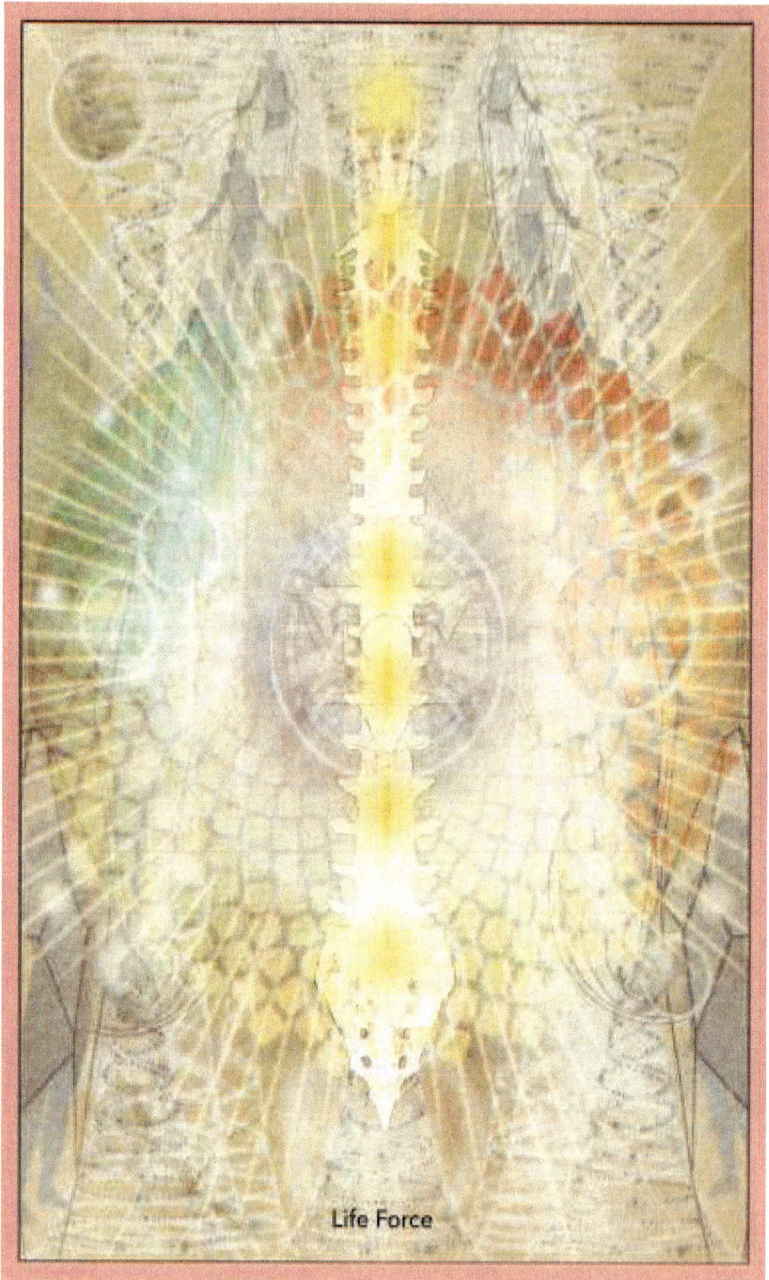

Life Force

116

Chapter 5: Main Courses

Healing is Possible

My first exposure to the amazing healing power of the human body took place during my early quarters at Sherman College.

Jackie was a classmate of mine in the pioneer class. Her father was a chiropractor, as well as her two older brothers. So all she knew, having grown up with it, was an inside-out approach and paradigm to health and healing. She trusted her body implicitly. One day she showed up for a class with a marked reddening, swollen skin patch on her face. We all noticed it, yet no one said anything. Within a few weeks, it had grown to a significant bulging mass, impossible to ignore. About half the class, still very much entrenched in the medical paradigm, was adamant that she should have it biopsied and removed. They were concerned and fearful that something very serious was taking place; it was nothing to be taken lightly. The other half of my class, having embraced a new perspective, was curious and supportive. They wanted to see what her body would do in trusting the natural inner healing process; certainly a stand easy to take when it is not your own body.

The mass grew to be a small lemon-sized growth. At that juncture, half the class thought Jackie was irresponsible, taking an unnecessary risk with her life. She should go to the hospital and have the tumor cut out. Many, on the other side, had a wait-and-see attitude. Over time the growth started to push itself outward, and a stalk, roughly two inches in diameter appendix of skin, formed. It became gruesome as now the stalk elongated itself under the weight of the growth, and the mass of tissue dangled back and forth as Jackie moved around. This was when most of the class encouraged her to have it surgically lanced. Fear was taking hold.

On a Monday, Jackie walked into class, and the stalk and tumor were gone. We were all thrilled. We all thought she finally relented and had the stalk and growth cut out. But she stated that she was taking a hot bath over the weekend, and the entire thing fell off her face. Amazingly there was just a reddish mark on her face, and over a few weeks, it vanished with nearly no mark or scar. Was it a freak happening? Was it the result of Jackie being so at peace and trusting the entire situation, thus delivering a positive outcome? Was this an unusual and isolated event? Could the body actually be smart enough to expel a tumor? We were all stunned by what had happened and curious to discover if this was a rare occurrence.

Walter was a classmate of ours. He had been a Vietnam veteran who had been a grunt, seeing active combat during his tour of duty. He was, like a few other G.I.s in my class, on a government scholarship. To supplement his living expenses, he worked as a night watchman at the Spartanburg Public Library. He loved books and was a bookworm with a bright mind and a superb photographic memory. He decided to investigate Jackie's healing by researching if such events were known and written about in anthropological books. He reported that the healing of tumors was not uncommon among native tribes the world over.

Tumors might heal the way it happened for Jackie; the growth is pushed outward, and a stalk forms that will either stay or fall off. In other instances, a tumor might be sequestered by being encapsulated in fibrous tissues, thus isolating it from the rest of the body.

Would such healing take place in everyone everywhere? Maybe; maybe not. Is the potential for such an amazing occurrence there? Yes, but we are all unique and different, with peculiar genetics, environment, eating habits, belief systems, energy flow, accumulated trauma, and mental states, amongst countless other factors, so there is no guarantee. This is key to remember. In facing such a challenge, one must decide for oneself what route one chooses to take. One can go the medical route and have a positive or negative outcome. Similarly, one may choose the natural healing journey and also have a positive or negative outcome. What is important is not to have a foot in each canoe while going down the river, or one is sure to fall in. What is essential is to be at peace with one's choice.

For Jackie, her experience was empowering. It had an impact on everyone in my class. There is a power and inborn intelligence within that can be trusted in healing to perform the seemingly impossible.

My second exposure to astonishing healing happened a few quarters later. What proved to be beyond belief took place for everyone in our burgeoning student body to witness.

I was working as a waiter at the Sizzling Steak House in Spartanburg, S.C., with Arthur and Allan. They were twins and also attended Sherman College. Both were short-order cooks. One of the requirements in operating a restaurant, commanded by the Health Department, was to thoroughly clean the entire kitchen regularly. This meant that the deep fryers had to be unlocked from their wheels and moved backward to access the back wall for cleaning.

While washing the floor, someone had removed the cap of the floor drain, a hole of about five inches in diameter.

You can anticipate what comes next. As Arthur pulled the deep fryer backward, one of the wheels dropped into the drain hole. The hot, nearly boiling oil spilled out onto Arthur's chest, abdomen, and forearms. The uniform we were all wearing was red nylon shirts and black Lewis cotton jeans. The burning oil melted Arthur's shirt into his chest and belly. He sustained third- and fourth-degree burns all over his torso and forearms. His flesh was burned, turning brown and black colors.

The restaurant manager wanted to call 911 and get an ambulance to take Arthur to the emergency room. Allan, Arthur's twin brother, after conferring with him, decided to decline the offer. Instead, they went straight home with me in tow. Arthur was in visible, severe, if not excruciating, pain. Once settled in a comfortable rocking chair, we decided to call Doctor Sherman, D.C., after whom the college was named. He had been the director of the then-famous B.J. Palmer Research Clinic in Davenport, Iowa. He was renowned for his expertise in upper cervical care. Doctor Sherman soon arrived. Assessing the situation, he palpated Arthur's neck, felt the atlas vertebrae being displaced, took a neurocalometer heat reading, and proceeded to adjust Arthur's atlas, the first cervical vertebrae, in the sitting position with a lightning-speed toggle recoil. This adjusting move delivers a powerful, controlled force with a torque, sending a thrust with a corkscrew-like winding, just like a spinning bullet into the atlas vertebrae. It is one of the most powerful and effective adjustments performed. When the practitioner is highly skilled in this approach, it clears the brain stem from obstruction.

Immediately following the adjustment, Arthur reported that the pain decreased markedly. How could this be? We had no knowledge or research data on such occurrences. Years later, Deepak Chopra wrote a book titled *Quantum Healing*. He revealed that the human body releases morphine-type substances, called beta-endorphins, 18 to 33 times stronger than morphine. Retroactively we reasoned that under the recoil-jerk reaction from being startled by the hot oil, Arthur had displaced his atlas vertebra. In turn, normal biochemical physiological endorphins had been dammed, blocked from being released. Once adjusted, the floodgate opened, and a load of beta-endorphins was released, sedating the pain to a tolerable level.

Over the months that followed, we witnessed the healing process. No ointment, no skin graft, no medication, no antibiotics, just rest, time, and nature while sitting and sleeping in a rocking chair. Once the healing was completed, there was no visible scarring. The body had removed the molten nylon from the shirt and all necrotic tissues. Am I, through this account, professing that burned patients receive no medical care? Absolutely not. I am only sharing what is possible and what I witnessed with 90 of my classmates because it speaks volumes about our healing capacities and potential.

It is clear that damaged tissues cannot heal. They have to be removed and replaced by new ones. A turnover of tissue cells is necessary. Have you ever seen the brown leaves of a house plant turn green again? Never. The dried- out leaves have to fall off and be replaced by new green ones. That is a law of life.

Since skin cells live for seven days, millions of Artur's burned cells had to be replaced. It takes time, patience, and trust to allow nature to work its magic. Subcutaneous tissues also had to be replaced. By not using bandages and dressings that have to be changed routinely, there was no peeling away of new tissues. This prevented infections while speeding up healing. What we had all witnessed was an eye and mind-opener.

In 1982, I dreamed of riding motorcycles with my wife Jane into the sunset. This was a romantic aspiration I was determined to make a reality. So I decided to teach Jane how to ride. In retrospect, this was a very bad idea — or maybe a good one, as the lessons learned have been valuable. Since riding had been my forte from an early age, I had little to no understanding that it might be a challenge for a thirty-something wife. We were returning from a ride, and I decided to pull into a quiet parking lot at Round Valley State Park near Lebanon, N.J. It was an early August afternoon, hot and humid. So we removed our riding gear. I instructed Jane on using the throttle, clutch, gearshift, and brakes. Sitting behind her, I reassured her that all would be okay, as I could reach for the controls if necessary.

She opened up the throttle, released the clutch, and off we were in a perfect wheelie, flying straight across the parking lot. We missed a parked car by a few inches that would have taken both of our right knees off and then hit the sidewalk ledge at full speed at the end of the parking lot. In an instant, we were airborne. Jane landed in the grass ahead of the bike. I landed on the rear of the motorcycle. Immediately I got up, picked up the bike, unfolded the kickstand, and inspected the bike for damages. A reflex action acquired from early racing times. To date, Jane still gives me grief for not first asking her if she was okay. She seemed fine, and so was I, until she said: "Oh my God, look at your arm."

My left arm was ripped open to the muscle from my left elbow to my shoulder. My arm had acted as a brake on the spinning rear tire. The gaping wound was almost the size of the tire's width, filled with gravel, sand, and rubber particles. Before Jane brought my attention, I had no pain. The moment I saw the wound, the pain surged. On the second inspection, I thought I better run my arm under a faucet to clean it. As I walked toward the bathrooms, the thought of placing my arm under running water made me cringe. The closer I got to the faucet, the more I recoiled. So I turned around and walked back up the hill toward the bike, listening to the message from my body. As the afternoon sun lit up the wound, I took another look. Now I saw that a gooey-oozing, thick fluid had already flooded the entire wound. Serum circulation, lymphatic fluid laden with immune cells, had protected and sealed the wound. If I had washed it away, now I would be open to infection. Hmm, it had paid off to listen to my instinct's message.

The bike seemed okay, so we rode the 26 miles back to New Hope, PA. By the time we got off, the extent of our injuries had shown. We both had sprained pelvises from the bike seat coming up between our legs while ejecting us. Jane's neck was sprained from landing in a heap on the grass. We went to bed seeking a reprieve. The moment I stopped moving my arm, the pain would surge. So all night long, I routinely moved my arm at the elbow back and forth. This actually allowed the oozing; now a thick layer of fluid began to coagulate in an elastic manner. If I had taken a painkiller and a sleeping pill, I would have awakened hours later, moved my arm, and ripped the edge of the wound apart, as the fluid would have dried up taut from lack of movement.

We both were very stiff when we got up. Body movement made it better, so we decided to go to the office. I cut off the left sleeve of my shirt and went off to practice. At the sight of my arm, clients launched into inquiries, concerns, and advice. This went on all day long for a week or so, "You need to go to the hospital." "Have you looked at it? It's full of dirt, gravel, and rubber; you need to have it cleaned." "You need a skin graft; the muscles are exposed." "Did you get a tetanus shot?" "Are you on antibiotics?" "You should be at home, resting."

The comments and advice sounded like a broken record. None of which I hid. I was at peace inside. I had no doubts. I had total trust that my body would heal and that I would be fine.

Over weeks, a ¼-inch thick scab formed. Then it began to detach itself from the shoulder down. Then the top of the scab started to coil on itself. At that juncture, people advised me to cut the coil. But the coil provided a spring that warned me when I came in close contact with a wall or a person.

It protected me from tearing the scab and creating a blood lesion that could be a problem or lead to an infection. Over time the entire scab disintegrated from the top down into a thin powder: no scar, no infection, nothing but perfect skin. From my muscles being exposed and covered with sand, gravel, and rubber, my body had remanufactured subcutaneous tissues and skin.

It healed the 10-inch by 2-and-half-inch wide wound perfectly. Over the years, I have shown my left arm to audiences worldwide while sharing the healing power of life. It carried the message loud and clear. Would this have happened if I had washed away the oozing liquid that had flooded the wound? I think not. The fluid provided the matrix to rebuild the subcutaneous layers and the skin and protect it from infection.

From the time of the crash, I had headaches. I did not know at the time, but my face had landed on the rear frame of the motorcycle, breaking my jaw and zygomatic arch, the bone below the eye, in a straight line. This was uncovered later by a dental X-ray. About seven weeks after the crash in September, I was bathing in the sun, and a shifting movement took place on the left side of my face with a clunk.

Headaches vanished. My body had reset my jaw under the soothing effect of the sun.

Both pelvises of Jane and I healed, as well as her neck, over the months that followed. We were both empowered in trusting our bodies, and so were countless of my clients who had witnessed the entire healing process, as most came in regularly for wellbeing care.

At the time, I was giving educational talks in my office on a bi-monthly basis. A week after the crash, I was due to give a talk on a Tuesday. Having pain in my jaw, I was mumbling with a thick French accent. The discourse must have been challenging for people to listen to and understand. At the end of my talk, a gentleman came straight up to me and stated: "I did not understand but a few words here and there, but seeing you up there with your cut-out left shirt sleeve and your wound, I believe you have something I want."

He happened to be the chairman of the board of Hamilton hospital in New Jersey. He and his wife became regular clients until years later when I left my practice for Colorado. I suspect that my passion, combined with the evident trust I had in the body's ability to heal, had a potent effect. It validated the words spoken in my talk. All this might seem far-fetched, almost beyond belief, yet it is the truth and the reality of what took place.

A few years later, we were on vacation in Antigua's Pelican Bay. Russ, my brother-in-law, and I were watching native kids doing flips, running toward the water, and cartwheeling into the green-blue Caribbean Sea. Jane was biting at the bit from her lounge chair. When they were done, inspired by their escapades, she decided to do it herself. Off she went, leaped in the air, and landed in slow motion in the shallow water headfirst.

I saw the entire event as if it were a movie, seeing every frame distinctly. The junction between her lower neck and upper back bent at 90 degrees; her body landed in the water, her legs jerked a few times, and she collapsed at the edge of the beach. Russ and I rushed to pull her out of the shallow water. She was alive but could not feel or move her legs.

The reality of the situation, isolated miles away from any hospital, with no phone or transportation available, led me to a fast decision with no hesitation. We laid her face down on a towel on the sand. I went right to where I had seen her spine bend at a 90-degree angle when she hit bottom. I put everything I had in the posterior vertebrae adjusting thrust, basically reversing what had happened. We then moved her carefully to a bed in the villa.

We knew the hospital in Antigua was very basic and miles away over rough, bumpy roads. It would have taken hours to get there, with no guarantee that care would be available. Jane rested as immobile as possible for a few weeks before flying back to the U.S. She was fine, with no sequels; her leg movements and sensations were restored.

Two years later, an X-ray showed she had broken her lower neck. If I had seen the fracture on an X-ray, I do not feel or think I would have had the courage to adjust her with the adrenaline-loaded force of the thrust I put into reversing what I had seen. I have to credit Dr. Clarence Gonstead, D.C., for my decision to adjust Jane. In sharing with audiences during his seminars that if you could get to a patient with a spinal injury or broken back within 24 hours or so, in what he called the golden hours, you could adjust and frequently prevent paralysis. Without that knowledge, I would not have had the impetus or courage to proceed. While Dr. Gonstead was alive, he had patients with spinal injuries fly in from all over the world to the Gonstead clinic in Mount Horeb, Wisconsin.

To piggyback on the above story, my friend Diego from Life University in Atlanta, Georgia, had a fairly similar situation. With his classmate Hernan, Diego decided to ride motorcycles from Georgia to Buenos Aires, Argentina, which was home to both. It was to be their graduation celebration after years of intense studies. While in Mexico, on a dirt road, Diego hit a large pothole. He was thrown off the bike and landed on his back on a rock. He broke his spine and was taken to a hospital. MRI and X-Rays revealed a fracture with spinal cord compression.

The orthopedic team wanted to operate immediately to ease the pressure on the spinal cord as Diego could not feel nor move his legs. He had also lost bladder and bowel control. Diego refused to undergo surgery. He asked Hernan to get in touch with Lou Corleto, D.C., from Tri-City, Tennessee. Lou agreed to jump on a plane on the condition that Diego would be clear that Lou was not flying there to fix him, just to adjust him. He could not promise a specific outcome.

Lou adjusted Diego every few hours incognito for three days. For a chiropractor to perform chiropractic adjustments in a hospital on a patient who had been admitted under the care of an orthopedic surgical team is unfortunately not usually allowed. So it had to be done in secrecy. After a few days of around-the-clock adjustments, the hospital neurologist was astonished at the transformation, stating the changes observed were medically impossible. He asked what was happening. Upon hearing that a chiropractor had flown from the United States to take care of Diego behind closed doors, he stated, "Wow, why didn't you tell me? Whatever you are doing is working. So no more secrecy."

Lou and Diego were grateful to be in Mexico, where turf protection was not prevalent. As much as the outcome seemed medically impossible, it had been chiropractically possible. Lou adjusted Diego for a few more days, then flew back to the United States. Diego used to be an avid soccer player. Over time he regained all of his sporting capacities. I personally visited Diego on three occasions in Buenos Aires while on seminar tours. He walked as if nothing ever happened, still playing soccer.

My experience in 1997, when I contracted the Hantavirus from doing extensive cleaning and work on the barn in the back of our property, showed me the power of my body to heal. We had just arrived in the southwest and were unaware of the potential danger of mice droppings. I worked inside the barn for weeks to prepare it to be transformed into an office. A few weeks later, I was bedridden with raging, chronic fevers that would cause my body to be drenched in sweat. I became delirious, hallucinating, had a chronic cough, and began to cough and spit blood. Not once did I question or doubt my body's ability to heal. I observed what my body was doing and how things were moving. I gained the knowledge, through inner observation, that my body began to release blood in my lungs and bronchial trees to flood the tissues with immune cells. I had the insight, yes *in-sight*, that my body was combating the virus by creating an immense area of interface between the immune response and the virus through fractal biology. Fractal biology is the process of using the infinite surface area available in the bronchial trees and lungs to attack a viral invader. The raging fever was destroying the viruses as they duplicated. Fever over 103, 104, 105, and higher kills viruses. Within six weeks, I was up, still coughing intermittently, and conducted my first six days of intensive training called Master Piece Training Camp at the stunningly beautiful Tamarron resort miles from our house in Durango.

That same month the *Durango Herald* reported the death of a well-known restaurant owner from the Hantavirus. The *Montrose Daily Press* reported the passing of a 38-year-old woman. Both had died from the onset of symptoms in a matter of days. What was the difference? Was it the virus or the resistance of the host? Was it the unwavering trust in my inborn healing capacity? Was it letting the fever run uninterfered with? Who knows? Regardless, I experienced a positive outcome.

I wonder how quickly I might have healed if my tonsils had not been removed when I was fourteen, in a two-for-one sale, a common medical offering of the 1960s. If one sibling had tonsillitis, the practice was to remove the tonsils and offer to cut out the other sibling's tonsils preventatively, all for the price of one.

The tonsils are not vestigial remnants of evolution, nor are they useless organs, as medically thought. They are actually the fuse box of the upper respiratory system, designed to battle infection in the throat rather than in the lower bronchial tubes and lungs, more vital yet vulnerable tissues. The ring of tonsils, called the ring of Waldeyer, is strategically positioned out of the way of the air passage. When called to action, they are designed to swell, and handle the infection, preventing it from moving into the lower respiratory system. Routinely removing them might not be wise. Who knows if the high death rate from COVID-19 in seniors could be due to the lack of tonsils in a generation where tonsillectomy was rampant?

Ask yourself: if all of the wealth and riches of nature are inside us when well, yet, suddenly outside when sick? Nature is boss, a wise man told me on a hike to the icefall of Ouray, Colorado. Its power and intelligence are with us around the clock.

We possess the greatest drugstore in the world within ourselves; we need to learn to mobilize its pharmacopeias. The combined output of the 86 trillion tissue cells is estimated to deliver over 37 thousand billion billion chemical reactions per second in our body. Yes, this is not a misprint: billion billion. Should anyone mess with that? Is a headache really caused by a lack of aspirin? Or could there be another cause, such as stress, biochemical imbalance, toxins, and neurological sympathetic muscular tension affecting blood flow? The inner drugstore is open 24/7/365 from conception to transition, and the prescriptions are free. This internal pharmacy produces more drugs and works more efficiently when we run a fever. In trusting the biochemist magician within, our power to heal resides.

Every organ heals at a different pace. Skin heals faster than muscles, ligaments, or bones, as it is more likely to be cut or injured. Bones heal slower than muscles due to the strength they display. Ligaments heal slower than bone because they have to heal with elasticity, a daunting task. Intervertebral disks take about nine months to heal independently of the presence or absence of symptoms. Replacing all the torn disc cells might take up to three years. Thus one needs to be very careful for years following a spinal injury to not reinjure themselves with contortions or heavy lifting. Spinal surgeons know that by experience.

Unless a disc is extruded with broken-off fragments that might have dropped into the neural canal, people with disc herniation will heal within three years. The stomach can heal very quickly as stomach cells have a high turnover rate. This is necessary as digestive enzymes breaking down food pour into it with every meal, affecting the walls of the stomach. Repair has to take place rapidly between food intake. Fasting facilitates the process. The same quick cellular turnover is true of the liver. Even if one-third of the liver is removed, it will regenerate in a few days.

We need to remember that most diseases or pathological processes are silent, going on underneath our awareness for years until they become symptomatic. Symptoms can be the last to come and the first to go. So if it took five or ten years to go downhill, decay, degenerate, and devitalize, it certainly might take some time to come back uphill. Most cancers and heart diseases may take fifteen to twenty years to become symptomatic, yet we expect to get well overnight; that is unreasonable. Surely time and patience are required to experience the seemingly impossible.

Biological healing takes time and is a wide departure from fixing, curing, and core healing. A shattered bone may need fixing with screws and a cast, but healing will continue for months thereafter. A cancer patient may be cured by chemo and radiation, yet little to no healing has occurred. The same circumstances, patterns, lifestyles, and behaviors remain unchanged. In other words, the car has been cured, yet the driver has not changed or healed at the core. By the same token, a cancer patient might not live yet in the process of declining and dying to heal at the core. In many ways, healing is always possible.

The biological healing process not only runs in cycles but is also affected by cycles. Cellular, circadian, lunar, menstrual, seasonal, and cosmic cycles superimpose each other, affecting our physiology and healing patterns. If you observe the pain pattern in the repair of an injury, you will experience the pain intensity rising at sunrise and sunset. As teenagers know, pimples get worse to get better. They have to come to a head to burst and then heal. The more we fuss with them, the worse they get. Of course, as a teenager, it is hard to resist not popping them. Once in the last stage of the cycle, to get the white, dried-up pus out, a little nudge appears irresistible. We all have been there.

Fluing is a process that first gets worse, only to improve once the fever has done its job. At the onset, we know something is coming on. Then we feel ill, weak, icky, and tired. Soon we want to rest and lie down, a good thing, as this is how we heal. Finally, the fever rages on. All our joints may hurt. Another day or so, and we are back to par, with a greater appreciation for our general health.

Sinus and respiratory infections will start with clear mucus, which turns yellow in a few days. With time, yellow mucus turns green. Then it is mixed with blood, a sign that healing is taking place, only to return with time to yellow and a clear color as the cycle completes itself.

I have observed our daughter Tanya going through bronchopneumonia, coughing for six weeks on end, only to crescendo into a healing crisis with a rapid-fire cathartic cough that lasted a whole day. That night she fell asleep exhausted. She woke up the next morning as if nothing had ever happened. These six weeks of a coughing spree healed something very deep inside her. We had adopted her at the sensitive age of two and a half. Three consecutive separations deeply wounded her. First from her biological mother, then from the orphanage staff, and finally from her foster mother.

Her behavior since her adoption had been to nudge constantly. She rejected happiness and affection. This was an attempt to test our love for her. Her emotional centers were shut down; her posture stooped forward and caved in to close her ribcage and chest, the treasure chest of emotions, to numb herself. The cough expectorated this postural pattern and emotional behavior by breaking open her chest. I saw that a physical illness was actually her path to emotional healing. If we had suppressed and interfered with the process, who knows what may have manifested for her? The trust and love with which we surrounded her allowed her to be at peace with what was happening. There was no fear or anxiety on our part to be perceived by her. The only care she received was love, adjustment, and gentle massage of her body and feet.

Going back to all the experiences I had with my own body and the ones I witnessed in others, were they isolated remarkable occurrences? Perhaps, but it demonstrates the amazing capacity we all have within.

Number One Priority

If there is one thing, one word that impacted my life more profoundly than any other, it is health. It turned me inward spiritually, mentally, emotionally, and physically once I understood its critical and vital importance.

At the risk of sounding like a broken record played by nearly all health and wellness practitioners, health is our most valuable asset. Health is, and ought to be, our number one priority and responsibility. All the riches in the world cannot buy anyone health. It is our most precious possession. It is and should be, if not already, our top priority. The PTA meetings, soccer games, and church services, among countless other priorities, have to take a back seat because, without our health, none of those important life events can take place. Health is truly number one.

Interestingly, when people lose their health, suddenly it becomes their top priority. There is almost nothing they would not do, places they would not travel to, money they would not spend; none are issues any longer if they could get but a glimmer of hope that their now precious health could be regained. Once we realize the truth of this, then it makes absolute sense to make health Number One on our list of commitments.

Now the irony is that even when we dedicate ourselves fully to our health, there are no guarantees, as countless unknown factors are involved. We can only do our best and hope for the best. Yet within the choice of making health our top involvement, a positive inner transformation takes place. We become intensely alert, aware, and conscious.

So what is health? It sounds ridiculous to have to ask this question when health has been talked about for thousands of years . . . or has it? What is quite sure is that there is much misconception and misunderstanding as to what health actually is. To clear the fog, it may be easier to start with what health is not.

Health is not the absence of symptoms, sickness, disease, or infirmity. In other words, we can be healthy and express symptoms, feeling quite miserable, as strange as this may seem. Of course, we can also be healthy and feel wonderful, vital, and energetic. In some ways, health is not really about how we feel. We could feel either fully alive or quite under the weather and, in both instances, be healthy.

The World Health Organization defines health as a state of optimum physical, mental, emotional, and social wellbeing and not merely the absence of symptoms, disease, or infirmity.

A person being challenged with flu symptoms can still be healthy, with a body functioning at the optimum level, doing its very best to handle the new genetic and/or immunologic upgrade. Someone experiencing the process labeled arthritis may be healthy. Their body may function at optimum potential, being on the upswing of reversing the *arthriting* process.

My friend Jason Holdahl D.C., paralyzed from the chest down after diving headfirst into a shallow river, is still healthy, independent of his handicap. Actually, he is so healthy that he uses only suppositories to allow bowel discharge. That is quite rare for paraplegics who use many drugs to deal with their situation. Indeed health is independent of symptoms, disease, or infirmity.

What health actually is, is a state of optimum wellbeing. For that to happen, all of the systems, organs, tissues, and cells of the body need to function at their best. So health deeply depends on how we function, not just on how we feel. Bodily functions are regulated by the flow of life energy-information coursing throughout the nerve system. This flow of energy-information is carried by life force.

The function of the life force is to animate, organize, control, coordinate, adapt, heal, and repair all body systems, organs, tissues, and cells. It does that primarily through the brain, spinal cord, nerve system, and genetic makeup.

Life force encoded with information flows over, through, and into nerves via nerve impulses that reach every tissue cell in the body. Nerve impulses end in neurotransmitters that can reach all cells via chemical messenger agents.

We are all given a deck of cards called our genetic potential. What activates DNA's potential is the life force flowing throughout our body. Contrary to popular belief, the nerve system and genetic makeup do not control the body. Life energy controls and activates the chromosomes and all other organs. If we were to doubt that, we just need to remind ourselves that once dead, we still have a brain, nerve system, organs, tissues, cells, chromosomes, and DNA, yet we are not alive.

So health depends on the amount and free flow of life force or chi. It is a product of the quality and quantity of message-laden life energy flowing throughout the body. A newborn, as a rule, is full of vitality and life. An elderly person, toward the end of life, is depleted of life force. The same skin scratch will take a day or two to heal for a baby and weeks for an older person; the healing rate depends on the amount of life energy or vitality available for the task. One of the primary keys to health is a free current of life force. A factor that most are unaware of.

Many will consider nutrition a key element in health, and it certainly is a very important factor. The devastating effects of fast and junk foods on populations are a vivid reminder of the crucial component that food has in the health picture. When I left France in 1973, obesity was rare. Ten years later, following the introduction of fast foods and sodas, the picture changed with a new demographic of obesity. This phenomenon repeated itself worldwide. We all have heard the slogan: You are what you eat. As with many slogans, this may not be the full truth. Actually, after what we eat, we are what we digest, absorb, and metabolize. The best nutrition in the world will be worthless if you have pressure on the brain stem, interfering with neural control of gastrointestinal functions. Actor Christopher Reeve, who was paralyzed from the neck down, is a perfect example of that. Most of his bodily functions were impaired as spinal-cord compression in his cervical spine interfered with messages from the brain. A clear pathway between the brain and body is a crucial component of proper function and health. Even Superman was not exempted from this fact.

There are basically seven essential ingredients to health: Food/Nutrition, Fluid/water, air/O2, exercise, rest, sleep, and life force. Humans can live about forty days without food. We can survive about ten days without water or fluids. Death may follow within about four minutes without oxygen. We can spend a lifetime without exercise, being a couch potato. Rest and sleep deprivation will begin to visibly break down the body within a month. But, one instant without life force, and we are a goner. Life force is the most essential ingredient of health and life. This fact is still mostly ignored by society and most health professions, as the life force is the most misunderstood force on earth.

Health depends primarily on the integrity of the system that fuels the life force in our body: the brain, neuro-spinal system, and nerves. Chiropractic, acupuncture, bodywork, energy work, reiki, Rolfing, and Heller work, among others, are all disciplines designed to free the flow of life force in the body. Many are used from an allopathic therapeutic model. Some are practiced from a proactive, vitalistic wellness model.

All would be better off serving humanity by practicing the latter. It is better to turn on the light than to fight the darkness. Much is saved in dollars and suffering by staying well in the first place. So much potential is available when we are thriving rather than being in defense, survival mode. Humanity is at its very best when fully expressed, vital, alive, healthy, and creative. It is well worth spending time, money, and energy to fulfill our commitment to make our health the ultimate priority.

In short, regularly engaging in truly positive, proactive healthy behaviors and wellbeing care are key to making health our first priority. This type of care is what humanity needs to move toward; it is the future. Pro-active wellbeing care is the next upcoming model, set to replace the present sickness and disease-care system. Everyone can benefit when embracing this new mindset and behavior, as it makes a world of difference in life.

Health Certificate

In 1983 Jane and I decided to adopt. Jane had had five miscarriages, most likely caused by a missing thyroid, which was removed at an early age. Her thyroid malfunction possibly was caused by a neurological impairment following a pommel-horse gymnastic fall. It damaged her lower cervical and upper dorsal spine with consequential nerve flow impairment to her thyroid from a subluxation. As a result, her slow metabolism would not allow her to sustain pregnancies.

We were not going to push nature. Neither of us was dead set on having our own child. We just wanted a child. We were not attached. As Kahlil Gibran wrote in the poetic verses of *The Prophet*: "Your children are not your children, they are the sons and daughters of Life's longing for itself. They come through you but not from you. And though they are with you, yet they belong not to you." We took that to heart. Why not adopt when so many orphans need parents?

The decision to adopt was made appropriately on Valentine's Day. We connected with an agency called Love The Children, located in Bucks County, PA. What a perfect name, we felt. Mary, an orphan woman herself who was never adopted due to her unusual looks, headed the Agency.

She was a heart worn on her sleeve woman trapped in an ugly physique. It is unfortunate that in choosing a child from an orphanage lineup, most will choose the cover of the book over its unknown content. Such is life. As it turned out, Mary was an extraordinary, exceptional, big-hearted, and loving human being who had dedicated her life to finding suitable parents for orphans. She had turned rejection and abandonment into gifts. She was a powerhouse to be reckoned with. An inspiration to transcend obstacles.

The adoption application had many choices and options to which we chose *any*. Any race, any age, any color, any sex, any religion, any physical condition, etc. For every question that was asked, we checked any. Why? Because we felt that once we make love, we have little to no choices as to what might come down the chute. There is a deep truth in that. So we decided to open ourselves to the Universe, giving us whatever may come. We chose to trust life implicitly and fully. We chose to surrender to life and what it might have in store for us.

In order to adopt children, one had to produce a Health Certificate officially provided by an M.D. So, for the first time since 1973, we entered the medical world and subjected ourselves to complete medical exams. Jane came through with flying colors. I, on the other hand, did not fare as well.

I had blood in my urine for a few months. I was not concerned. I was at peace with it. When it came time to handle my urine sample, it looked like pink grapefruit juice. The nurse took it without comment. When the M.D. finally entered the exam room, he asked right away: "Have you noticed anything unusual in your urine lately?" In that instant, my mind flashed to a comic book caption with a man taking a leak, looking down at the reddish urine stream, as this is how men urinate, and thinking: "No, nothing unusual, just bloody urine coming out." So I replied with restrained laughter, "Yes, I have been urinating blood for a few months now."

Hearing that, the M.D. took an actual step backward with a frightened look on his face. "What? Do you realize it could be due to a tumor in your bladder, kidneys, or prostate cancer that has metastasized? We first need to do an IVP or Intravenous Pyelogram as soon as possible. I cannot sign a health certificate until we get to the bottom of this." I left somewhat concerned when I had previously been at peace with what had been happening, with full trust in my body.

So an IVP was scheduled at the Flemington, N.J. hospital a week or so later. An iodine-containing contrast material was injected through a vein in my arm. The contrast material collected in my kidneys, ureters, and bladder sharply defined its appearance in bright white on the X-ray images. Radiographs were taken of my kidneys. First, the usual front-to-back and then a side view. A long interval took place while I remained on the frigid X-ray table. The technician returned with props, wedges, and pillows, stating that another view was necessary. I was then propped up in a quite unusual position. Instantly, I thought they had found something. *There must be a tumor*, I thought. I asked to view the X-rays, for after all, they were of my own body and as a D.C. I had training in radiology. This was in 1983, and I was aggressively denied the request. The result will be sent to the referring physician, I was told. The medical world back then was still antagonistic to chiropractic. Thankfully, the new generation of M.D.s is, as a rule, much more open.

So Jane and I left the hospital and drove back to New Hope, PA. On the way, we were a bit concerned and in a downtrodden mood. We sat for breakfast at Mother's Restaurant, a local favorite, on charming Main Street in New Hope. On the ride back, we had made a joint decision that, if indeed it was cancer, we would sell our home, stop practicing and move to a tropical island. We would eat great fresh, healthy food, play, have fun, enjoy life, make love, and let the outcome be whatever it might be. We were not going for chemo, surgery, or radiation.

Weeks later, we received a phone call. The voice asked if I was Arno Burnier and, upon confirmation, stated, "This is Doctor so-and-so from the Lambertville medical clinic." My heart began to beat faster. Then the M.D. stated, "Your results are negative." I sank for a moment. Negative, that's bad. Then I caught myself. *Wait! Negative, of course, that is good, positive news.*

At that very moment, as I was elated, the doctor's voice came back and stated, "Yes, but this is not conclusive; we need to schedule you for a cystoscopy." This is a test where a scope is inserted through the urethra of the penis to take a look inside the bladder. At that point, I replied, "Before I met you, I was fine. Since then, I have been down and depressed; I feel a presence in my lower abdomen and am still urinating blood. You decide whether or not I have the right to adopt children." And with that, I hung up the phone.

Right there and then, I took back the very power I had surrendered to an outside authority. A few weeks later, we received the health certificate through the mail. The adoption application process was complete. I kept urinating blood until June of that year and never had another episode.

I will never know what had been there. But what I know is that, medically, doctors were concerned. I was not. What I know is that in medicine, there is a constant search for what might be wrong. It is, from their perspective, a legitimate chase. It can be a seemingly endless expedition, with inconclusive multiple diagnostic options. Medically, they nearly always leave you with fear or put the what-if doubt into your mind with the follow-up, *Just in case...* What if it is serious? Just in case it is this or that, we shall dig deeper and do these tests. These results are not conclusive; we need to do more tests. I was not going to have any of that.

I trusted my body and its inner capacity to heal and experienced a positive outcome. Many reading these words might think this was irresponsible. To me, in contrast, this was taking full responsibility and accountability for my life and health choices. My body is mine and mine alone. I have a fundamental right to decide how to take care of it. This is called freedom of choice, a basic human right. A right that has come under attack many times, taken away by court decisions, and more recently wiped out with the COVID-19 pandemic vaccination enforcement.

Who knows where that other road might have taken me? Maybe there was a tumor in my bladder; maybe there was early cancer. Yet, we know today that most of us have cancer in our bodies nearly all the time; nothing to worry about because our immune system has the knowledge and capacity to deal with it outside our awareness. If my body created my kidneys and bladder out of one cell, the fertilized ovum, without any outside professional help, then it is logical to me that it might have the capacity to heal and repair it. Having chosen trust over fear, I experienced the outcome, physiology, biochemistry, and immune response of trust.

What gave me such trust in the innate intelligence of my own body? The very thought that every part of me was designed, created, and developed from a hyper microscopic dot invisible to the naked eye. All of me; all my cells, tissues, organs, systems, and parts originate from that one single cell, the human egg. This is truly a bewildering process, mystery, and miracle, no matter how science has been able to explain the embryological steps and processes involved. The fact remains it is an unimaginable feat far beyond our intellect to comprehend.

To me, this spells that the knowledge, intelligence, and power to design an entire human being was locked inside that hyper-microscopic dot. Surely that power did not abandon me the moment I was born by suddenly leaving my body. Certainly, that intelligence has the capacity to repair and heal me. Actually, it does it all the time in what is called cellular replacement, as all our tissues, cells, and organs replace themselves constantly.

It's funny how we do not question a cut, a broken bone, a torn muscle, or a sprained ligament to heal over time, yet when it comes to internal organs, we frequently deny that capacity. Is it possible that the fear or trust created in my mind could alter the physiological outcome? The mind is powerful and can be directed in either direction: negative or positive, with potentially different outcomes.

Regarding the health certificate necessary for adoption and frequently other situations such as immigration and marriage, I really questioned its validity. We all know of people being given a clean bill of health only to fall over a few days later from a heart attack, a stroke, or some severe pathology undetected during the check-up. Most of what is happening in our body is beyond the detection of a physical exam. Many pathologies are silent for years before becoming symptomatic. Of course, I understand the desire to be cautious and avoid a potential adoptive parent with an infectious or terminal disease with the imminent risk of death. Yet should that prevent one from marrying, immigrating, or adopting? Do we know what the future holds? Could a vibrant, healthy, and vital adoptive parent die in a car crash while one with a pathology heals quickly? No one knows what life has in store for us.

Here, I am questioning the special authority granted exclusively to the medical profession to produce health certificates along with other certificates. Who and when was such legal power given to them? Is it possible that other healthcare professionals might have a better insight into the inner state of health of a human being? Could it be that those health professionals who focus on true health and wellbeing have a better handle on assessing the health level of a person? If we want light in our homes, should we go to people who study darkness? If we want health, shouldn't we go to professionals and doctors who study health? Shouldn't this legal authority of producing a health certificate be at least extended to other so-called alternative or holistic health professionals rather than remaining the sole privilege of M.D.s?

Adoption

It was late May of 1983 that Jane and I received a phone call from Mary, head of the Love The Children adoption agency in Quakertown, PA. We were in the middle of a busy morning at the office. Jane, being at the front desk, took the call:

"Hello, Mrs. Jane Burnier?"

"Yes."

"We have children," said Mary.

"Children? But we had asked for a child, a baby, not children." Jane replied, stunned yet elated.

(*You don't always get what you want; you can always get what you need!* Lyrics from the Rolling Stones.)

After a pause, Mary's voice came back, "The babies are brother and sister; we do not want to separate them. Would you take them?"

"Let me ask my husband," replied Jane, being very considerate.

She walked over to the adjusting room and, with excitement, said, "They have children, a boy and a girl; they are siblings!" I looked up from my stooped adjusting position as I was checking the cervicals of a client and paused. Then I said, "Wow, ask if one of them is out of diapers!"

After all, as a man, you need to have some control over the situation. To this day, I can't even believe that I asked that question. But I was as stunned as Jane was. Two children at once… that was a surprise. The prospect of jumping right out of being a couple, with all the freedom it gives, into being the parents of two babies was a bit concerning and overwhelming. I know that regardless of the answer from Mary, we would happily take those two little

Souls. Jane did ask and came back with a huge radiant smile, "The little girl is out of diapers and potty trained."

"Great, we will take them," I said.

At that moment, I felt a shiver up my spine and a blast of energy filling my entire body. I still can't remember what I did next with the person on the adjusting table. What I recalled is that she got up from the table, beaming with joy, and gave me a big loving hug. I floated with a bursting heart, full of love, for the rest of the day. The thought of rescuing two little babies, siblings to boot, filled my deep hunger to protect and rescue the less fortunate. Again being open to life brought unimaginable blessings.

Vacation Time

At that juncture, Jane and I decided to take our last vacation as a couple, unattached to children. We regularly took two weeks' vacation every three months from the practice. I found that such a break was highly beneficial in breaking patterns and resetting communications, always leading to a refreshed start in my practice. Paulo Coelho wrote in *Manual of The Warrior of Light*: "He [The warrior of Light] withdraws his forces from the battlefield and allows himself a respite." A very sound insight that we took seriously.

So we left in late August for a two-week motorcycle trip throughout France. At the time, I was riding a crotch rocket, a Yamaha 350 RZ water-cooled two-stroke fury of a bike. The entire luggage we had was the tank bag, a 12" x 8" x 5" filled with some tools, cleaning products, one sexy outfit for Jane, a toilet kit, and tightly folded rain gear.

Jane was not so thrilled to spend two weeks on a bike with no luggage. I could not blame her. After some deliberations and compromises on my part, she relented on the condition we would stay in Castle Hotels. Those are beautiful estates entirely refurbished with modern amenities into exquisite 6-10 bedroom hotels on stunning grounds, dating from the time of the Kings, Dukes, and Queens of France. Of course, I accepted, thrilled at the prospect of staying in gorgeous romantic places. No problem; we had the best of three worlds: Riding with Jane through the beautiful French countryside on my bike, staying in Castle Hotels, and eating fantastic food. Can it get any better? What's not to love?

We had perfect weather, an amazing trip, gourmet meals, and memorable accommodations; we were flying high at the prospect and anticipation of receiving our babies. We had one picture of them given to us by the adoption agency. Every time we looked at that picture, our hearts melted. Two little tender beings. The little girl, with one fist closed tight, standing fierce, determined, protective, shielding her little brother who looked so pure, innocent, and vulnerable, yet powerful. Still, today, when we look at that picture, we tear up with a swell of love in our hearts.

Every evening, Jane turned heads in the dining rooms of Castle Hotels. She had a black mini dress off the shoulder, fishnet stockings, high heels, and a beautiful necklace and earrings. I sported my grey riding jeans, a black t-shirt, ankle-high boots, and a silver necklace. Since we moved to a different Castle every day, it was all we needed to look elegant and sexy, like celebrities. I have to say that these Castle Hotels staff sometimes looked perplexed as we arrived on a crotch rocket with barely any luggage. They did wonder about our magical transformation when we arrived for dinner. We were living it up.

On the last day of our trip, we were at my mother's apartment on 5 rue Mirabeau in the elegant 16th district of Paris. It was midnight when the phone rang. My mother answered but did not understand the person on the line speaking English. She handed me the phone. It was Love The Children, the adoption agency, telling us that the children were in the air. We were shocked, almost panicked. Prior to our departure from the USA, we had specifically told the Agency we would not be back until September 7th, therefore, only to send the children anytime thereafter. The voice on the other end of the line replied: "Yes, we understand, but it is already September 7th in South Korea!" Pure grace and hyper synchronicity were about to befall us.

Our babies were now flying from Seoul to Chicago, then JFK airport in New York. We attempted to sleep that night but were too excited to drop off. On the morning of September 7th, we took our scheduled flight from Charles de Gaulle airport to JFK. We arrived at our gate about 40 minutes before the babies, in the same concourse and gate where our children would arrive.

We had gone to get a bite to eat and to meet the rest of Jane's family, who had driven from Bucks County, PA, to join the happy reception. The location of the concourse's nearest restaurant to our gate was near the room assigned for the transfer of adopted children to their respective parents.

Quickly, I left our table to walk, with my father-in-law, back to his car at the airport parking lot. I wanted to drop the tank bag to have my hands and arms free to receive the children. When we closed the car trunk, my brother-in-law, Russ, and his wife, Mary Ellen, pulled into an open spot two spaces to our left. Needless to say, I was blown away, considering the tens of thousands of cars parked there. What about the timing of it? They had driven two and a half hours in traffic to get there just as we had gotten to my father-in-law's car. Pure luck? Coincidence? I think not; just the pure magic of the flow of life.

Now the four of us walked back into the concourse and sat down for refreshments. The big moment was near. We were all beaming with excitement and anticipation. Jane and her sister Mary Ellen went to the lady's room. While in the bathroom, a Korean woman, holding a little girl in her arms, recognized Jane from the picture on the adoption file and turned to her, saying, "Mrs. Jane, your daughter has to go shishi." Which in Korean means: "Your daughter has to go pee!" And that is how Jane was introduced to our daughter, Tanya. She was two and a half. Scared, traumatized, tense, jet-lagged, having traveled across more than half the world, looking at strange faces with eyes and Caucasian features she had never seen, speaking a language she could not understand. We must have looked frightening to her. Total strangers. Alien beings.

Of course, Mary Ellen burst out of the bathroom to wave at me, sending the message, "They are here. They have arrived. Go get them!" We all sprang up to rush to the allocated reception room. As we entered, another Korean woman walked right up to me. She was holding a bundle in her arms. She faced me, pointed at me, and said, "Booboo, this is Appa." Pronounced Oppa, which in Korean means, "Booboo, this is your dad."

My new son gazed right into my eyes for a moment. Then in a calm gesture, he took his pacifier right out of his mouth and put it into mine. I melted in that instant. Tears of joy, love, tenderness, compassion, and empathy, all wrapped in a flood of emotions, poured out of me.

I sobbed hard with a giant grin on my face from the rush of pure love that sprang from my heart to this tiny being. I felt the large empty black hole in my abdomen closed for the first time in five years. Since my break-up and divorce from my first wife, I felt like a cannonball had shot through me, leaving a gaping hole, which left me emotionless. Yes, I could think of my emotions, yet not feel them.

That single act from this innocent one-year-old healed five years of emotional wounds. To this day, it is this picture, this moment, that I flash in my mind to open my heart and enter a loving space while adjusting in my practice. I knew then that the physiology of unconditional love could entrain others' physiology vibrationally. Indeed love is powerful. Whether it was the love I self-generated from my heart toward our new son or the love this tiny being extended to his new father is irrelevant. Pure unconditional love was in the field. It bound us together and healed me.

Love is The Power

Love heals. Love is the answer. All you need is love, love, love is all you need, as the lyrics of the Beatles remind us. Too often, those are statements we take for granted or shout in such a way they become mundane, cliché, or even corny. Yet I have experienced first-hand the reality of the power of unconditional love, innocently expressed by our adopted son, Mr. Boo, as we came to nickname him. This one-year-old, who happened to arrive on his birthday in the innocent act of sticking his pacifier in my mouth after peering into my Soul for a long moment, had restored wholeness to my emotionally broken being. He had never seen me. I must have looked to him like a total stranger with unfamiliar Caucasian facial features. He had traveled halfway around the world after being abandoned three times. Once by his birth parents, once by the caregivers of the adoption agency, and lastly again by his foster mother. He was traumatized, to say the least. His gesture was an act of trust, acceptance of me as his new father. It cracked my heart open. In that instant, emotional healing took place within me as love poured out of me toward this innocent child. Love had been inside all along, yet it was locked behind protective armor.

A pacifier unlocked it through the hand of a one-year-old. What a metaphor! A pacifier restored peace within my being. What I had read in books on healing and spontaneous remission, what was still theoretical to me, no matter how good it sounded, had become a lived experience and reality. Love is what heals.

Today science has shown that the human heart's electromagnetic field forms a Taurus, a butterfly-shaped field that extends three to ten feet outside the human body in all directions. This field is 5,000 times greater than the one of the brain. It is the most powerful source of electromagnetic energy in the human body. The heart's electrical field is about 60 times greater in amplitude than the electrical activity generated by the brain and more than 100 times greater in strength. Interestingly, the shape of the heart's electromagnetic field is identical in shape, yet not in size, to the electromagnetic field of the earth and then of our solar system, our galaxy, and the universe. In brief, when our heart is fully blown open, we align with the Universe or Universe. In this alignment, the depth of the reality of the power of love to create a miracle is amazing.

Among many others, I had such an experience in the summer of 2019 when my heart overflowed with love, empathy, and compassion for a deeply broken and destroyed woman. Among all the thousandths that I have met, known, worked with, adjusted, played with, and journeyed through life, I have yet to meet a human being who was so utterly damaged.

For the first time in her 70 years of life, she experienced a ray of sunshine in her being. The sun of unconditional love was piercing through the dark clouds that engulfed her. That ray of light became a soothing warmth that began to melt the ice of her heart that was shattered at the tender age of three. This broken woman, with astonishing courage, plowed through life in spite of her demons. She endured rejection, blame, and toxic venom from her children. She faced the deep sorrow of being prohibited from visiting her grandchildren. She endured witnessing her own children's painful and broken life. The guilt of not having been capable of caring for and supporting them in their childhood, as the mother in her would have loved to, had been eating at her for years. The toxic rage, angst, and anger that oozed out of her body, covered with open, gaping emotional wounds, impacted all who came in her proximity. She endured not knowing love, not experiencing love, and not being able to receive love for 67 years, as her being and heart were shattered as a young girl. To her, love was only a word, a mental construct, and an act to play.

The only two romantic relationships she had experienced triggered epileptic-like trashing the moment sexual penetration took place. This was followed by an immediate repressed urge to stab and murder the man she had just bedded. As a prostitute, fully dis-associating, she bore the harsh judgments, debasing looks, insults, finger-pointing, brutalities, violations, and abuses that prostitutes frequently are subjected to. She had the courage and fortitude to keep on living when darkness was her only companion.

On her 70th birthday, she was touched by a ray of love, a new beginning. The first brick to reconstruct her shattered SELF. I had taken her to a quiet hotel outside Berlin for a few days together. We reconnected after being apart, as I was living in the USA and she was in Germany. She opened up and spoke incessantly. She had been living alone for years on end. She needed a listening ear. It was wonderful to be able to provide her with one.

What frequently men can do to women is hard to comprehend. Women, the embodiment of the mother from which they were born, the mother who raised them, breastfed them, loved them, listened to them, comforted them, are the subject, the world over, of violence, abuse, mistreatment, rape, bestial violations, degradations, enslavements, and murders. The ripple consequences of such actions are frequently trans-generational.

Whatever men have done to women, they have done to their own mothers, sisters, and daughters. So much healing is needed in this world. Men must wake up to the reality of what a woman inherently is. They need to look into the innocent, tender, delicate, open, loving, joyful, trusting, caring, and sensitive eyes of any three-year-old girl. They must connect to the inner divine energy of the feminine, absorb it, ingest it, and remember it. By searing their brain with the hot iron of that connection, they will never forget. They will approach women with the utmost respect, care, gentleness, and tenderness. They will awaken within a volcano of love that will dissolve all primal, primitive, and bestial impulses. True love will be the reward.

This woman is my sister Florence, my heroine, my best friend, my unconditional love, and, unbeknown to her, my mentor from the moment I began to perceive but crumbs of her history when I was young. On those days outside Berlin in the summer of 2019, I ate the entire cookie, not just a few crumbs. Flo revealed to me all her violations, in great detail, in a cathartic release triggered by love. I choose to ingest her pain and suffering, digest it in the fire of love, compassion, and empathy that sprang from the inner chamber of my heart.

LOVE, LOVE, LOVE is the ointment and salve, the enzyme that began to heal my sister. Over the course of the following years, she blossomed. Relationships with her children and grandchildren were restored. Her life and herself began the healing climb out of the valley of her despair.

On the third evening of our stay, as we were lying in bed, she turned toward me and asked, "Is my face ugly? Am I ugly?" A piercing, blunt pain plunged into my heart when her question landed. How to answer such a question? Being dishonest and denying the truth to avoid further harming her did not feel right. Internally, silently, I saw her as the gorgeous young, vibrant girl she was in our childhood. With tears falling down my face, I replied, "Yes, you are ugly when your face is distorted with demented facial expressions that surface whenever you are triggered." The room stood still. A thick silence permeated the space between us. We fell asleep with deep, sad, and heavy energy hovering in the room.

The next morning, the silence was palpable between us. After our showers, I asked her to lie on her back with her head at the feet of the bed. Kneeling on the floor, without a word, and with all the love in my heart and hands, I gave her the softest, most gentle, soothing, loving facial massage I could bring out of me. I wanted to infuse her with the touch of angels if at all possible. The whole time I held in my mind the memory of Flo as a young girl with a radiant face full of life. When we were done, we stood up, and I walked her, with my arm over her shoulder, to the full-length mirror in the corner of the room. She was glowing. Her face was relaxed. It radiated light.

"This is you. This is who you are inside; a beautiful, loving, radiant being of love. Always remember that. You are so beautiful. This is how I have always seen you, your entire life," I said. Touch and soothing, loving words morphed into a healing transformation, a metamorphosis. Love heals. I know that at the core of my being.

In that moment, in that hotel room, core healing began for my sister, triggered by the unconditional love that sipped out of my wide-open heart.

LOVE, LOVE, LOVE, is indeed the only answer.

We know that Christ would walk amongst a crowd, and people would heal. The paralytic could walk, the blind could see, and the deaf could hear. So many so-called miracles would take place, which is actually the normal consequence of being bathed in the field and the energy of pure unconditional love emanated by the hearts of enlightened beings. It is said that Christ's field of energy extended for miles outside his body. People were attuned to him and could feel his presence at a far distance. Many naturally born healers and health professionals can entrain, through loving presence and a wide open heart, the physiology of those seeking help and healing.

When we truly get to experience and witness the truth of those love slogans or clichés, the depth of the reality of the power of love to create a miracle is amazing. In my early years in practice, I read the beautiful novel by Thea Alexander titled *2150 A.D.* on the power of love to transform. I think it came back to me in full force years later.

Whenever I witnessed a so-called miracle taking place in my office, I could always associate it with my state of being.

I was fully open-hearted. Usually, people have brought me a compelling, tragic story about their journey in the healthcare system. Their trials and tribulations, combined with their suffering, often brought me to tears. I felt deep empathy and compassion. My heart would open wide. I was more present than ever. I felt love pouring out of me toward them as I adjusted them.

In allowing the flow of love, I told my clients I could not heal them; only their own bodies had that power. This clarification empowered them with their own healing potential. It fully liberated me from any expectation on their part. It removed all pressure on me to attempt to fix them. I was clear to myself to be unattached to the outcome. This allowed me to be unstained by outside influences. I could be pure in my intention and assessment of clearing the neuro-spinal system.

I refused to let any expression of symptoms by clients enter my consciousness. I knew that if I did, it would influence my analysis, perception, and care. We are not our symptoms or disease. It might be what is happening in us, yet not who we are. By seeing them as a whole rather than broken parts, I could hold a loving presence.

The flow of love between a practitioner and clients is crucial. Unfortunately, many health practitioners are great givers yet poor receivers. They feel in charge and in control as long as they are giving. The vulnerability necessary to open up and receive frequently scares them. When the cycle of giving and receiving is broken, we violate natural law. When I identified this problem in myself, I realized it was a block to serving humanity. I started to work on myself to open up. I began to let others give to me when appropriate.

I authentically showed my humanity and vulnerability. Soon thereafter, my practice took another leap upward. Doing so removed an invisible block to my capacity to care for and serve my clientele. The pressure to always be up, jovial, happy, and excited, encouraged by many consultants, coaches, and seminar leaders, has value. Yet, if used without vulnerability and authenticity, it becomes fake, hindering growth.

The free flow of love is essential to healing in and out of the office. Kelly, my sister-in-law, and I would drive every morning to the office from New Hope to Yardley, an 11-mile drive. On the way, we would talk about people we hadn't seen in a while. We were truly curious, interested, and concerned about them. We did this in a genuine way, with love and caring. Invariably that day or within a few days, these people would call to ask for an appointment. Some would just walk in, in spite of the fact they may not have been in for months or years. We used to call this psychic recall. The love, concern, and care we have for them reached them at a distance.

Many of us have experienced thinking lovingly about a friend we had not spoken with in a while, only to have them call that day. The reverse is also true. How many of us have reached out to a friend or relative only to hear, "I was just thinking about you; too funny you called."

Love is not a one-way street. It is not just the love that doctors and healers give out that facilitates healing in others. It is also the love we may self-generate and give to others. Elderly people, who have been ridden with arthritis to the degree that their hands were clawed nearly shut, have been seen fully opening their hands in a supple way while given a pet to caress and love.

I want to impart again the words of Ida Reed, my brother-in-law's mother: "Love, Love, Love." In the last year of her life, it was all she would welcome us with and leave us with whenever we visited her. One of my good friends, an amazing chiropractor, Annie Claude, D.C., who practices in Lake Saint-Jean, Quebec, signs all her letters and emails with: Love, it is easy to love. She is a bundle of radiant love.

Love can easily be expressed through touch, an open heart, and genuine words. The late Jim Parker, D.C., the charismatic leader of the chiropractic profession and a visionary, repeatedly shared, "Love and Service is my first technique." What a simple and powerful concept. In healthcare, it hits the nail on the head. Yet it does not have to stop with health practitioners. This approach to life can permeate every aspect of society, especially in the workplace, within businesses and corporations where it is greatly needed. Each one of us can live with Love and Service as our first motto. We can all ask ourselves, "What would love do in this moment or situation?" Easier said than done, yet a worthwhile mantra and aspiration to follow.

Birth

Chapter 6: Greens and Fromages

Hyper Synchronicity

Many travelers have experienced a higher level of synchronicity while on vacation. Could it be that we are living more in the present moment, free of worries, concerns, or routines? In that state of being, we live on the edge of discovery, with curiosity and alertness. We surrender to life and the moment. We access life's flow.

In regard to the numerology and timing of the arrival of our adopted children, was it all luck? Just a mere chance? Or was it life perfectly orchestrated by hyper synchronicity?

- We had surrendered fully to whatever the Universe would give us.

- On the adoption application, we checked *any* to all the questions. Physical condition: any Race; any Gender; any Age; any Etcetera.

- The children were abandoned on my birthday.

- They arrived on September 7th, our adopted son Boo's birthday and also Jane's mother's birthday.

- Our daughter Tanya's birthday is also Jane's younger sister Kelly's birthday

- They arrived at the same concourse and gate as our plane from Paris.

- They arrived on September 7th, the same day as our scheduled return flight from Europe to the United States.

- Russ, my brother-in-law, parked his car two spaces away at the very same time we had just closed the trunk of the car where I had dropped the tank bag.

- The children arrived 40 minutes after the arrival of our scheduled flight. Not too soon, not too late that we would have to wait anxiously for hours. Just enough time to settle, get something to eat, rid ourselves of our tiny luggage and be ready to welcome and embrace them with wide-open hearts and arms.

The very best yet is that throughout childhood, and now in adulthood, they both love all the things we love: travel, adventure, sports, health and fitness, fashion, gourmet food, the outdoors, life, and spirituality. They are both, like Jane and me, entrepreneurs with a love of nature. They could not be more our children than if we had conceived them.

Jane and I feel that these two little ones came through us by the grace of the Universe. Was the way they came to us pure hyper synchronicity? Was the perfect timing and numerology due to our full acceptance of Jane's condition, preventing her from sustaining pregnancies to full term? Was it because we had opened ourselves fully with total surrender to the Universe in the adoption process?

I believe so. How many times have I rerun these events in my mind?

What would have actually happened if we had called the Adoption Agency and told them:

"We want to adopt a child, but make sure it is abandoned on my birthday, and if there is more than one child, make sure the other baby's birthday coincides with my sister-in-law's birthday; she is sensitive about that. Also, if there is more than one, we want a boy and a girl. One out of diapers, please. We are going on a vacation in Europe. Can you please arrange for our children to arrive on the day of our return, forty minutes after we land, in the same concourse, at the same gate, as this would be very convenient for us since we live two and a half hours away? It will save us a trip. Thank you.

And by the way, make sure they arrive on September 7th, because that needs to be our future son's birthday, which is also Jane's mother's birthday. That would make Helen, Jane's mother, very happy to have her grandson celebrate his birth along with hers until the day she passes. Thank you for doing this for us. We appreciate it greatly."

Fat chance of that happening. Good luck with that one. We all have heard the saying: "If you want to make God laugh, tell Him your plans."

The message here is that total surrender and trust in the Uni-verse may not deliver exactly what we want, yet it delivers what we need and what is best for us. Universal Intelligence organizes the Universe for a reason. It is more than a philosophical construct. It is a practical reality in everyday life.

One of the most astonishing synchronicities, amongst the countless that have blessed my life since 1973, took place in Helen, Georgia. My long-time friend, Jay Komarek, D.C., and I were scouting the hills of the Unicoi State Park in Georgia to find an ideal situation for an outdoor event called The Edge.

We were preparing for a six-day intensive program for health practitioners, students, and laypeople. We had bushwhacked for 48 hours in a dense forest, searching here and there for an ideal place. My bladder was full, so I stopped to pee. Right there in front of me was carved on the tree trunk the word Boo, my son's first name. Jay and I were deep in the forest. Over the last few days, we had passed thousands of trees, zigzagging between them with barely a shoulder's width to go between.

What were the chances of me stopping right there and then? How can I specifically face the side of that one tree in a way I could see the carving? A few degrees off, and I would have never seen Boo written. There was not a single marking anywhere to be seen. This one might have possibly been carved during the Civil War. Who knows? What an extraordinary confirmation it was to both Jay and me that we were in the flow of life.

That afternoon we found the ideal spot on top of a waterfall with a good 40 feet drop. When the event took place, and the roped-in participants had to lean over the void at ninety degrees while straddling the stream, a butterfly would consistently land on their shoes. The sign of transformation. You had to be there to believe it. Again what are the chances of that happening? You can't make that stuff up. Trust, presence, and surrender allow for such synchronicity to show up.

At times hyper synchronicity is baffling. Jane and I were in Italy, entering the city of Florence in the late afternoon rush hour. It was bumper-to-bumper traffic. When traveling, we chose to stay, if at all possible, in non-touristy eclectic boutique hotels. Just in front of us was a VW Jetta with a bumper sticker saying, I'd rather be sailing. We knew nothing about Florence, so I thought the driver might speak English despite the fact he had an Italian license plate. I stepped out of our car, walked to the Jetta, and tapped on the window. It opened.

"Excuse me, do you, by any chance, speak English?"

"Yes, I do. What do you need?" the man replied.

"We are looking for a small hotel that local people would go to for a romantic stay. We are not into touristy hotels."

"Well, right here to your left is an area with boutique hotels. Just take a left at the next corner and look around."

"Thank you, I so appreciate you," I said.

So we took a left, and there it was: Hotel Arno. I went in, but it was full. So we drove another block, and low and behold, here was Hotel Jane. Of course, it was available. I know it feels as if I am making this up. Nope. This is the actual truth.

Many do not experience the perfection of life because to see it being revealed, a great open awareness of all the factors, details, numerology, timing, places, and people involved is needed. One needs to be open, perceive clearly, and act instantly when the message from within comes. Any delay in stepping out of the car would have gotten us out of sync with life's flow. We would have missed the left turn; we would have been way down the road. If I had not listened to the inner voice calling me to ask the man with the I rather be sailing sticker, I would have missed the Jetta!

Life, Light, and Shadow

In my experience, there are two possible ways to live life: in fear or in trust. Of course, one can vacillate from fear to trust and trust to fear; that is a normal pulsation. Yet to always return to trust once the inner battle has raged means embracing trust rather than fear as a touchstone.

Sitting for what seems like an eternity on a bench outside the Nice Airport amid a nervous breakdown/depression solidified for me the choice to embrace trust. My mind went up and down like a yo-yo swinging from fear to trust. I had to have the courage to step into trust, a terrifying edge into the unknown at that moment.

Living in trust requires unwavering surrender and acceptance of whatever comes our way. Acceptance of what is becoming a requirement for such a life. One cannot argue with the reality of what is. We are sure to lose every time. The refusal to accept what has happened leads us into drama with ample wasted energy and emotional pain. The past is the past; the sooner we embrace it, the quicker we unburden ourselves. In this world, whenever we fight reality, we suffer needlessly.

Loving what is happening becomes the mantra of a Soul-driven life. A life lived in trust demands listening to the heart's inner voice, intuition, and gut feelings. Such a life is laden with flow, bliss, joy, unexpected twists and turns, lessons, and challenges. There is ease and guidance in all of it, even in the face of difficulties.

I feel Nelson Mandela has given humanity a clear message in acceptance of, and surrender to, what is. His 27 years in prison, split between Robben Island, Pollsmoor, and Victor Verster Prison, along with his exemplary behavior while gaining the ears and respect of his guards, won him the presidency of South Africa in 1994. This is a piece of history to keep as a reminder of the power of acceptance of life.

I believe we all have three lives we can live and choose from:

The one we were given-our own river of life that is ordained by our Soul, the life we live for others, and the life we intellectually design for ourselves. No right or wrong path. Just the one we choose and the consequences of our choice. I feel blessed that I have chosen the path of the river of my life.

The question is, what part of us chooses? The educated intellect or the innate mind? Of the two, who knows more?

B.J. Palmer, D.C. estimated that millions of brain cells are utilized by our educated intellect and billions of cells by our innate, inborn intelligence. Einstein attributed his intellectual giftedness to using more than 10 percent of his brain. Where does that place the average person? We must decide for ourselves where the answer lies when it comes to listening to the voices within: our intellect or our innate wisdom. One voice is talking relentlessly, and the other whispers when stillness and silence prevail.

To access the life we were designed to live demands an act of volition in which one surrender fully to a power greater than oneself. The power of our Soul. It needs to be accessed, accepted, and given over to. The great spiritual books speak about *Leave everything behind and follow Me.* To live our Soul's life, we must be willing to give it all up to follow the guru within. Giving up our plans, expectations, attachments, desires, and goals allows us to flow with the river of our life. Guidance, signposts, messages, directions, and obvious opportunities will show up, usually in sets of three.

I was returning from a long weekend of travel with multiple public speaking engagements and a two-day seminar. I was full of energy and high on life, yet physically tired. As I was saying goodbye to a friend who had driven me to the airport, we were engaged in conversation. Every time I shifted my body posture during our interaction, the word 'rest' came into my field of vision. The words, interest, restaurant, and restroom appeared, yet only 'rest' was visible as the remaining words were blocked from my sight. What was the message? Pretty obvious!

So frequently, a word will jump out of a page when opening a book, only to show up again a few more times within a short period of time.

Many times it will be a word from the lyric of a song that again will leap a few more times in our awareness as we move down the road of life. These clues are hints to pay attention to. Following the markers of the highway of our life requires alertness and awareness.

Many, if not all, will be put to the task on the path of living our Soul's life. Most will experience the *dark night of the Soul*. Life will test most of us to our very limits to see if we are worth it and can handle such a life. There can even be *crucifixion and resurrection*. There might be a rebirth, so to speak, after everything has been stripped away. Everything we think we are will be removed. As it has been stated, "Seek to be nothing, so you can become everything."

On a moment-by-moment basis, there is expansion into union with spirit and contraction out of union with spirit, just as a photon is one instant a particle and the next a wave of energy. One moment, there is total faith, and the next, suddenly, doubt invades. It is as if a power drill is coming in and out yet still going deeper into the wood. The persistent drilling requires trust, perseverance, and surrender to access the very inner core of our being.

As I have learned and observed in introspection, doubt is the life behind faith. It is doubt that allows a deeper reflection of beliefs and faith; doubt causes our faith to grow. Doubt demands a deeper inquiry into truth. Doubt is the enzyme of transformation from beliefs, to faith, into a state of knowing.

As we come through this door of transformation, we leave certainty behind and stand in clarity. Clarity is brought forth by the light within. Certainty is forceful, intellectual, and laden with ego and hidden doubts. Clarity is powerful, anchored in deep knowing. It is a reflecting pool, free of ripples. Feel the tone, energy, and vibration of *I am clear on this. I have clarity.* Now attune to this, *I am certain about this. I have certainty.* There is a great distinction between the two for the discerning mind.

The Soul-driven life is lived from within. There must be an alignment of Soul, heart, and body. Every aspect of our being must be exposed, known, accepted, and loved, the light as well as the shadow. As the light gets brighter, our shadow grows stronger. To become a whole human being, we must know our darkness and our light. As the circumference of a circle of light grows, so does the contact with the darkness, an inquiry into the dark closets of our being. Soon we uncover that all the darkest traits of humanity live within us in potentiality, a shocking and sobering realization.

After years on this journey, when the Soul is in alignment, shining directly from above, the shadow is no longer visible, just like the summer sun at its zenith, right above, will not allow our body to cast a shadow.

What about our feet? Won't they cast a shadow? Yes, but it is a shadow one cannot see because it is under our feet. It is the grounding part that keeps the spirit shining bright. That is in full alignment with our light.

The journey of awakening is similar to a full cycle of day and night. We awaken with the light of the dawn. Facing the sun to the East, we cast a long and large shadow. Our shadow is fully present, yet behind us. It is time to choose how we are going to live our day, with a clear visualization of our being in action.

Who am I choosing to be today? How will I conduct myself? What do I need to focus on, be aware of, to keep my center and connection? How can I bring out the best in me? Can I hold the blessings, gratitude, and joy of being alive as a constant companion?

As the day progresses, the shadow recedes until full alignment takes place by midday. At noon, with the sun above, we become aware and empowered by the totality of our light. Then, with the sun setting behind us, the shadow comes back, creeping up in full force, right in front of our eyes.

At dusk, the shadow engulfs us; it is a time of introspection and self-reflection. It is the time for core healing.

What were my wins in holding myself to my chosen way of being? Where did I slip? What did I learn from my blunders and losses? How can I reset? Where do I need to place my attention?

Restorative sleep overcomes us, and in the depth of the darkness of the night, the light of morning once more arises.

As Paulo Coelho wrote, "It is when one is dying of thirst that the palm trees of the oasis appear on the horizon." So the morning of every day is a new beginning. We are indeed a renewed being, filled with new tissue cells, new understandings, new knowledge and experiences — and perhaps with age, new wisdom. It is a time to embrace life fully like a lover, fueled by the growth, learning, and healing that took place in the recent past. We can meet the new day with joy, curiosity, enthusiasm, and passion.

As the day progresses, we can live and act like a warrior of light with focus, commitment, courage, and intention. It is a time for action and contribution to the world. At dusk, we reflect on our day and how we lived it.

Healing and learning from our failures, mistakes, and trespassing can take place as rejoicing in our wins and successes.

These are the archetypes of the cycle of our days. When integrated, it allows us to stand in life like a king or queen, overseeing our land populated by our family, friends, clients, patients, acquaintances, or constituencies. We can walk in the world with a presence that, in and of itself, has an impact and influence. We can make a difference as powerful, healthy, and spiritual beings.

As much as I had surrendered my life to Life and a purpose greater than myself in 1973 when I embraced my calling and path, I did not grow to understand, articulate, and utilize the navigation of these archetypes until I stumbled into M.K.P, the Mankind Project.

M.K.P was created to bring back a process and rituals that had been part of nearly all indigenous tribal cultures: a young man's rites of passage into manhood. I am deeply grateful for this worldwide organization and its founders, who teach men to become safe and responsible. This way of being can only happen when one uncovers and knows the darkness that lives deep within all of us.

Women also have their rites of passage into womanhood. However, for women, it is built into the design of life. Inherent to menstruation, the breaking of the hymen, pregnancy, miscarriage, birth, lactation, breastfeeding, and menopause, life has created powerful rites of passage for women. What women experience binds them together emotionally, in mutual understanding of their common reality. By nature, women are more open-hearted, communicative, and emotionally aware, seeking connections, kinship, and support with other women.

Men have much to learn by knowing their dark side, the very root of sexual violence, rape, brutality, and enslavement of women worldwide. How can men have lost sight that they invariably were grown, hosted, birthed, breastfed, and nurtured by a woman, their mother? Utmost respect toward women arises when men have made the journey to discover their own shadows.

Gratitude

A few years ago, I was on a long motorcycle ride throughout the western United States. It was a majestic clear blue day. It was late afternoon, and dark clouds were forming on the horizon.

A thunderstorm was brewing, and the sky opened up as I neared the town of Cody, Wyoming. Within minutes I was riding in two to three inches of water. Needless to say, as soon as I got to town, I pulled over into a motel. The street and parking lots were flooded with four to five inches of rain. The next morning, the air was crisp, the sky perfectly blue, not a cloud in the sky. I took off at about 6:30 a.m. There was no one on the wide-open road. The prairie was covered with last night's moisture and dew. The sun was reverberating in thousands of water droplets like diamonds shimmering all over. I had a full epiphany. With a huge grin, I was overwhelmed with joy, bliss, and gratitude. My mind raced, one thought tumbling to the next like falling dominos to engulf all humanity.

Gratitude for my Honda Valkyrie and for Mr. Honda, a Japanese inventor who started building bikes in his garage. Gratitude for the oil companies, the Arab workers manning the oil wells, and the truckers and tankers crew carrying the precious liquid from the Middle East to the shores of America. Gratitude for the engineers, the assembly workers, the mechanics, the electricians, the chemists, the dealership staff, and the owners. As I was riding, completely elated, my mind traveled throughout the world and the past, extending gratitude to countless human beings who contributed to this blissful moment of me riding my motorcycle. My body was filled with the emotion of gratitude for my life, my body, my health, and my parents, wife, and children. At that moment, the whole world and humanity became one interrelated and interconnected whole. I was one with it all, bound by gratitude.

Prior to sleep, by reflecting on the day, we can practice gratitude, my daily routine for years. Starting with our parents, grandparents, ancestors, aunts, uncles, siblings, children, spouses, and extended family, then expanding the circle of appreciation to all our friends, teachers, mentors, acquaintances, and all beings, until sleep befalls us is a worthwhile practice. It is said that gratitude gives Life to life. How true that is. One single thought about enjoying a cup of tea will transport us on a never-ending journey of gratitude. Gratitude for the earth, the sunshine, the water, the nutrients, the bacteria, the tea farmer, the packaging, the transportation vehicles, the designers, engineers, the factory workers, the ore miners for steel, the oil industry, the tanker builder, the merchant mariners, the radars, GPS developers, the navigation satellites, the port authorities, and the list goes on ad infinitum, showering people, past and present, from all nations, creeds, colors, and genders. Indeed as had been stated by Zen masters, "In a grain of rice, I see the entire universe."

Gratitude links us all in oneness and interdependence.

Every time I go to the bathroom to empty my bladder, I am overwhelmed by gratitude. A simple act of awareness bears great dividends. How can it be that my body, without dripping, holds half to two cups of urine? Have you ever attempted to carry water in an upside-down bag, tightly bound by a rubber band? It leaks. Yet our bladder, with its sphincter, can do that while we stand, sit, run, snowboard, or jump rope. The Designer has placed a sensor to let us know it is time to empty our bladder. An internal alarm goes off during sleep to wake us up to urinate. That, in and of itself, is astonishing and a true blessing to be grateful for.

Gratitude can be performed nearly around the clock when we tune in to what our body does for us every moment. According to Candice Pert, Ph.D., an internationally recognized neuroscientist and pharmacologist, every emotion we feel or generate is an actual chemical reaction in every cell of our body. Could chronic gratitude become a healthy diet of neurotransmitters in our cells, tissues, organs, systems, and entire being? Could such a simple action engender huge health benefits?

I do not have to wait for some scientific study to be published in a prestigious journal to know that gratitude is a healthy habit with great rewards for our being. Gratitude is truly a difference-making in life.

Two Paths in Life

It might be my own delusion, yet I believe there are two paths in life—that of the ego and that of the Soul. One arises from the higher realm of being, the other from the lower realm. One meets flow, ease, serendipity, providence, synchronicity, and grace. The other meets challenges, resistances, difficulties, obstacles, and dis-ease. One is fueled by the boundless energy of inspiration, the other by the limited energy of motivation. One is manifested by force; the other emanates from inner power.

No right or wrong choice… only the consequences of the choice we make. The choice is ours at every moment. So we ought to choose wisely.

In choosing the path of the Soul, vulnerability is essential. Vulnerability does not mean weakness. On the contrary, it requires strength, courage, and openness. Vulnerability allows for a greater listening to the silent inner voice. Most of us have experienced new vulnerability, listening, understanding, and comprehension coming to us with a broken heart when a romantic relationship dissolves.

Now that our heart is open, we have access to the wisdom of vulnerability.

Back then, in the comfort of a taken-for-granted relationship, we could not hear, listen, or understand our partner's pleadings, viewpoints, and requests. We were locked into a protective shell. We were not vulnerable. We could not see the forest for the trees. With the new opening, softening, and vulnerability, a new channel gives us insights we did not have before: How can I have been so blind? I can't believe how stubborn and closed I was to my partner's observations. What was making me so clueless? What prevented me from being open to observations and pointers from my partner? What was I guarding and protecting? What was I afraid of?

A broken or open heart welcomes vulnerability and the insights to which it gives birth.

The flip side when falling in love creates a portal of openness and vulnerability, which gives us a deeper level of listening, curiosity, and attention. The early honeymoon phase of a relationship is blissful due to us being open and vulnerable.

With awareness and surrender, the Soul-driven life can be accessed. By being in love with the higher dimension of our being, we make a difference in the world.

Relationships

"Hi, my name is Justin. I have wanted to meet you for quite some time."

"I am Mikela. I am so happy you came over to talk to me. I wanted to meet you also, but I was not as brave as you." Then within days, they fell in love. Countless couples enter romantic, passionate relationships, clueless that what they really just got themselves into is a relation-shit. This might sound crude and cruel, but it is the truth.

A more realistic dialogue could have been:

"Hi, I'm Justin. I have wanted to meet you for quite some time. You are stunningly beautiful, attractive, and outright gorgeous. How much shit do you have? I know this sounds rude, but I have plenty of shit myself, and I am wondering if you have plenty of it, too."

"Wow, Justin, I'm Mikela. I am glad you brought this shit up from the get-go. I think that's healthy. Yes, I have some shit, too. Actually, to be honest, I have a lot of shit. Do you want to talk about your shit, or do you first want me to talk about mine?"

"Well, Mikela, I'd like to hear about your shit. To be frank, I hope our shit is manageable because I really would like to work our shit out before doing the deed, if you know what I mean."

"That sounds good, Justin. I certainly would not want to do the deed with you before I know what kind of shit I am dealing with. You know, because if we can't work our shit out, we will find ourselves in deep shit. Some shit is just too much for me to handle. It scares the shit out of me."

You get the picture. This would be a healthy, honest, trustful dialogue, one that makes a difference.

New relationships that many of us move into with great passion and enthusiasm could be better renamed 'relation-shit' due to the reality that, in time, we will be faced with our partner's shit as well as our own. Truly, life's design is magical to entice us to grow through relation-shits.

The sooner we are vulnerable in exposing our mutual shit, the quicker we can move on, avoid disaster, and build a solid, honest, authentic relationship.

I do not know about you, but I wish someone had opened my eyes early in life about the reality of relationships and the shit they bring. It would have led to healthier relationships from the get-go. Our overall health is intertwined with the quality of our relationships, whether friendly, amorous, conjugal, or social. This awareness makes a difference in our lives.

From Religion to Spirituality

Having been born and raised in a mostly Catholic society (France), I was exposed to the church's teachings. As a young child, the solemn grandeur, decorum, and rituals of mass impressed me. On the other hand, I was quite bored with bible studies.

My innocent and young mind knew intuitively that most bible tales were metaphors, not to be taken literally. These oral stories were spoken to mostly illiterate, uneducated crowds who could neither read nor write as an appropriate way to communicate with them. They are not to be embraced as literal truth in today's modern world with the present conjecture, literacy, worldview, and scientific knowledge. Only with age and spiritual experiences did I understand those metaphors' brilliant and genuine value.

The accounts of the life of Christ certainly made a mark on me. It fed my idealism. It was both inspiring and elevating. Unconditional love, forgiveness, and sacrificing oneself for something greater than oneself for the greater good of humanity resonated deeply within my heart as an example to follow.

God was said to be omnipresent, omnipotent, and omniscient; the Creator and the Cause of all that was, is, and ever will be. That I could accept as an explanation for the mystery of life. The idea of a God who lives somewhere in the Universe to keep watchful eyes on every one of my deeds, thoughts, and actions to punish my trespassing did not add up in my young mind. I could not fathom a God that had to be feared and who was at once punishing and ruthless but also merciful and loving. I yearned to experience union with God, yet I only had an intellectual understanding of it, which did not seem to add up.

The sexual abuse I experienced as a young child at the hands of a priest sealed the deal. I was out of there. Many years went by with a void and no connection to religion or spirituality, despite the subtle presence of an internal longing.

Then, while studying Chiropractic Philosophy, the concept of Universal Intelligence sounded truer than a man-made human-like God. It stated that there is a Universal Intelligence in all matter and continually gives its properties and actions, thus maintaining its existence. For the first time, I could grasp the fact that there was an ever-present Intelligence that permeated all matter, space, and time. That is what omnipresence met. That Intelligence was also omniscient and omnipotent by the sole virtue of being the cause and source of all that is. It is the creative Intelligence of the Universe.

Chiropractic Philosophy also spoke of Innate Intelligence being that part of Universal Intelligence that resides within living things. That also made sense to me. If indeed Universal Intelligence is omnipresent, it has to be present in every cell, fiber, and speck of matter of my being. Indeed, I was made in the image of God, a part of the hologram, which contains the whole.

Now the image of God has disappeared into thin air, replaced by a more realistic concept of an invisible, intangible Universal Intelligence. God vanished just like the many Gods of antiquity, from when Poseidon, Zeus, and Eros, ended up in a puff of smoke under the progress of science.

As science states, "Locked in every speck of matter is the knowledge for the creation of the entire universe." Now things began to make sense. Something inside began to oscillate within me. Over the years, my spiritual connection to Innate Intelligence within and Universal Intelligence without became more profound.

Innate Intelligence had become a practical and real internal knowledge, power, and know-how I could trust fully to run, control, operate, coordinate, heal, and repair my body. Innate Intelligence became my moment-by-moment companion. Total trust in it has not yet failed me in my life to date.

I have come through many physical experiences, some quite severe, that most people would not have handled without seeking medical assistance or visiting the hospital ER. My body and the Inborn Intelligence within delivered with flying colors every time. Consequently, I felt increasingly empowered as I progressed through life. Each experience built a greater trust.

I became aware that as long as I surrendered to being used as an instrument of Universal and abided by the voice of Innate Intelligence within, my life was in the flow.

I had found a deep spirituality within, free of rituals, dogma, limitations, and external controls. It was all about my relationship with Innate Intelligence, the guru within, from this point forward. No hoops to jump through, no ritualistic steps to climb, no religious hierarchy to follow, no doctrine to abide by, no one to submit to on the path, just myself and my SELF. Freedom to listen within and choose. A wide departure from the dictatorship and enslavement of religious directives, guilt, and shame I had experienced early in my life with the Catholic Church.

Where is the freedom in being told what to do and how to behave? In reflection, the land of the free is not so free for the countless entrapped in religion. Being forever free does not come by following a leader or joining a cult, sect, or religion.

I had found freedom and my spiritual life. Freedom to listen or not to the whispering voice within and to trust my innate Intelligence.

I believe religion may well have been one of the most destructive forces for humanity. Like many organizations, it started with good intentions. In time, however, it became distorted from the original message and soon thereafter became self-serving, plagued by control, power, corruption, secrecies, egos, political maneuverings, and perversions.

I cannot reconcile Christ's message of Love with the crusades, the inquisition, witch-hunts, the torturing, murder, and genocides of indigenous tribes, the burnings at stake, the satanization of homosexuality, and all the wars waged in the name of Christ. None of it sounds to me like "Love thy neighbor as thyself!"

This beautifully expressed passage by Meggan Watterson, author of Mary Magdalene Revealed, sums up my feelings about God and religion: *"I feel sorry for you that your god is so small. That your god has such a fragile ego, he'll send us all to hell if we don't believe in him. And that your Jesus only loves his own followers, people who have surrendered over everything to him, like some power-hungry, twisted cult leader.*

I think you have missed the whole point. You've mistaken god for power [control]. I think whoever the hell Jesus was, he was about love. I think Jesus was about a love that's the opposite of power [control]."

I believe spirituality is the next step and upcoming hope for the world. The information age is bound to come to a close, as all is soon available to everyone on a chip or wristwatch. The next step and economy for humanity is the age of consciousness and spirituality. As we enter the digital age and the world of artificial intelligence, spiritual connection to our inner self is becoming critical if we are to still express what makes us human beings.

Spirituality is void of dogma, control, and doctrine. It is experiential rather than academic rhetoric. The Divine within is to be experienced rather than talked about. The connection to the spirit can be reached through breathwork, meditation, contemplation, yoga, bodywork, adjustments, communion with nature, and numerous other avenues. In rare instances, it is attained spontaneously through unusual circumstances. As Michael Talbot mentioned in the Holographic Universe, it happened to a construction worker taking a break, leaning against an air conditioning unit. The vibration of the AC unit entrained his body into letting the coiled serpent of the Kundalini energy spring out of its sacral base cage and rise like a rocket up the central canal of the spinal cord to explode into the brain into pure light. He experienced enlightenment!

Once the light within is experienced, there is union and communion with all other human beings and living things. The heart is cracked wide open while the mind is silenced. Pure bliss and ecstasy reign supreme. There is little to talk about. Silence seems to be the only appropriate communication.

I feel the Quakers might be onto something along with meditators: sitting in silence with no other authority than the one of our own being. Sitting in a state of open-heartedness, love commands just being. Present-time consciousness is experienced.

To those who have never been there, it may appear a mystery. To those who have been there, understanding the power of silence when love arises out of a blown-open heart is immediate.

As Elton John's The Love Song reminds us: "Love is the opening door, Love is the key we must turn, Love is what we came here for, do you know what I mean, have your eyes really seen?" Love is the light of life, the light of the world, and the illuminating presence within.

Today, I know without a shadow of a doubt that, for me, Nature is humanity's original church. This church dwarfs the greatest man-made cathedrals, mosques, temples, and synagogues. I have been to many of the crown jewels of religious edifices, from Notre Dame in Paris to the Blue Mosque of Istanbul, to the Sagrada Familia of Barcelona, along with the Chartres Cathedral, to name but a few. Jane and I have traveled in more than 49 countries, entering religious edifices in towns and villages. None rival the grander magnificence, power, and dynamic beauty of Nature: from the majestic mountains of the Swiss Alps, the Rockies, Canyon Land, Valley of the Gods, Monument Valley, Bryce and Zion, Lake Powell, and the Grand Canyon. That is not to mention the Canadian Rockies, British Columbia, or Alaska. Nature is an ever-present church; it teaches the natural laws of life to anyone willing to observe and listen. No need for scriptures, popes, priests, rabbis, mullahs, or preachers.

Nature does not demand donations or attendance one day of the week. It is a church that welcomes all at all times. A church that nourishes billions daily with the bounty of food, air, and water.

A church that does not seek control or power because it inherently possesses all power and control. A church whose door is always opened, a church that commands rather than demands respect and humility and engenders awe and mystery.

It instills awareness and awakens consciousness. It confronts us with the polarity of life, the yin-yang, as nature can be harsh, devastating, destructive, nurturing, kind, soothing, and giving. Nature exposes us to balance, discernment, and adaptation. It requires us to go deep within while revealing life force or spirit. This church is Universal, as the cosmos is part of Nature, and Nature is part of the cosmos.

Life is humanity's true religion, embracing all human beings. For centuries, if not millennia, life has spoken to those open to receive from Christ, Buddha, Mohamed, and many other great beings. It has taught shamans, medicine men, healers, witches, and countless lay people, from the uneducated to university graduates. This religion directs communication with all life and human beings alike. It is the great equalizer, leveling the playing field and erasing all disparities. It has no intermediaries between Universal and human beings, plants, animals, all of nature, and earth.

Life is a religion that teaches around the clock, not just on Sundays. It offers lessons for all those paying attention and willing to learn and grow. There are no misinterpretations or distortions. Nature speaks a direct, universal, clear, silent language to all equally. The messages, laws, and commandments are the same for all who listen in silence. Nature reveals the immutable laws of Life to those who contemplate in quiet observation.

- Law of Survival. (Dominant law driving physiology)
- Law of Cycles (Circadian, seasonal, lunar, cellular, menstrual, cosmic)
- Law of Equality of Exchange in pairs of opposites. (Dynamic balance)
- Law of Impermanence. (Everything returns to source)
- Law of Limit Cycle. (Self-regulation in nature)
- Law of Opposites. (Male-female, venous-arterial, sympathetic-parasympathetic)
- Law of Adaptation. (All living things seek to adapt)
- Law of Energy Flow. (Greater the energy flow, the slower the decay)
- Law of Life. (Life is the trinity of intelligence-matter-force)
- Law of Time. (Every process requires time)

- Law of Interconnectedness. (All is one)

The laws that govern nature outward govern nature inward. The macro-cosmos and the micro-cosmos within us are subject to the same laws. Can we control the movement of celestial bodies, galaxies, and stars? I think not; no more than we can control the inner workings of the 40 trillion cells of the body, with their multitude of biochemical factories producing dazzling arrays of natural pharmaceuticals and biological fireworks. All of it is a mystery, governed and orchestrated by an Innate Intelligence. Universal laws are universal.

Having studied the life sciences of the human body, both in my years of medical school and then again in chiropractic college, I believe that, viewed from a deep perspective, the books of biochemistry, biophysics, anatomy, physiology, neurology, cardiology, myology, osteology, biology, and all other -ologies are, in reality, sacred spiritual texts about life and nature. They reveal, by allowing us a tiny glance, the incomprehensible magnitude of the mind and creative power of the Architect, the Designer, the Blueprint, and the Intelligence behind all that makes up who and what we are. They bring an extraordinary feeling of awe at the mystery of it all. They humble us to the core.

Trust is the true faith of humanity. In many ways, we all trust more than we may realize. We, mostly unconsciously, trust the elevator, the planes, the cars, the food we buy, the water we drink, and the sun rising.

All of Nature has to trust and adapt to thrive, grow and survive. Aren't we all also part of Nature? Could humanity even be here without the support of Nature that provides all? Matthew David Hurtado, in his book, Trust, stated, "Trust is the most powerful force in the world." Total trust, not a sustained moment of wavering, not a lasting flicker of doubt; isn't it how the natural world lives?

Life Force, the Light, and Spirit within are the object of worship for humanity in the religion of life. Life force is the power within, the animating light of our life. The energy of life itself, called vital force, chi, élan vital, prana, ki, mana, elixir of life, bio-essence, or life energy, needs to be studied and understood in health and healing. Without it, we are looking at dry, devitalized versions of human beings. Going within means connecting with and tapping into the elixir of life, our own Life Force.

Love is the ingredient of Universal synthesis and is the unifying factor of humanity. As humans, it is the sword we want to carry in life. When our heart is fully open, we are in a state of love. We connect with the magic of life. We experience the alchemy of life. Many speak of nectar, the nectar of love. This subtle essence radiates from within out. In the state of love, we have a profound connection with the breath. By being aware of our breathing through conscious focus, we can sustain a loving state with the silent mantra, "What would love do in this moment?"

For me, nature is my church, life is my religion, trust is my faith, and love is my sword. This is an invitation for those who are open to it, those seeking true health, connection, and presence —a simple way of living in the world.

The Path to the Experience of Enlightenment

With my first adjustment in 1973, my life shifted drastically from being lost on a dark, self-destructive path to being inncr-guided. It was a slight shift at first, but a monumental transformation took place over time.

It is said that a one-degree deviation by a ship over an ocean crossing can be enough to produce a radically different destination. Airplane pilots have to make regular small adjustments to stay on their flight path. Failure can be triggered by a hairline departure from the original path pursued over time. By the same token, a minor spiritual adjustment can reset us on our Soul's path.

B.J. Palmer D.C., the Developer of chiropractic, stated that a minute change in the timing, quantity, and/or quality of the mental impulse coursing through, into and over nerves, over time, can transform normal physiology into first, a silent mal-function called dis-ease, then into patho symptomatology and finally into pathology and possibly early death. This subtle change in mental impulse creates a minor dis-connection with our inner light. In time, it can lead to a perceived separation from spirit. The sole purpose of the adjustment is to unite the physical with the spiritual.

Because the neuro-spinal system is the main pipeline for the life force, keeping the channel clear and the energy flowing freely is crucial in health, healing, and wellbeing. This passage in Autobiography of a Yogi by Paramahansa Yogananda drives the point of the crucial key residing within the human spinal column, "One half-minute of revolution of energy around the sensitive spinal cord equals one year of natural spiritual enfoldment."

Getting checked regularly by a chiropractor and adjusting if needed became part of my lifestyle. At times, I would receive care from different practitioners, with various levels of artistic adjusting skills and levels of perceptions in reading the body and clearing the neuro-spinal system of interference. Most of the time, I experienced more than a physical feeling of release and ease. I felt energetic changes as well as a deeper inner connection.

In the mid-1980s, I connected with Dr. Donald Epstein, D.C., at a hotel in Newark, New Jersey. We were both giving seminars in adjacent conference rooms. Rose Pannuccio, a vibrant elderly woman who had been a chiropractic advocate for years, introduced us to each other. For me, there was nothing accidental in a Rose connecting the two of us. Such synchronicity and serendipity had and have blessed my life regularly.

It is my experience that life speaks in various ways. There are signs on the highways of life. When we are in the flow, those signs seem obvious. When our heart is wide open, these signposts are even stronger; manifestations of our desires into actual reality become nearly instantaneous. I have had a burning desire to share my love and expression of chiropractic philosophy far and beyond my practice and the venues I had. Rose provided this new opportunity.

As a result of my connection with Donald Epstein, D.C., I began to speak at his Network Seminars, sharing the philosophy and principles inherent to our profession. At that time, he was in a creative state: the birthing of a new approach and paradigm to chiropractic care. He was downloading information so fast that his mouth could not keep up with the input flow from his spirit. It seemed that if you had placed all the English words into a blender, it was sort of like his speech had become. As fascinating as they appeared, his discourses were nearly incomprehensible to me and, for that matter, to most of his audience.

Yet everyone present could feel he was onto something big. What was coming through him was so big that later on, I stated, "Donald Epstein, D.C., is to Chiropractic what Einstein was to physics."

It took me a few years to understand what he was up to, even though we had become friends with deep mutual respect.

One day, we were both at a convention in Atlanta called Dynamic Essentials when a woman came up to me during the banquet dinner, asking if I could step outside. She wanted to talk to me. Her tone was both commanding and insistent. Her name was Helene; she had been a client of Donald Epstein for a number of years in Brooklyn, N.Y. Once in the hallway, away from the noise of the crowd, she implored me to get adjusted by Dr. Epstein. She was assertive beyond resistance. I promised her I would, thanked her, and returned to my table.

That evening on my way back to my room, Dr. Epstein was adjusting people in the convention center's hallway. I sat on an open adjusting table and waited for him to approach. He adjusted me, and I went to bed thinking, *Why did Helen make such a big deal out of me getting adjusted by him?* Nothing special had happened. It felt like most other adjustments.

The next morning, I went to the conference sessions and, by mid-morning, stepped out on my way to check out of the hotel. There he was, adjusting people again. Something inside me led me to again sit at an open table and wait for him.

When he stepped behind me to check my neuro-spinal system, I vividly remember turning to him and saying, "Take me home."

Within seconds of lying on the adjusting table and feeling Dr. Epstein make light contacts with my spine and adjust me structurally, an intense energetic pressure began to build up from my coccyx and sacrum and moved up my spine to explode into a deep primal roar and scream.

At that moment, I felt like a rocket had been placed at the bottom of my spine, taken off, and had risen the entire length of my spinal canal at lightning speed to explode into my brain. Another way of expressing this would be to say that it felt like I was plugged into a socket with 100,000 volts of electricity running through my spine and body without a bit of discomfort. My body was figuratively pulverized by white light. I felt every cell of my body turning to pure white light and being transmuted by it. I experienced my whole being vibrating at an extraordinary frequency.

I remained there on the table, motionless, in bliss and deep communion with the light and spirit within. After an undetermined amount of time, my awareness of having to catch a plane returned, and I got up. I walked from the convention center toward the front desk feeling myself being about five feet above my body, watching my physical body walk for me. I was very much out of my physical body and into my spiritual one. I had no perception of my physical body; I was just engulfed by white light.

By pure synchronicity, a student whom I knew saw me taking my room key out of my pocket and asked me if I needed help. In an unspoken way, I just handed him my key. Without a word, I told him his help would be greatly appreciated. He went to get my luggage out of my room, and later met me back in the lobby.

It was a Sunday at the Waverly Hotel in Marietta, Georgia, and a lavish brunch had been set up for churchgoers, tourists, and hotel guests. People were coming in droves. I was standing there in the lobby, arms by my side, hands wide open, facing the elevators in bliss, my back to the main entrance, waiting for the student to return. By then, I realized my hands were so full of light and energy that I could not close my fingers nor make a fist. I was standing there passively, just Being while waiting.

Three times young children came from behind me and stuck their heads under my hands, like docking to light pods, remaining there for a moment as if they were filling themselves up with the energy that emanated from my hands. My hands had become energy-charging devices. It seems that only the young children were aware of this, as none of the parents scolded their children for their unusual behavior with a total stranger.

As I was waiting for the student to return with my luggage, there, in my field of vision, was Michael Kale D.C., a prominent chiropractor from Spartanburg, S.C., who had had a falling-out with Sherman College. I remember that, while in school years earlier, I had spoken some inflaming words against him to the student body, in anger and frustration, because the recognition process of Sherman College was being blocked by the South Carolina State Board, on which he was a member. As a result, graduates would not be allowed to practice in South Carolina. He wanted to protect his turf since his practice was in Spartanburg, the same town as Sherman College. As a result, some students threw rocks in anger into the window of his clinic. I had not thought of the inflammatory words I had spoken in more than ten years. In that state of being, however, they came flooding back into my brain.

I walked up to him and said, "Michael, you may not remember me; my name is Arno. I was a student at Sherman College during the challenging years with accreditation. I had, through my words, inflamed students' frustration, and some did vandalize your clinic windows. We were young, passionate, in love with this vocation, and only wanted the legitimate right to practice. Most of us were willing to go to jail for practicing illegally. I am so sorry and ask for your forgiveness."

His wife was standing next to him, listening. She bolted away, screaming in a scornful voice, "We lost the baby over this." I was stunned. I had no idea the stress involved might have caused her to have a miscarriage. Nonetheless, Michael extended his forgiveness, and we parted.

As I turned away, still waiting for the student to return, I saw an ex-classmate who had been a snitch. His denouncing me led to my being kicked out of Sherman College for six months. The reason being I was adjusting people outside the school, which was against school policy.

I walked up to him, letting him know that I had no anger, had fully forgiven him, and actually had been grateful to him because it allowed me to practice for six months while out of school to further refine my skills and gain experience.

Within a few minutes, I had asked for forgiveness and given forgiveness.

I felt the strings of tension melt away. Past emotional cords I had not been aware of were released. Impeccable synchronicity was at work. My heart was wide open. I felt no needs, no desires, and no wants. I was just being in the purest sense of it for the first time in my life. Unless something caught my awareness, I had no thoughts. My mind was blank and still. I was bathed in pure inner bliss.

Without me asking, the student checked me out of the hotel, having returned with my luggage.

I cannot remember how I got to the airport, but someone took me without me having to request a ride or call a cab. By the time I landed in Philadelphia, I felt so complete within myself that any need to speak had vanished. I was without words. Silence had become total communication. Presence was all I needed. I was in heaven on earth.

I got to my car, intending to start it, but the battery was dead. I had jumper cables, and someone stopped right away to give me a jump. This event spoke so clearly to me, "Your life is getting a jump start. You are being 'hooked up' to Universal Energy."

As I began to drive home, I could not close my hands on the steering wheel. They were so full of energy that I had to steer with my wrists. I had done the trip from the airport to our home in New Hope, PA hundreds of times, yet that day I went southbound on I-95 and had to turn around to go back northbound. One would think I was out of it and out of my mind, which in many ways, was exactly the state of being I was in. The U-turn brought to my awareness another sign showing up on the highway of life, "Your life is taking a 180-degree turn." And indeed, it had.

By the time I arrived home, I felt a subtle current of energy moving up and down my spine with every breath. It was as if each breath would pull up a very fine silk thread of energy and light from my coccyx to blossom in my brain. In my throat and chest, I felt a delightful nectar with each breath that expanded to connect my heart to my throat. The tip of my tongue had risen spontaneously to gently touch the roof of my palate. This was not only comfortable but also soothing. A very faint humming was occurring with every breath.

My awareness had expanded to notice all those subtle changes. I realized later that the chi was circulating up my spine's central canal, into my brain, through my tongue, to the front of my body in a gentle, subtle cycle.

Arriving home, my wife Jane welcomed me. I embraced her without a word. None were needed.

She had prepared dinner. We sat down, me in silence. I must have chewed my first bite of chicken for what seemed like ten minutes, only to spit it out. It felt like chewing gum. The message from the inside out was clear, "My body is refusing meat." In that state of being, I received information that meat was no longer appropriate food for me. The message and guidance came from within. This was different from becoming a vegetarian from the outside, hoping to attain a higher state of being. It was an inside-out job.

That evening, as tired as I was, I felt compelled to meditate. For years, I had sporadically meditated for periods of time with little perceived rewards, except for frequently falling asleep. This meditation was so deep, profound, and nurturing to my being that I had no desire to stop. I was just being in complete bliss. I had to force myself out of it with all my willpower.

Jane and I went to bed. We fell asleep quickly. Hours later, I was awakened by a commanding voice, "Arno, get in your sweats, go downstairs!" The voice was so loud and real that it felt like someone was in the room. My rational mind refused to obey the order and dismissed it as being crazy, a psychotic breakdown. Within minutes the voice spoke for the second time in a stronger tone, "Arno, get in your sweats, go downstairs!" Again my intellect rejected the command. When the voice spoke for the third time, the commanding presence was so powerful it jolted me out of bed.

I got in my sweats and went to lie down in the downstairs guest bedroom. Within seconds a presence, a force of enormous magnitude, pinned me down to the bed, my arms and hands driven upwards by my head into the universal posture of surrender. The presence spoke again, "In the morning, get up, do not take a shower, walk to your office barefoot, and wash the feet of everyone in your waiting room." All I could say in blissful surrender was: "I will, I will, I will."

Then waves of gratitude overwhelmed me, so much so that I was forced to prostrate myself back and forth in the universal gesture of gratitude and thanksgiving, with joined hands over my heart center. This posture was organically generated in me from within.

Then a huge feeling of inner peace took over my entire being. I lay there on my back, with my arms and hands which had been driven open by my side in the universal gesture of inner peace. It was an involuntary gesture. My body was vibrating light. I was bathed in the light and by the light.

I later reflected on the gesturing that happened spontaneously and organically in my body and recalled the gestures of Catholic priests during mass: open arms and hands, then joined hands, then hands and arms by the side. These gestures are combined with the Latin liturgy of: "Dominus vobiscum or Pax vobiscum, Et cum spiritu tuo…"

I now understand that those gestures arise organically during a spiritual experience as one surrenders, feels gratitude, and bathes in inner peace. They are performed ritualistically by priests, possibly outside of a spiritual experience, but through the dictates of the church. These universal gestures and postures can be witnessed all over the world in people experiencing profound love and gratitude with an open heart. In some cultures, joining the hands over the heart center is part of their way of greeting one another. It might have lost its connection to deep gratitude, becoming a cultural mannerism like in Thailand or India, yet I believe it originated from there.

As I was bathing in the light, Jane came downstairs, aware that I had left our bed, and lay beside me to check if I was alright. As she did so, she was engulfed by the light. She felt a deep inner peace and bliss. My field of energy had bathed her in the light.

That morning, I was again compelled to meditate. Again, the inner light was pure nourishment to my being. In deep meditation, I entered a state I did not want to leave. But my office hours were calling me; I had to extract myself out of meditation to get ready.

As I opened my eyes, words jumped out of a pile of books sprawled on the floor catching my attention: History in the Making, the title from a pamphlet written by B. J. Palmer, D.C., rose from the cover to jump into my awareness. Next, the word fragile leaped out from a sticker on the side of a box that was still unpacked from our recent move. I got it loud and clear: "The energy was fragile, and it was history in the making."

A ground-breaking evolution in the delivery of the chiropractic adjustment to clear the neuro-spinal system and free Life Force had occurred.

There was not a single doubt in my mind that I had what we call chiropractic subluxations that had interfered with the free flow and expression of my Life Force. Subluxation, or sub-lux-ation, means less light in expression. I had received two consecutive adjustments or clearings within a span of ten hours, and for me, it was all it took to free the totality of my light.

The neuro-spinal channel, the life force pipeline, light, and spirit, had been cleared and opened fully. The Kundalini energy that lies dormant, like oil underground, had surged through my body like a geyser surging in oil drilling when the pipes finally pierced through the soil to the rich liquid below.

Now I was in a quandary. Should I actually follow the command and walk 10 miles to my office, unshaved, un-showered, and barefoot, and wash everyone's feet in my waiting room? I was ready to do it, but I needed confirmation and reassurance. Jane was more skeptical. After all, Yardley, PA, where my practice happens to be, was a conservative, upper-class, a bit stiff bedroom community for Wall Street and the Route One Corridors of pharmaceutical companies. Not exactly your friendly New Age community that would openly accept such behavior. So I conferred with Jane. She suggested we call Barbara, a close friend of ours and ex-wife of Carl Tomkins, D.C., from Peekskill, New York.

Barbara had recently watched the PBS series called The Power of Myth by Joseph Campbell and had also read his book by the same title. She immediately said that the washing of the feet was a universal metaphor for relinquishing the ego. Yet she was going to call a monk friend of hers living in New York and get back to us just to confirm. Within a few minutes, Barbara called back to confirm it was a metaphor. With two confirmations, I was relieved, took a shower, and drove to the office.

I had always seen new people at the end of my morning hours and/or evening hours to have ample uninterrupted time with them. If I needed more space for new people, I would see them first before my afternoon hours or, at the last resort, before my morning hours. In all my years in practice to that day, I had never had to see someone before my morning hours. That day, a new person was waiting for me on the porch without an appointment. I always did get to my office at least 30 minutes before opening time.

That morning, I had a silent first visit. I did not need to speak. I felt everything that was happening with this woman. I knew her journey in life and could read her like an open book. I felt no need to explain anything.

I sensed that my presence alone and our mutual connection were all that was needed. She was an ex-nun in her mid-fifties and wore a large, highly visible wooden crucifix around her neck. The meaning of the cross represents death and resurrection; the death of the ego as the light of spirit floods our being. It also symbolizes living from above-down and inside-out, when connected to our Soul with a fully open heart. The cross reminds us of the example of Christ who authentically lived, fully connected to the spirit above and expressing it from his heart outward, having fully surrendered to the will of his Father. During that visit, this woman's cross stood out and came to my awareness as a guiding reminder.

For the next three months, I practiced in a nearly constant silent state. I would acknowledge people with a nod, check them, adjust them if needed, kiss them on top of the head, which was my signature, and move on to the next adjusting table, where another person was waiting.

I meditated compulsively every morning and evening. I had to extract myself from these meditations by truly willing myself to exit.

During those months, I saw amazing healing by laying my hands on people. Sometimes healing would take place before I even adjusted them. My coherent field of energy had entrained their physiology back to wholeness.

A woman named Mary came with her daughter Amy about 15, who had been anorexic for years. As I touched Amy, to begin a neuro-spinal assessment, her mother, Mary, who was sitting in the corner of the adjusting room, erupted in tears and into a full-body sob. I did not get to adjust Amy that day. We were all complete. They left the office, and that was the last of Amy's eating disorder.

Mary also brought her daughter Selena, who was wearing Coke-bottle-type eyeglasses, those thick lenses that prevent an onlooker from seeing her eyes. In one visit, the glasses were gone, not to return.

Mary began to receive care on a regular basis with her two daughters. Within a few weeks, Mary had become psychic with horses, a horse whisperer — or better stated, a horse listener. She lived on her farm in Bucks County and cared for horses she loved so much. She was now able to communicate telepathically with them, non-verbally, just by sending out thoughts and attuning to them. With telecommunication, I witnessed her direct a horse into her house and have it sit on its hind legs in her living room. A few years later, Mary left Bucks County to open a massage school for horses in Virginia. Both her daughters were still clear of their prior conditions by the time the family moved south.

During that time, Kelly, my sister-in-law, re-lived her birth trauma while getting adjusted and was without breath for a few minutes, enough time for me to get very concerned. I immediately called Donald Epstein, D.C., in his office in Bellmore, N.Y., asking him for some guidance. He instructed me to hold gentle contact on the posterior aspect of the second vertebrae in the neck, and her breathing resumed. We later discovered that Kelly had had a difficult birth with prolonged apnea. Cellular memories of the traumatic birth, which had been held for years, were being released.

Another woman appeared to be drowning while getting adjusted, making intense gurgling noises as if she were inhaling water. Upon questioning her mother, it turned out that as a young child, while taking a bath and slipping underwater, she had nearly drowned in a tub. The adjustments were clearing the cellular memories of that trauma. She had been plagued with respiratory problems for years. Consequently, those breathing conditions vanished.

During that span of time, I witnessed healing and resolutions of health problems in my clients at a very rapid rate, way beyond the norms of my prior years in practice.

For the following three months, I had no sexual desire. To the dismay but acceptance of my wife, I had become celibate. Sexual abstinence has come organically from within, not dictated by the church, as it is for Catholic priests. My sexual organs had actually retracted inward. My penis was no longer or larger than a young child's or like men's penises in cold water. All my energy had moved up my spine into the upper realms or chakras.

I became a vegetarian following the inner request of my body. I lived those months in constant bliss and inner peace. I still managed to give regular health talks every other week. They had a totally different tone and content. There was no need for me to prepare talking points. I spoke extemporaneously in present-time consciousness.

One evening, on September 17, 1988, Jane begged me to watch the opening of the Seoul Olympic Games on television, as a family, with our two adopted Korean children, Tanya and Boo.

I had lived a secluded life for three months with a monk-like discipline. So I honored her request and sat down in front of the television. The instant I locked on to the TV, a vacuum cleaner-like virtual energetic tube sucked the energy out of me from within the television. In an instant, I had come down to a lower vibrational state of being. It was not as low a stage as prior to that adjustment in Atlanta, but the change was marked. Since then, I feel I have organically grown and raised my stage of being, yet I have not re-entered that same state of being. Could television keep the masses in a lower vibrational state of being? My experience speaks to this possibility.

Indeed the energy was fragile. With hindsight, I regret not having guarded it better. If I had known its fragility, I would have done what David Hawkins, M.D., the author of Power vs. Force, did. I would have secluded myself away from the modern world for a year or so at a retreat center or in nature. I would have integrated and grounded this state of being deeper into myself to a firm and stable stage of being.

Ken Wilber, transpersonal psychologist and author of many books, including A Brief History of Everything, clearly distinguishes between stages and states of consciousness. One must go through all the stages, like climbing the rungs of a ladder, to attain and retain the highest level. The higher states of consciousness that can be experienced by those using psychogenic substances, other drugs, or alcohol are a result of suppressing the lower energy fields so people can experience the higher ones. The presence of what is already within us is simply revealed. These heightened experiences can lead to openings and insights into what is possible. However, there is a cost that everyone needs to weigh for themselves. As David Hawkins states in Power vs Force, "The permanent high-state experience, which may be legitimately attained only through a lifetime of dedicated inner work, can be reached temporarily by artificial means. But the balance of nature dictates that to artificially acquire that state without having earned it creates a debt, and the negative imbalance results in negative consequences."

The experience of a higher state of being can be the impetus to rise to a new stage. Stages of being are permanent until the next stage is reached while climbing higher and higher on the ladder of consciousness. However, throughout it all, our basic personality remains with all its quirks and shortcomings.

Unfortunately, the window of time that had opened in the mid-1980s closed off. Donald Epstein, D.C., was aggressively attacked by some of the powers that be within the Chiropractic profession.

A few state boards and colleges made his approach to clearing the neuro-spinal system illegal. Many chiropractors who observed him adjust, without themselves experiencing his adjustments, ridiculed him. They felt threatened by the power of what they saw. They felt inaccurate and inadequate in the care they were giving in the face of what they witnessed. Egos were being challenged. Most scorned him, making derogatory comments in light of what they saw: people being adjusted, manifesting involuntary wave-like movements, adopting spontaneous yoga postures, or emoting loudly. All were forms of release of trapped energy, stored memories of trauma or postures, to direct the life force where the body needed it most for healing.

Few became curious. Most had no context to make what they saw fit into the limited box of their education. It was ground-breaking work.

Dr. Epstein soon withdrew and shelved that adjustment process. He tamed it and made it more acceptable while engaging in scientific validation. For a time, his heart was broken. He suffered from heart problems. He was deeply hurt that his beloved vocation and profession could not embrace the gift he had birthed.

I witnessed and took part in a peep preview of what was possible. I had a glance at the maturity of chiropractic adjustment, its potential, and what it could deliver to the world in the future. For the first time, I fully understood the words of the Developer of chiropractic, B.J. Palmer, D.C.: "The sole purpose of the adjustment is to unite the physical with the spiritual."

At first, I did not fully comprehend what had happened to me. Of course, I knew I had entered a higher state of being. But what state? It was not until I read the books titled *I* and *The Eye of the I*, by David Hawkins, M.D., Ph.D., that I understood.

In those books, he described his experience with enlightenment. I can honestly say that the ways he described his state of being could have been my own writing. I could not have formulated it better.

I had experienced enlightenment-a state of being I held for three months. The adjustment had opened the channel for the Kundalini energy to rise from a coiled serpent at the base of the spine to blossom into a thousand petal lotus flowers in my brain.

Years before, I had read a book by Peace Pilgrim called *Peace Pilgrim: Her Life and Work in Her Own Words*. She was a luminous older woman who had walked more than a hundred thousand miles for peace without asking for food or lodging until it was freely offered. Friends of Peace Pilgrim is the organization that was founded after her example to carry on her legacy. In some of her writings, she charts her path to enlightenment as being a series of spikes to higher levels of consciousness, only to drop back down. At times she experienced deep lows. Toward the end of her life, she spiked up again and retained the enlightened stage.

This gave me great comfort that the journey is not over and possibilities still abound. Moving through the stages requires sustained inner work to plow the field to make it fertile. Ultimately, the occurrence of enlightenment appears to be outside our control. We cannot force, push, or will ourselves into it. Attachment and desire will stand in the way. One can only be open to the possibility.

Since my enlightenment phase, following the adjustments from Dr. Epstein, D.C., I have shared with many audiences what I had experienced. Frequently, people came to me and revealed that they had similar experiences during or after getting adjusted by him or by the few chiropractors he had taught. These sharings were mutually validating. It gave me solace that I had not gone off the deep end and that my experience was real and communal with others.

During these extraordinary times, I brought my family and in-laws to get adjusted by him in Bellmore, Long Island, New York. Both my sisters-in-law Kelly and Mary Ellen began to channel angelic beings following their adjustments. Today Kelly is a well-known channel in Bucks County, PA., and beyond. She was recently invited by a prominent breast-cancer surgeon in Sedona, AZ, to channel for hundreds of her patients. When the nerve channels open fully, through the release of blockages along the neuro-spinal system, we become more open to higher energies and realities.

Since 1989 Dr. Epstein has been holding Transformational Gates throughout the USA that later extended to Europe. These are two-day events where participants are being adjusted every few hours, giving them time to process and integrate the energetic and neurological changes. Instead of attempting to treat symptoms or disease, people must experience the power of innate forces that heal, transform and awaken us. It engenders a greater connection to our inner SELF. He adjusted, with his staff, thousands of lay people, chiropractors, and students. What I witnessed was astonishing. It often defies the rational mind and the reality we live in.

What I am about to describe might sound to some as made up, impossible, and even downright insanity. Insanity often appears when we have reached the limits of our rational minds. Going to the moon might have seemed pure insanity to the brightest scientific minds in the eighteenth century.

One may want to stay open to what follows.

At a teaching seminar, I observed, along with my wife Jane and many other participants, black smoke coming out of a man's mouth and lungs while he was being adjusted. It turned out that, years ago, this man had been in an airplane fire with consequent smoke inhalation. Through the adjustment process, he released the stored trauma of that experience by virtually releasing the smoke in retrograde.

Needless to say, respiratory problems that plagued him for years cleared up.

I witnessed, at a seminar in Florida, the brother-in-law of Monroe Schneider, a chiropractor from Pennsylvania, moving his paralyzed limbs at will while Dr. Epstein held a contact on his second cervical vertebrae. As long as the connection took place, Dr. Epstein, who was standing behind the man in the wheelchair, could move his own leg and cause the paralyzed man's leg to move in unison. Both had become one, as the neurological blockage had been bypassed.

I saw surgically fused toes breaking loose and regaining full movement at all the metatarsal joints. The Light released had transmuted matter, as well as time, by reversing the surgery. Hard to believe, but we know today that matter is nothing but energy in motion. Just as a blast of energy can transmute solid ice into water and then vapor, a blast of life energy can transform articulations. We need to remind ourselves that the past, present, and future all happen simultaneously. Traveling in the past to heal the present is as possible as traveling into the future to heal it.

I observed a previously rigid older woman adopt a spontaneous yoga posture and move her body with amazing flexibility as a result of the life force released by an adjustment. All movements were completely involuntary and inner generated, as the vital energy was moving through her body, being Innately directed where needed. She had never before done yoga in her life.

My wife Jane and I traveled numerous times to Dr. Epstein's office in Bellmore, N.Y.

We were moved to tears when an older woman got off the adjusting table in excitement, crying out: "I can stand, I can walk, I can walk, I can dance!" She had been a young child in a concentration camp during World War II. The Nazis had had her legs bound at the knees by wires. This was done to many children in the later days of these camps. The gas chambers and crematoriums were running at full bore around the clock while trains loaded with Jews were arriving. The Nazis, knowing that the Allied were approaching, wanted to eliminate all evidence of their heinous crimes.

When the G.I.s liberated the camp, they saw many children walking on their knees with bound limbs. The Nazis did this to save space by stacking the young children on shelves while waiting for the gas chamber.

The G.I.s clipped the wire and held the children under the armpits while another G.I. yanked the legs out to bring the knees into extension. In some children, it caused damage to the growth plates of the head of the femur and hip socket.

As they grew up, those children could not bear their own weight. The ball and socket joints of the hips never fully formed and thus were not functioning normally. Incredibly, in this older woman, the life force healed her body.

If it were not for the presence of my wife and the Jewish family, I would have thought that I had conjured that up in my mind. How was this possible?

In my office, I witnessed a woman with cervical fusion and wiring of the transverse processes, the lateral bony protuberances on each side of vertebrae, regaining all movement following adjustments I gave her during that three-month period of my heightened state of being. She regained full motion of her neck and brought spinal X-rays showing that all the wires had broken loose.

All these events could be labeled miracles, yet they were just the outcome of great adjusting skills combined with an open heart, love, and a selfless desire to serve and help others. These so-called miracles were the works of the power of the Light released and moving freely through the body.

Richard Bartlett, D.C., in his book The Physics of Miracles, explains how miracles are the result of touch, love, and the practitioners being a vehicle to be used by the divine to do the healing. Non-judgment of the person's condition, symptoms, or diseases is essential to access the field of all possibilities. Christ certainly was not a diagnostician. Non-attachment to the outcome is also a critical ingredient in healing. If we want to be an instrument of healing, our attachment to the outcome has to be zilch, absolutely nil, zero, the big zip. As health professionals, our efficiency escalates as we become healing facilitators rather than believing we are the healers.

I believe we are now only years away from the Science of Miracles. I believe that in the near future, nearly all healing will be done by light, love, sound, and touch. Sound healing, cold laser, ultra-focus sound therapy, Reiki, vibrational healing, adjustments, and many other forms of hands-on healing are emerging with a promising future.

During my phase of enlightenment, it became inconceivable for me to go to a mall. Neon lights and blazing music became intolerable to my senses. One feels more rather than less in that state of being. In many ways, chiropractic is not about numbing pain or the senses. It is about opening up perceptions and feelings. As one feels more, one is more aware. The brain-body itself is also more aware and attuned to what it needs to heal and/or ought to avoid. As perception increases, so might pain, yet pain can be an enzyme for growth and transformation as well as a path to healing.

It allows the body to learn new strategies for living. Pain is, in many instances, a message that the body needs to reveal the do's and don'ts of living. Pain has been labeled the Western way of meditating. It can be a guiding mechanism to alter the way we treat our bodies. Many of us have experienced the severe pain associated with uncrossing our legs when one limb has fallen asleep, causing numbness. As the blood circulation returns, intense pain is felt, yet healing is taking place.

As it turned out, my personal experience with enlightenment was shared by many others who were adjusted by Donald Epstein or his staff during the mid-eighties. What I had lived could be validated by others. I was no longer standing alone on this journey. I no longer felt like a lone freak wolf with a weird story to tell.

I want to clarify again that there is a wide distinction between the state of enlightenment and being enlightened. One is enlightened during the experience, yet as that vibrational state of being recedes, enlightenment fades. However, the profound experience becomes a touchstone as to what is attainable.

Uniting the physical with the spiritual has been the ultimate purpose of B.J. Palmer, D.C., the Developer of chiropractic. After 125 years of existence, still in its infancy as a profession, the desired goal is starting to pierce through. What a powerful difference a single human being can make in lifting humanity upwards.

Understanding Symptoms

One may ask, "Why spend so much of this book on various facets of health? What does it have to do with the mosquito principle and making a difference in the world?" Being healthy and having a health-focused mindset demands being awake, alert, and conscious. It requires living moment by moment daily with heightened awareness. This alone makes a difference. Every being engaged on such a path contributes to the health of humanity. We are cells in the body of humankind. With that in mind, understanding symptomatology is critical, as it changes how we interact with them.

Symptoms have gotten a bad rap. They have been cast as villains by modern medicine. Let's face it; no one seems to enjoy pain or symptoms. Billions of dollars are being spent and made every year on their suppression. Most people seek relief, even if temporary, because no one wants to feel bad. This is very understandable. Yet there might be a hefty price to pay. Such behavior usually costs our overall health dearly down the line. The advance of drugs and medications has molded the human herd into numbing whatever aches us.

This pattern of behavior is deeply encrusted within the human psyche. It is quite challenging to rout it out. As with most undesirable habits, it takes repeated efforts to change them.

As a collective, humanity seems to have endorsed the belief that life should be at an even keel, a nearly sensation-free ride, without physical and emotional fluctuations or ups and downs. So most of society has bought into numbing itself with drugs and medications. But is that the nature of life?

Now the question arises: "Why on earth would we want to feel our symptoms and not suppress them?" Could the short-term comfort gained not be worth the debilitating long-term effects we will irrevocably endure later on? The Western world likes to play Chess, a game with the objective of killing the king. The Orient enjoys the game of Go, a long-term strategic game in which the two players aim to surround more territory than the opponent. In the West, we seek immediate gratification and relief, but not so much in the East. Health is a long-game endeavor. Suppressing symptoms is nearly always short-sighted.

If anyone needs convincing, just go spend a day in a nursing home. What you will witness there are the survivors of the suppressing symptoms mentality. Older people staring into space absently with a whole smorgasbord of prescribed medications within reach. The actual yearly casualties from adverse reactions to symptom-suppressing interventions in the USA are equal to all U.S. casualties in WWI and The Civil War combined, according to Gary Null, Ph.D., in his book titled *Death by Medicine*. Could it be that most people would fare better long-term without suppressing their symptoms?

We need to rethink symptoms. Symptoms are part of the inborn language of the body. They are part of the language of innate intelligence within all of us. As human beings, we must decide whether the body, with its myriad of functions, chemical processes, and adaptive capacities, is dumb and stupid or intelligent beyond measure.

For me, this isn't even a question I need to ask myself. All the evidence points to the fact that the human body is super smart and intelligent above comprehension.

With all my education in the life sciences, from biology to neurology, I could not run one single liver cell of my own body. Yet my body runs an estimated 100 billion tissue cells extremely efficiently. Thank God that it does this all by itself, outside my intellectual control, because it is hard enough for me to keep track of all my daily tasks. I cannot imagine having to regulate my heart, liver, kidneys, brain, and lungs, amongst all other organs, while driving my motorcycle. I would quickly crash and not be long for this world.

Would that kind of super intelligence create symptoms with no purpose? Would the inborn wisdom of life lose it when it comes to symptoms? Would symptoms happen for no reason at all? Is all the wisdom of the universe gone when we express symptoms? I think not. The inner wisdom is ever present; its capacity to express itself and communicate properly via the nerve system may have been impaired, yet it is always potentially available around the clock.

Symptoms communicate different messages depending on what is happening. They can signal that something is array within, a sort of warning light. They let us know that some parts have been injured, broken, disconnected, or damaged. They may strictly be a natural expression of adaptation to a changing environment. They may also be the final expression of a long-standing silent dysfunction that has moved into pathology with associated symptoms. In some situations, medications might then be appropriate. Yet not always.

Pathology also means the path of logic. Why do pathological symptomatic expressions take a logical path? Because innate wisdom is guided by the laws of life. One of the dominant laws of life is the law of survival. Consequently, the body will make all the sequential adaptations necessary to preserve life and safeguard the most vital organs to remain alive as long as possible.

Frequently symptoms are messages to change behavior or lifestyle. We may view symptoms as abnormal responses to what we consider a normal lifestyle when, in reality, they are normal responses to an abnormal lifestyle. By suppressing them, we totally shut down the impetus to change our way of life. Long-term consequences surely await us. Suppressing symptoms is, in most instances, like rearranging the chairs on the deck of the Titanic, as my friend Ted Koren, D.C., would say.

Most humans have poor knowledge of the language of the Innate. They know the beginning of the alphabet of the body's inner language, usually from A to J: I am hungry, thirsty, tired, sleepy, I have to do number one, do number two, I am cold, hot, uncomfortable, and clearly I am horny. Past that, listening to the Innate is often sparse. Yet the body constantly speaks if we can just slow down, tune inward and learn to listen.

Our inborn, Innate Intelligence guides us as to what foods agree or disagree with us: pasty tongue, dried mouth, stomach ache or bloating, flatulence, loose bowels, constipation, rashes, hives, irritability, lethargy, a sudden drop of energy or sleepiness, the list of messages to listen to goes on and on as we tune inward. Those symptoms nudge us to make changes. Could it be a good idea to listen and act upon those messages? The body's intelligence moves our hand instinctively to cover an aching back, a toothache, a headache, or a hurt. The discipline of Reiki has proven the healing power of laying of hands. We are Innately guided to scratch an itch. The guidance is constant as the body processes an estimated 30,000 environmental inputs per second. Indeed it might be wise to relearn — or — remember the meaningful language of symptoms.

There are basically six categories of symptoms:

- Cleansing symptoms:

Vomiting, diarrhea, pus discharge, pimples, rashes, perspiration, and in some instances, coughing are ways the body purges itself to eliminate and push out unwanted by-products of the body's physiology and/or toxic substances. If you were to have a dinner date with a friend and both of you ate spoiled foods leading to food poisoning, your bodies may respond differently. You may vomit within a few hours while your friend may feel fine, wondering what is the matter with you. Medically, you would be the sick one, while your friend would be considered healthy. You might actually be the healthy one, as your body quickly identified the poison and effectively discharged it.

Your friend's body might be so numbed out that it did not even pick up being poisoned. As a result, it ingested the toxic substances deep within its tissues with potential damage. Medically we have it upside down and backward when it comes to most symptoms.

In some instances, vomiting, diarrhea, and fever are signs the body may be working very well, hard at work ridding itself of various toxic substances or unwanted bacteria. The fever associated with food poisoning is the built-in mechanism to kill and inhibit bacterial reproduction. In any case, not having any symptoms might be alarming and a sign that the body is not functioning properly.

A close friend of mine, Joshua, started vomiting chronically. Unbeknown to him, he was experiencing renal failure. So his body, through vomiting, was attempting to discharge the toxins the kidneys were no longer removing. He soon recognized that he needed medical help. Suppressing the vomiting could have indeed brought on sudden death.

Coughing, the deep kind of cough where the diaphragm and intercostal muscles are involved, along with the bronchial tubes' muscle contractions, drives the air out of the lungs at a speed of 90 mph. The purpose of such coughing is to air-blast the respiratory system, pushing upward and outward all kinds of unwanted materials such as synthetic fibers, undesirable bacteria, toxic fumes, dust particles, or cancerous cells. Usually, some mucus will come up, trapping particles of lead, fiberglass, dust, and synthetic carpet fibers, among others. Suppressing such a cough would work against the body rather than for the body. After years of suppressing this type of cough, whenever it comes back, which is the body's attempt to clean itself, one may develop lung disease, a growth, or a tumor. Just as an air-conditioning system has a filter that needs to be cleaned or replaced regularly, the respiratory system has a built-in mechanism to clean itself periodically.

When my son Boo left Korea for his new home with us in the US, the immigration department required him to receive all his immunization shots before leaving Asia. Despite our objection, there was nothing we could do; we had to comply against our will. He arrived at JFK airport in New York on his first birthday. Within a few weeks, he became restless. He would squirm intensely when we would change his T-shirt that had to pass over his head. This behavior lasted for a while. Then one evening, he was sitting in his high chair at the kitchen counter and began crying uncontrollably. My wife Jane and I tried everything we could to calm him, from giving him a bottle to holding him, distracting him, to checking if his diaper was full; nothing would soothe him. At the time, he had long Korean hair that covered the side of his face below his ears. After what seemed like a long time, I felt compelled to hold his face between my hands, seeking to comfort him. As I reached for his face, I brushed away his hair and uncovered in horror that his left ear had swollen and coiled out of itself like a snail out of its shell. In fright, I took a step back. All I could see was the inside of his ear hanging out. It was gruesome.

Then, I caught myself, realizing I was in fear mode. I took a deep breath and relaxed, regaining my composure and trust in his body's wisdom. Immediately my eyesight shifted from a narrow focus to an open vision. I now saw the greater picture. With every cry, his face distorted, and the side of his face was contracting, engaging the masseter muscle of the left jaw and the temporalis muscle of his left temple. These mastication muscles were working in unison, pushing toward the ear. I gained an insight; a thought flashed that his body was working at increasing pressure on his left ear. Within ten minutes, the bulging ear burst out, and foul-smelling pus shot out. All I did then was brush a finger gently upwards against the side of his face, and more pus came out. By the next morning, it was as if nothing had ever happened. His ear had retracted within.

To date, at age 37, Mr. Boo, as we call him, has perfectly normal hearing. I know beyond any doubt that it was his body's way of ejecting the poisons present in the numerous vaccines injected into him. These toxic chemicals are called adjuvants. They are laden with mercury, formaldehyde, aluminum salts, and dead fetal cells, amongst other toxic substances. (Amorphous aluminum hydroxyphosphate sulfate (AAHS), aluminum hydroxide, aluminum phosphate, MF59 an oil-in-water emulsion composed of Squalene, AS01B made of Monophosphoryl lipid A, Cytosine Phosphoguanine (CpG) motifs, a synthetic form of DNA, potassium aluminum sulfate (Alum), Ethylmercury, antibiotics such as neomycin, polymyxin B, streptomycin and gentamicin). None of these can be good for anyone's body, even if promoted by the FDA as being safe due to the small amount of adjuvants.

Returning to Mr. Boo, I cannot help but think about what might have happened if I had panicked and called 911. Most likely, he would have been taken to the nearby hospital, given a painkiller and antibiotics, and the doctor might have lanced his ear. By stopping the pain, Boo would have stopped crying, and the bursting would have had to be done by a puncture to release the pus. Since we were in the early stage of adoption, Boo, like all adopted children, for the first year was in the legal custody of the State of Pennsylvania; social services might have viewed our non-interference approach as child abuse and taken our son away from us.

The curious thing is that if I had brought our son to the hospital and he had died while under medical treatment due to an anaphylactic reaction to an antibiotic, or by contracting an iatrogenic disease, no action would have been taken by the State of Pennsylvania against the doctors. This scenario happens from time to time. Parents are charged for not providing standard medical treatment, but not the medical personnel, when standard medical treatments cause injuries or death. This double standard needs to be addressed, as the issue of inside-out versus outside-in approach to healing and health is not clear to everyone. Decisions around which approach to take need to be evaluated according to each specific situation. We have sovereignty over our bodies and, as parents, those of our children. Freedom of choice is everyone's fundamental human right. I believe this right is being eroded at a fast pace, as we have observed during the COVID-19 pandemic.

Over the 40 years that I practiced Chiropractic, I have seen countless babies who were fine, then got vaccinated, only to return to my office within days or weeks with severe ear infections. Of course, to my dismay, those ear infections would be frequently treated with antibiotics. Even the American Pediatric Association recognizes that antibiotics are not an appropriate treatment for ear infections. The typical scenario was a quick resolution of the infection from the effects of the sulfa drugs, only to return soon after with greater intensity. In time parents were medically convinced by well-meaning pediatricians to place tubes in their children's ears. Often, the child's body would reject the tube. So then T-tubes were inserted that the body could not expel.

Is anyone listening to what the body is saying? "I do not want the tubes" is being spoken loud and clear. The fear of hearing loss is driving parents to comply with the standard approach when in reality, that fear is mostly unfounded. Whenever I could encourage the parents of a child with ear infections to trust the process and keep the baby's neuro-spinal system checked regularly and adjusted if needed, the outcome was quite different. The typical course of events was a crescendo, the peak path of the infection, combined with high fever, then would come the climax, the healing crisis and a resolution on its own. The cycle was complete. Thereafter the child did not have any other ear infections. Cleansing symptoms need not be suppressed; they need to be expressed so the body can do its work without the interference of us getting in its way.

- Healing symptoms:

Fever is probably the best healing mechanism the body has. That knowledge grew out of my own experience over the years. Multiple times I experienced raging fevers, as well as witnessed my wife and two children healing as a result of high fevers. Common sense tells me that if it is happening, there must be a reason and a purpose. Bottom line: the body is innately intelligent. Fever has been defined as "a state of elevated core temperature, a defensive response to the invasion of live microorganisms or inanimate matter recognized as pathogenic or alien to the body." That is an interesting definition, yet we are pushed to suppress fever.

In doing so, aren't we just working against ourselves?

Fever inhibits the bacterial life cycle. Whenever there is an infection caused by low tissue resistance or overwhelming exposure to harmful bacteria, the fever will rise to prevent their reproduction. Since bacteria have a short life span, with an average of 12 hours, their population dwindles quickly, and the infection is handled.

Fever kills viruses. Virologists estimate that at any given time, our body harbors around 380 trillion viruses, all living on and inside the body. The immune system keeps the peace, as we would not know that we are hosting so many submicroscopic guests. Most viruses will lay dormant until ready to deposit their genetic material. There is a scientific consensus that is seldom being heard; it stipulates that viruses are like messengers linking the entire DNA chain of life. They drive the evolution of cells to a greater extent than other environmental conditions. Their purpose is to update our own genetic pool so as to allow us to evolve and adapt to life's constant evolution.

Whenever a virus becomes active, the news update may threaten a non-flexible or stuck biological system. In other words, the organism cannot handle the news. It may even cause death. In most instances, with a balanced and flexible nerve system, along with a strong immune system and raging fever, the news update is accepted. Fever will kill the messenger who, having done its job, is no longer needed. In some situations, the temperature needs to rise to 103-106 degrees to eliminate the carrier.

In order to reach 103 to 106 degrees and above range, convulsions may be necessary. Convulsions are not the result of the high fever but their cause as it engages muscle contractions, thus generating additional heat.

The concern about brain damage and high fever is mostly unfounded. Fever does not cause brain damage except in some cases of over-exposure to the sun. With hyperthermia, indeed, the body needs to be cooled down progressively. That is common sense. The body might be super intelligent, yet it has limitations. Most of us are not bulletproof or extreme heat and fire-resistant. What causes neurological damage are harmful bacteria or viruses that are able to bypass the natural defenses of the body. How? Because fever was suppressed by drugs at the very onset.

These microorganisms want to survive like anyone else, as the law of survival is the strongest law of life. Since the early fever did not stop them, they went on to hide deep in the system, actually at the very core of it, by getting into the meninges, spinal cord, cerebrospinal fluid, or brain. Now we have spinal meningitis or encephalitis, which will be labeled as the cause of brain damage. The fever did not cause brain damage; it was more likely caused by interfering with the fever.

When fever rises, our inner pharmacopeia increases its production. For every $2°$ C of temperature increase, the metabolic rate rises by 20%. This means more drugs are available in greater quantities wherever and whenever needed. Interleukin I and II, anticancer agents, are being released by high body temperature. Cancer cells are being destroyed by high fever. Suppressing a fever might very well buy us cancer later on in life. We know today that nearly everyone has cancer cells present in their body on a regular basis, yet we have nothing to worry about. The immune system handles it daily. If necessary, a good fever will handle whatever was not taken care of by routine immune patrols. The walls of blood vessels open up with high temperatures to let larger macrophages enter areas previously closed to them, allowing them to seek out invaders.

Fever is by far one of the best biological healing symptoms available to us. Wise and aware people cover up with blankets and let the fever burn, sweat, shake, convulse, sleep, dream, space travel, and come back healed. A hot toddy appears to be comforting during the process.

Pain is frequently a healing symptom. It is said that pain is inevitable, yet suffering is optional. Pain can be a healing symptom when it guides us on what we can and cannot do. It may restrict us from doing something harmful, such as lifting too heavy a load or twisting in an abusive position. In that sense, it is a preventive symptom, protecting us from harm. It may limit our movement to allow a torn muscle, spinal disc, or ligament to mend. The antalgic position held by back-pain sufferers is designed to cast, brace, or immobilize the spine while the damage is being repaired over time. As the healing takes place, freedom of movement may return, managed by the decreasing pain.

Pain may also prevent us from eating, forcing us to fast to heal a GI tract problem and save energy spent on digestion for healing. Animals seem to know Innately that fasting is a great path to healing. We, humans, seem to have forgotten the healing power of fasting. So much can be learned by observing animal behaviors. I have read that pain is the Western way of meditating. I believe there is some truth to that. Pain allows us to slow down, rest, be still, and listen. Listen to the inner voice speaking, telling us important messages about our life and the way we live it.

Surely when intractable pain is a constant companion, sedatives are more than welcome. Blocking the pain can actually allow a person to rest, sleep, and heal. Post-surgical narcotics are certainly welcome. But this is neither the norm nor what we are addressing here.

Bleeding can, in some circumstances, be a healing symptom. A cut inflicted by a sharp object may bleed for a while in order to clean the cut. To restrict the bleeding is to invite a potential infection by blocking the cleansing process. Actually, sucking on the cut not only pulls more blood out as well as extracts any impurities. The salty saliva is a natural antiseptic as well as a healing formula. Saliva can change its chemical composition from poisonous venom when we bite someone out of rage or while under a life-threatening assault to a love ointment in love-making to a healing salve when licking an injury.

Women may bleed between periods as a way to erode and clean the walls of the uterus. This process may dislodge an early growth, abscess, tumor, or some pre-cancerous tissues. Clearly, if the bleeding becomes chronic, it is an indication that something has interfered with the natural, normal functioning of the body. Medical intervention might be necessary. Yet the cause of the underlying malfunction needs to be determined. Removal of the uterus may solve the immediate crisis, yet it does not address what has gone awry in the first place and how to remedy it. If not resolved, consequences will emerge in some other organs at a later time.

My little dog Mia vomited significant pools of blood every few hours for a full night and a day. She became weak and lethargic, refused food, and drank little water for the next 24 hours. The next day she refused all water. She lay still, and I thought she might be dying. By the following day, though, she perked up and took in a small amount of water. By day's end, she ate a tiny bit. I will never know what she purged out of herself; was it the stomach or liver that she cleaned out? Was it cancerous tissues she got rid of?

The blood was bright red, and some of it was darker, with membranes and gobs of mucus in it. We loved her, caressed her, and soothed her through the process. Jane and I were saddened and grieving, yet we were willing to let go of the outcome and not interfere. As it turned out, she healed, all on her own, by respecting the messages she was getting about eating, drinking, and resting.

It would serve us right as humans to learn from animals. I noticed that all the dogs I ever had purged themselves regularly by eating grass and cleaning their GI tract by drinking muddy water out of a puddle. Mud and clay have been an ancient and effective mode of cleansing the body. Clay has inherent magnetic properties as well as the capacity to draw out toxins and coat wounds or ulcerated areas. I wonder how city dogs manage to purge, as they are always walking leashed on concrete sidewalks.

- Symptoms are messages to change:

There is no question that many symptoms nudge us to alter the way we live. So often, I met overweight people complaining of pain in their feet, knees, or lower back. The message is quite clear, yet not always easy for people to follow.

People who are not exercising frequently experience shortness of breath and heart and blood pressure problems. They may even develop tendonitis of the wrist from overuse of the TV remote by being couch potatoes. Even that message may not come through to them. In a society where we have been led to believe that life should be lived at an even keel and where pain can be suppressed at any time with drugs, it is no wonder that so many people cannot listen to the messages for change.

- Adaptive symptoms:

When fall is here, and the cold season is rapidly approaching, nearly everyone, at one point or another, will have a cold. In one year alone, Americans spend the equivalent of the national budget of all the Central American countries combined on cold remedies, a whopping $6 billion, trying to alleviate or cure their colds. All this is in vain, at the expense of the liver, kidneys, overall body chemistry, and potentially long-term health problems, not to mention the pocket.

In a futile attempt to gain temporary relief, we destroy our long-range health. All drugs, whether over-the-counter or prescribed, have side effects. Our society still regards a cold as an illness we catch from someone who had it before us. Not so. A cold is a normal, natural adaptive process. It is our body's biological way of adapting to environmental changes that occur in the fall as we move into winter and then again in late winter as spring arrives. Colds occur at times when all of life outside goes through profound changes. In the fall, trees are shedding their leaves, lawns are turning brown, animal furs are becoming thicker, and bees are moving underground; the list goes on as all of nature undergoes a transformation. By spring, the resurgence of life can be seen everywhere, as trees and shrubs bud, grass turns green, flowers spring up, and animals shed their winter coats. As human beings, we are *part* of nature, not *apart* from it. We are alive and, just like the rest of nature, are going through similar changes. We label this a cold. The symptoms we experience — stuffy nose, sneezing, coughing, scratchy throat, runny eyes, and sometimes fever, are normal processes our body goes through to clean the sinuses and upper respiratory tract.

In other words, a cold is the menstruation or shedding of the mucus lining of the sinuses and upper respiratory system. That lining needs a different coating for a changing situation. No amount of medication will stop the process. Instead, it temporarily suppresses the symptoms while rendering the body more toxic. As the late Dr. Robert Mendelsohn, M.D., put it in his book *Confession of a Medical Heretic,* "A cold with medication lasts a week. Without it, it lasts seven days!"

Yet by suppressing the symptoms of a cold down the line, we may be paying dearly. Recent findings have uncovered that during a cold, the body activates protein P53, an anti-mutagen agent instrumental in preventing cancer. Who knows if the pandemic of cancer may be partially due, among other causes, to something as simple as society interfering with a normal biological process?

Contrary to popular belief, colds are not caused by viruses. Viruses may be present while we are *colding,* but this does not make them the causative agent. England's Common Cold Research Unit, established in 1946 in Salisbury, has been a pioneering institution in the worldwide study of transmission, treatment, and prevention of colds. Every year 400 volunteers spend weeks at the lavish research facility where they are given nose drops that contain Rhinoviruses. As of 1993, 47 years and 18,800 volunteers later, only one-third of the tested subjects ever caught a cold. And that is because the one-third who reacted to the artificial, unnatural swabbing of Rhinoviruses may have a weakened immune system. Viruses do not cause colds; no more than flies bring garbage. Any proactive avenue that allows the body to function better and expresses life more fully provides greater resistance to sickness and disease, ensures a better immune response, and facilitates the shedding and cleansing process of the cold.

So the next time you are *colding*, remember, you did not catch it from someone who had it before you. If you did, someone would have caught it from someone who had it before them. This would mean that Adam, the first man, must have had a cold to pass it on to others throughout history. However, there was nobody before Adam he could have caught it from! A little common sense beats the common cold theory.

The teething process in children can be painful to both the child and parents. We all know of the crankiness of babies in that phase of life. Associated with the process of growing teeth are very specific sequential symptoms. Once understood, concerns and suffering vanish. First comes irritability, then drooling, discomfort, pain, mucus discharge from the nose, fever, rashes around the mouth, loose bowels, diarrhea, and diaper rash. That is a lot for a little one to handle. However, it is natural and normal. Yet it seems that it is the parents who are having the harder time. They usually want to eradicate the symptoms, thinking their child is sick.

The biological reality is that every symptom that comes with teething is perfectly orchestrated. The irritability is normal since drilling through young bones is not so pleasant. The drooling does moisturize the drill bit, which is the upcoming tooth. It also tenderizes the gum and provides saliva enzymes to begin digesting the broken-down tissues coming from bones and gum. Pain causes the child to want to chew on something to pressure the gum against the growing tooth, thus facilitating the perforation. The mucus results from bacterial action that is munching on the dead tissues. A lot of mucus will be discharged outside by drooling, yet some will be absorbed through swallowing. As the mucus, loaded with dead tissue and bacteria, hits the stomach, the body moves fast to discharge it to the intestines. In turn, the peristaltic movement, the contraction of the gut muscles, will move the package down and out. The irritation around the mouth is due to the saliva partially digesting the skin on the face. Diaper rashes are due to the acidity of the bowel that has moved so fast through the digestive tube.

There is also a reflex action between the mouth and anus, as both ends are part of the same tube, the gastric tube, in embryological development. If you haven't noticed, pay attention when you bite on a very pungent or bitter food and witness what contracts at the other end! All those teething symptoms are perfectly normal, healthy, and necessary. There is not a thing to worry about. Rest in peace, while the medical profession is raking in millions of dollars because of well-meaning parents viewing their teething toddlers as sick, seeking to suppress the symptoms.

Blisters and calluses are common-sense responses to prolong irritation. When the rubbing is acute and chronic, the bubble will form. I have seen Dr. Val, D.C., a woman who attended a six-day training in Colorado, come back from an extreme mountain hike with a blister bubble that covered the entire length of the sole of her foot. She was quite overweight and got the message loud and clear. She was the only one with such a huge blister among over a hundred participants.

I am sure a few others had some blisters, but she won the trophy. The amazing thing is that she was a passionate chiropractic teacher on staff with us; she managed to teach the rest of the training, standing on her feet for hours. Subsequently, she reduced her weight and remained fit for years to come.

Calluses will form when the friction is chronic yet moderate. It is an adaptive process to render the area of use tougher. It happens not only in the hands of manual workers but also in the bones of martial artists. The shins of Muay

Thai practitioners are hardened like a baseball bat after years of beating their legs against tree trunks, a useful adaptation to their sport.

I have seen emotional calluses on the hearts of soldiers and veterans from ongoing exposure to very painful and gory war situations. I have also seen an X-ray of a bullet that could not be removed due to its proximity to the heart, being flattened by years of heart pounding. An amazing feat of adaptation.

It's similar to the way bursitis, tendonitis, myositis, gastritis, colitis, and many other -itises normally adapt to overuse and/or abuse. They are warning signals that things better change in the way we have been living, eating, or using our bodies. The inflammation will settle, in time and at various speeds, depending on the tissues involved. Tendons and bursa heal slowly. The stomach and other muscles heal faster.

In my late forties, I acquired bursitis and tendonitis in my shoulder and elbow from doing too many push-ups at an extreme angle. It took me nearly a year to heal from it. Granted, I continued to do push-ups as part of my daily routine, yet modified the position to adjust to the pain. The pain guided me, yet it did not stop me from training. Even as we age, the body is still healing, especially if we treat it right.

- Pathological symptoms:

These symptoms arise from long-standing mal-function or dis-ease. The body has not been working right for years and has been mostly asymptomatic except for a hardly perceptible and gradual loss of energy. Milder symptoms may have been present off and on, yet, in most instances, they were suppressed with over-the-counter drugs or medications, therefore, not tended to. It is important to understand that there is a chain of events taking place from health to disease: the path goes from normal physiology to dis-ease physiology that is either asymptomatic or mildly symptomatic, to silent pathology, to expressive pathology, to disease, and potentially an early death.

These symptoms follow a logical path. They move up the chain of interfered physiology, scarifying the least important parts, such as limbs and non-essential organs while preserving the most vital organs, lungs, heart, brain, kidneys, and liver. At times, after repeated abuse, a specific organ, even a vital one, may fail. A heart attack is a good example. It is easy to know that the heart will never attack itself. What kind of intelligence would design the human body and then cause the heart to attack itself? We know that such heart pathology starts as early as childhood through the use of junk food, lack of exercise, poor nutrition, and through long-lasting interferences to the nervous system. An added stress on the nerve system can precipitate the heart to fail, the straw that brakes the camel's back.

- Retracing symptoms:

The last categories of symptoms are those experienced while embarking on a natural healing journey. Somehow that just doesn't seem fair. Here we are doing good things for ourselves and getting all kinds of symptoms. Who says life is always fair? Have you ever gone to a natural organic health food store? Did you ever question the value of eating such good food when you look at the pimply workers and cashiers? Good healthy food will kick the junk out, and it won't look pretty at first. Persist, however, and things usually turn around.

The same retracing process frequently takes place with people starting chiropractic care by mid-life or later. It is common for these people to experience symptoms they had in the past and had been silenced with medications. The good news is that the process will be over in time, and a new vitality will emerge. The U.S. Marines have a saying that pain is weakness leaving the body. To some degree, there is truth to that. As we become stronger, more vital, and healthier, there might be some symptoms or pain to endure on the way.

It becomes clear that symptoms are not a valuable gauge to assess our health or wellbeing. However, they can be a valuable gauge to assess our injury or disease state. One may be healthy and have no symptoms. One may be quite ill, silently malfunctioning — and have no symptoms.

By the same token, one may be healthy and have symptoms, healing and adapting. One may be quite sick and, of course, manifest symptoms. As pertinent as symptoms might be in sickness and disease, they become almost irrelevant when we are interested in promoting our health, vitality, and wellbeing.

This little-known common sense knowledge about symptoms significantly impacted countless lives. It can transform yours as well.

The Normalcy of Sickness

When focusing on health as a path to transformation, understanding how we approach illness has been crucial on my journey. It has significantly impacted my return to health when faced with an illness.

What if, contrary to what most believe, sickness were to be our God-given birthright? Would that change our mindset and approach to it? Could sickness actually be normal? Such a proclamation is destabilizing, yet a proposition worth investigating.

As shocking as this might be, hang in there, open up, and see if a new perspective may be viable.

Because of the belief that illness should not exist, society has launched an all-out war on it. The language used by modern medicine echoes warfare images: we wage war on disease, eradicate leukemia, wipe out multiple sclerosis, zap cancer, go on a seek-and-destroy mission, bombard the tumor, cut out the growth, and combat the infection. Overall, we are propagating a philosophy of *against* instead of *for*. We are against symptoms, against sickness, and against disease; we are even against death. This approach has been insidious and is such a part of our social and cultural domestication that we no longer question it. We have responded physiologically with fear at the news of a diagnosis, which only contributes to a weaker immune response, biochemistry, physiology, and often a poor outcome.

It is well known that people who experience spontaneous remission operate from unwavering faith, trust, and clarity while frequently dismissing the news of a serious illness, as reported by the diagnosis. They operate outside the norms of most.

Anita Moorjani, now famous for her TEDx talk, should have died from end-stage lymphoma on February 2, 2006.

Weighing 85 lbs., she was in a coma after fighting cancer for four years with lymph node lumps the size of lemons. Nearly all her organs were failing. Her doctors told her family she had only hours to live. After leaving her body, she experienced expanded awareness, connecting to everything and gaining clarity that her fears were the cause of her disease. Previously unbeknown to her, she had been a participant in her disease. She returned in physical form to heal and be cancer free within five weeks. Her disease was a gift for her transformation.

The late Norman Cousins, professor, political journalist, and world peace advocate shares in *Anatomy of an Illness* how he outlived his prognosis of ankylosing spondylitis - a degenerative disease of the connective tissues. He disregarded the diagnosis and created his own laughter therapy, now known to boost the immune system and relieve pain and stress. He ended up attending the funerals of many of his own younger doctors.

Andrew Weil, M.D., in his book *Spontaneous Healing*, gathers ample evidence that positivism, trust, and faith in the natural ability of the body to heal are vital ingredients of spontaneous healing. In most instances, people who experienced miraculous healing and remission will explain that it was not the new treatment protocol, diet regimen, or nutritional supplements but rather a deep-seated change in beliefs, consciousness, and state of being that triggered the healing. They vividly recall a shift that took place internally at a specific moment in time. A sort of inner awakening had given birth to spontaneous healing. An in-depth realization, an epiphany, had occurred that was transformative. Deep-seated patterns were abolished. Clarity about their responsibility, participation, and fears in creating their condition had surfaced. It led them to dissolve fears, clear destructive internal dialogues, and patterns to embrace trust in the life force powering them. The biochemistry, immune and positive physiology of trust can be activated as we embrace illness as an offering and a normal path to healing at the core.

When my left elbow spontaneously shattered in a movement I had done hundreds of thousands of times, I knew through pathology this was very likely the result of four years of nerve compression in my neck that led to disorganization, disconnection, and the devitalizing of the bone cells in the elbow.

This was caused by a few hours of mountain biking, riding with my right hand only while holding a heavy bag in my left arm. The chronic contracture on the left side led to my neck being locked. In spite of frequent adjustments, it remained locked for years until it finally cleared. By then, decay had taken place, with associated cancerous damages.

X-rays from the hospital emergency room in Barcelona, Spain, showed a five-centimeter shadow on my left humerus. Subsequent needle biopsy at the fracture site, taken by the oncology orthopedic team in Denver, CO, came back positive for unspecified pathology of either osteosarcoma or osteomyeloma. Following the diagnosis, the oncologist orthopedic surgeon told Jane and me: "We need to do chemo and radiation. If you do not do it, you will be back in three months, and we will have to amputate your arm to save your life." Those were his exact words. Jane and I looked at each other, a silent mutual understanding passing between us, and we both got up and walked away. We drove back seven hours to Durango, concerned, yet feeling empowered by our joint decision. We were not going to give in fear. We decided on a different path. My elbow was reconstructed with a titanium prosthesis by an orthopedist at the Animas Surgical Hospital in Durango.

Right away, I designed a natural healing protocol for myself to shock my physiology out of whatever pattern it was stuck in. I took full charge of my situation. From the moment I shattered my elbow and received the cancer diagnosis, my mind was running a continuous tape in a loop.

All I could think about was cancer, possible metastasis, and ensuing death. I was depressed and in a dark mood. Finally, after a month of the dreadful internal dialogue, I caught myself. The words from my first chiropractor that I had shared with audiences all over the world for years came back to me: "You cannot fight darkness; you must turn on the light."

I abruptly shifted to an internal dialogue of life, vitality, healing, and health. From that moment forward, it became my sole focus. From that inner decision on, I could talk with others, friends, and acquaintances about the bone cancer in my arm, yet it was no longer mine. I found myself completely detached from it. It lived outside of me. I stayed on my new routine and protocol for a year and a half, monitoring my blood markers every month. Within a year, my body had healed.

Certainly, it was wise to drastically shock my physiology. Doctor Terry Wahls' diet protocol, cryotherapy, daily breath work, white light meditation, exercising naked in the Colorado early morning cold weather — no matter what the temperature — infrared sauna, zero sugar or alcohol, Vit D, C, E, and omegas were contributing factors; yet the internal shift in mindset seems to me primary in my healing.

Rather than focusing on the disease, I focused on the healing process. If my body had created cancer, it could un-create it. I did not have cancer; I was *cancering*, a living, dynamic process created in my body by my body that could be reversed. Total trust was my daily companion.

So how was the disease normal and the cure? The elbow is a joint of transition and change in direction. Just look at your arm, bend the elbow, and you will see not only the transition but also the capacity to change the angle and direction of the hand. When my elbow exploded in pieces, I was at the door of a transition in my life. I was about to pass on my teaching seminars to senior staff. Yet I loved so much what I was doing that I kept delaying. I could not let it go just yet. The destruction of my elbow sent a clear message: You can no longer teach adjusting seminars. The disease was the cure, forcing me to let go and put me back on the beam of my life. Truly a blessing in disguise.

So could disease actually be normal? If so, being at war with it might not be the wisest approach. In the book Entropy, Jeremy Rifkin explains that disease was always part of humanity. Every era, from the cave people to the hunter-gatherer to the agricultural and industrial revolution to the present-day information age, always had specific diseases associated with it.

Cancer is the true pandemic of modern times; nature's response to a polluted, toxic, stressful, and radioactive environment. Our capacity to heal from it depends greatly on the strength of our immune system, the balanced state of our nerve system, our overall vitality, as well as our attitude, lifestyle, internal beliefs, and emotional and spiritual state. In the Southwest, one can observe disease as a normal phenomenon with prairie dogs. Their natural predators, the white ferret, have vanished. So their population regularly explodes. Then, spontaneously, the fleas that live in their fur trigger the black plague. Soon they are devastated by the disease, their population declines, and the balance is restored. The normalcy of disease helps engender balance in nature.

I am not suggesting ignoring a disease process and letting people die like prairie dogs to restore balance. Instaed, I am proposing that rather than attacking diseases we view as abnormal, we might be better off promoting health and facilitating healing, thus allowing the body to restore itself. Certainly, medical intervention might be necessary, yet being a fully active participant focusing on vitality, health, and healing is essential, if not critical.

Could sickness be an essential part of the health picture? Is it possible that health could not be viable without sickness? Could our body need the challenges of illness to reorganize itself and develop new and more appropriate strategies for living? Might the order of health be challenged by the dis-order of illness and indeed be necessary to create disruptive chaos? Chaos is the precursor to emerging creativity. As the poet Wallace Stevens wrote in *A Connoisseur of Chaos:* "A violent order is a disorder, and a great disorder is an order. These two things are the same." Is it then possible that sickness is a disruption needed as an ingredient of health?

Health and disease are like the positive and negative of electricity, the male and female, night and day. One cannot exist without the other. They are opposite forces of the same process. Could the weather exist without its high and low-pressure systems? Of course not. In The Treasure of Kahlil Gibran, Kahlil Gibran tells the story of a priest returning to his home in the evening after preaching at his church. Homebound, he encounters a human form lying by the side of the road, severely wounded, moaning in pain, and asking for help. As he approaches the man, he recognizes Lucifer, the Devil himself. The priest immediately recoils, turns away, and begins to walk home, feeling that the Devil's fate was now sealed. The Devil mustered some strength, though, yelling: "Priest, priest, do not let me die here, for next

Sunday, you will have nothing to preach for." In the oneness of life, there is polarity.

There is a Universal Law called the Law of Dipole, The Law of Opposites. The Chinese refer to it as yin-yang. When looking at the human body and the magic of its design, we can readily observe that law at work. The right and left lungs, although made of identical cells and tissues, are different in size and weight. The heart has four chambers with two small atriums and two larger ventricles. The nerve system has a parasympathetic and a sympathetic branch. There is venous and arterial circulation. In the pelvis, the auricular surfaces of the sacrum are longer and narrower than the one of the ilium. This phenomenon goes on ad infinitum.

Health and disease are parts of a dynamic equilibrium. Problems exist when our physiology is stuck anywhere along the spectrum or at one end or the other of the pendulum swing.

On one side of the swing, there are chronic and acute disease processes. These processes can be degenerative or inflammatory. There can also be tumors (two-more), malignant or benign, which really are hyper-growth processes where two more cells are produced per unit of time.

Degeneration is hypo-growth physiology, where fewer cells are born per unit of time. What is interesting is that the Innate wisdom of the body commonly creates an acute inflammatory disease process to ward off, heal and resolve a chronic degenerative process. If we suppress with drugs and medications the acute inflammation, the healing process may be blocked, interfered with, and degeneration might follow.

At the other end of the dynamic equilibrium of wellness, there are two interesting states: One we all know as *hypochondriacs*. These people constantly believe something is wrong with them and generate psychosomatic symptoms when none are actually present. The other state, less known to the public yet witnessed by health practitioners, is what I have coined to be *healthochondriacs*. These people are so overly concerned about being healthy, so obsessively self-focused, that they virtually medicate themselves into health. Their common conversation could be: "I feel this little pimple here is because I did not eat enough garlic. This slight dryness here on my skin is because my third chakra is leaking on the right side." The dialogue goes on into hilarious and comical statements.

When stuck, radical changes in patterns, and beliefs, a healthier lifestyle, shocking our physiology, and clearing the nerve system of interference provide a better chance to get unglued and heal. It might be challenging to break established behaviors and heal when we are locked in a dominant sympathetic nerve system stress pattern. When we are loaded with chronic stress, in fight-flight mode, our physiology is in survival, not in healing, growth, or transformation.

Hans Selye, Canadian Medical Hall of Fame M.D., advanced the theory that stress plays a role in every disease and that failure to cope with or adapt to stressors can produce *diseases of adaptation*, including ulcers, high blood pressure, and heart attacks. He called his theory the General Adaptation Syndrome. How often are we being told that this or that illness is more likely due to stress?

What may be problematic is not the disease itself but the inability to heal. A consistent and regular reset of our neurological state into ease, relaxation, and flexibility might be a welcome approach to promote healing, yet it is still frequently ignored.

Could sickness be an essential challenge for our immune system to reach a new level of responsiveness and efficiency? Look at babies and children who are what I call biological vacuum cleaners. As they crawl, everything in their tracks, from dirt to garbage, poop, and snot, will go into their mouth. This process is normal and healthy as it trains and schools their immune systems when the thymus gland is most active. The babies will display ongoing sniffles, coughs, and occasional fevers as their immune response matures. The apparent sicknesses generate healthy children.

Of course, there is a healthy balance and common sense to maintain; one may not want to let their children play in a septic pool. Although in India, as shown in the movie *Slumdog Millionaire*, children find themselves waist-deep in a latrine or rummaging through garbage dumps. Large groups of scavenger children, by the millions, live and feed in garbage dumps, as is the case in Brazil and Cambodia, among many other countries. Somehow they manage to stay healthy or survive.

Maybe those germs are not the sole cause of the disease after all. Could it be that it is adaptation, the strength of the immune system, along with the resistance of the host that are the leading determining factors in infectious diseases? Just as seeds need fertile ground to sprout and grow, so do potentially harmful bacteria need a weak host to thrive.

It is well documented by Jeremy Rifkin in his book *Entropy*, by Ivan Illitch in *Medical Nemesis*, and by Leonard Sagan in *The Health of Nations* that the decrease in infectious disease had little to do with immunization programs, as believed by the masses. The decline was mainly caused by improvements in housing, sanitation, nutrition, and water purification. The sudden emergence of infectious diseases in refugee camps where sanitation, housing, water, and food are sketchy is a great reversed example. It is interesting that whenever immunization programs are introduced in third- and fourth-world nations, infrastructure improvements, nutrition, sewer, and water supplies come along as a prerequisite policy.

In nearly all instances, the decline in infectious diseases occurred before the microorganism was identified. By the time vaccines were developed, the diseases had lost social interest. Why and how? Because of the diseases, natural herd immunity took place. Illness is a normal path to a new level of health.

When we view illness as a *necessary evil*, we can approach it with new eyes. Illness and disease are not *events* but rather *processes*. They are not something that happens *to* us (victims) but rather processes created in the body by the body *for* us (participants).

The victim mentality leaves us powerless as we surrender all our power to the professionals who are supposed to know and take care of it for us. Most doctors may have the best intentions, yet they could not run, with all their intellect, education, and learning, one single cell of their own body, a body in which they have lived for years. Still, we are led to believe that doctors can run someone else's body. When we understand that disease processes have arisen from within the body as dynamic processes, we see ourselves as participants. We are empowered to make changes, trust, and listen within. Even if professional help is deemed necessary, we are not to surrender our power to any of them. They might be welcome as allies to support us on our journey rather than dictators to submit to.

Most people abuse, misuse, and overuse their bodies when symptom-free, then get sick and add more abuse in the form of drugs, medications, X-ray radiation, anesthesia, radiotherapy, and sometimes surgery, yet in many instances still manage to get well. Do we really believe that sickness and disease are due to a lack of medication, radiation, and chemotherapy and that a strong diet of it is the solution? Unbeknown to many, we frequently get well despite, rather than because of, the treatment, as most diseases are self-limiting.

Illness is a dynamic process, not a thing we have. It is fluid, constantly changing, and evolving, being influenced by our daily activities, our emotional, mental, energetic, and spiritual states, as well as the cycles of life. The Innate Intelligence of the body will do everything possible to slow down and/or reverse the disease process, which is actually a lack of life and disconnection of specific parts or areas of the body from the whole. This is where reconnection plays a critical part in the healing process. There is a hierarchy of order in creation. If you reflect on it, all creation stems from the spiritual into the mental, emotional, and finally, the physical. The primal underlying cause of dis-ease is a separation from spirit, a deviation from life, and a disconnection from our inner calling and heart. This is mostly hidden from most human beings' awareness, buried deep within. This primary cause can be retrieved and corrected through deep inner listening, introspection, contemplation, meditation and reconnection. It takes slowing down to hear the silent voice within to take the hint. The next level in the hierarchy of creation is the mental realm. This is where believing an illness or a disease is something abnormal or static might be critically flawed. It crystallizes the physical and makes it much more difficult to change. The mental flow of thoughts is not out of our control as the *I* in us has the power to choose which thoughts to self-generate.

In the *Tibetan Book of Living and Dying*, Soyal Rimpoche tells the story of a Llama who moves, at will, his cancerous physiology around to teach his western doctors a lesson about the dynamic, energetic nature of our being.

As participants, we become active, engaged, in power, and capable of steering the course of our disease process. There are no illnesses that people have not recovered from. There are no incurable diseases, only incurable patients. This means that the body's capacity to heal from any and all diseases resides within us. A comforting fact and realization.

Once we embrace illness as normalcy, our judgment of illness or disease processes transforms. We are now witnessing and observing it, rather than minding it with a judgmental dialogue frequently deepened by the news of a diagnosis.

The subtle distinction between minding and witnessing is consequential.

With this new perspective on illness as a normal occurrence, we are empowered. It allows us to be patient observers and active participants in our healing process. In all instances, we can optimize our capacity for healing when we have engaged proactively in ongoing wellness care as early in life as possible. Wellness care is an individual responsibility. It must come from the ground up, made available by health practitioners from doctors of chiropractic, physicians for responsible medicine, acupuncturists, nutritionists, and naturopaths, to energy and bodyworkers, amongst countless others. They need to lead the charge by inspiring and motivating the public to the worthwhile endeavor and benefits of regular positive wellness care.

When the public is empowered with the knowledge of Innate Intelligence within all of us, a change in mindset, attitude, beliefs, and behavior takes place. Consequently, mental and emotional interferences to healing are cleared. Add to this outlook proactive wellbeing care, lifestyle, and exercise, and we might have a winning formula. We can then face illness with a fully loaded positive health account. A game changer.

A Marvel of Design

Deep within every human being lives the inner wisdom of life evidenced over and over by the beauty, complexity, and ingenuity of astonishing designs. With over 1000 ligaments, 134 articulations, 24 movable vertebrae, and 23 shock absorbers residing at our very core, our neuro-spinal system is the most complex and amazing biomechanical structure ever invented. The human backbone is a marvel of creation, unmatched in countless ways by anything man-made. It is often ignored, abused, and taken for granted until back pain brings the spine to one's awareness.

Our 10lbs skull and brain stand like an acrobat held in precarious balance on top of the spine. The brain stem, Houston Control, regulating all bodily functions, descends through the foramen magnum, the large hole of the Occipital bone at the base of the skull.

The first vertebra of the neck, the Atlas, named after the giant of Greek mythology who carries the world, allows the skull to move in a wide directional range due to the unique concave shape of the superior articulating facets that cup the convex condyles of the Occiput above. This peculiar design predisposes the Atlas to be a wobbler, the most frequently misaligned, displaced, and subluxated vertebrae in the neuro-spinal system.

Just below the Atlas rests the Axis or second cervical vertebra. The only vertebra with a tooth-like structure called the dent.

Like the rudder of a ship, the Axis acts as a pivot. Depending on its position, our neurological processing shifts from a balanced state to the left or right brain dominance or denial of one's true essence. The so-called military neck posture forces the Axis into a posterior position, leading to a neurological pattern that allows a human to be taught to inflict violence or kill another. This feat could not be entertained when the Axis is in extension during the bliss phase of orgasm or in the surrendered ecstatic posture during a spiritual experience. Could the fight-flight stress posture and the loss of the cervical curve be the unseen cause of our violent society? A possibility worth investigating.

The Occiput-Atlas-Axis Complex is the Center of Life in the body or the Mouth of God. It is in that small section of the neck that the Medulla Oblongata or brain stem resides, making it the most vital center in the body. According to the Science of Yoga, it is at the Occiput-Atlas-Axis site that Universal Energy enters the body.

Neuroscience holds the Reticular Formation located in the brain stem as essential in all major functional activities of the nervous system. Locomotor, homeostasis, cardiovascular, respiratory, and gastrointestinal control centers are located in the Reticular Formation. This makes it the major informational processing center of all vegetative functions.

This crucial and vital portion of the upper neck has been the primary focus of experts in the field of Death, through executions, as well as in the field of Life in Chiropractic through the adjustment.

- In the field of killing: the French use the guillotine, the English use the gallows, and the Japanese use the sword to terminate life briskly by severing or compressing the spinal cord at this most vital and strategic place.

Martial Artists Kun Fu Sansui use the bare knuckles of the hand to hit the back of the Occiput, sliding down its slope to land on the posterior projection of the Axis, driving the tooth-like projection of the Axis straight into the spinal cord. Death occurs instantly.

• In the Field of Chiropractic, the upper cervical adjustment and/or the Occiput lift have proven to be a powerful restorer of life and physiological function. Upper cervical adjusting was brought to world fame by B.J. Palmer, the Developer of Chiropractic in the 1900s, and continues to be practiced to date.

Actor Christopher Reeve, known as Superman, the world's greatest hero, having fallen from a horse, proved to humanity that the upper cervical region is crucial for life and bodily functions. A slight intrusion on the spinal cord from a broken neck is enough to interfere with organic function and performance. Superman was confined to a wheelchair with a respirator and a feeding tube. In time, life could not be sustained, and Christopher Reeve transitioned into the great beyond. As tragic as his accident was, it served to remind the world what Hippocrates, the father of medicine, stated centuries ago: "In the care of human ailments and health, first look to the spine."

Traveling further down the neck, the remaining five cervical vertebrae ensure the amazing neck mobility we enjoy. C3, C4, and C5 are referred to as the respiratory centers' vertebrae in Emergency Medical Technician or EMT courses. Those vertebrae are frequently damaged or subluxated through whiplashes leading to a wide array of respiratory disorders.

Many neck problems, not directly caused by physical trauma, arise from feeling emotions yet being unable to express them or thinking of feelings but incapable of feeling them.

The seven cervical vertebrae correspond to the seven steps to knowledge. This energetic journey leads to the descent from the intellect in the brain to access the intelligence of the heart. It is the longest shortest distance most of us will have to travel to leave our heads to live from our hearts.

The dorsal spine, made of twelve vertebrae connected to the rib cage, forms the posterior wall of the treasure chest of emotions. This is where so much of our emotional wounds are stored behind us, especially the ones we do not want others to see, like stacking our junk on the back porch to present a clean appearance in the front of our home. The twelve dorsal vertebrae correspond to the twelve stages of healing at the core level. Core healing involves resolving our baggage, letting go of our armoring, and healing emotional wounds. It requires open vulnerability, introspection, and self-reflection while reconnecting with our deeper selves.

When we emerge from a caved-in, shut-down body position to a fully vibrant, expanded, openhearted posture; or experience one postural shift from depression to the joy of being in love, the correlation between posture and emotional state is quite evident.

We are energetic beings. As our energy metamorphoses, so does our structure, and by the same token structural changes lead to energetic shifts. Structure and function are interrelated. Structure allows function, and healthy function requires proper structure. The functional integrity of the neuro-spinal system affects the quality of the vascular supply to the spinal cord and meninges, the membranes wrapping it in three protective layers. Altering or restoring its structure affects the state and performance of the nerve system.

The lumbar spine is the site where most support issues are imprinted. Some lower back problems are actually the result of a lack of emotional, financial, familial, or social support. The five lumbar vertebrae correlate to the five basic wounds of humanity: humiliation, abandonment, betrayal, injustice, and rejection. Interestingly enough, lower back problems are one of the most common ailments of humankind.

The Sacrum, from the Latin sacred, constitutes the foundation of the spine. The Sacrum is considered holy by many native cultures and spiritual and mystical traditions. Some cultures do not place the Sacrum on the ground while sitting and simply squat or sit in the traditional lotus position of the Yogis. This allows the gentle, rhythmic sacral movement to take place freely, in harmony with the in and out flow of the breath. The Sacrum acts as a pump to push the cerebral spinal fluid, or CSF, up and down the spinal cord. The normal flow of CSF is essential for proper nervous system function and nutrition.

Sacrum malfunction can be the cause of severe disorders, as proven clinically by Chiropractors and Cranio-Sacral Therapists. It is in this sacred place that lies dormant the Kundalini energy, which, when awakened, may lead to enlightenment. Energetic changes along with shifts in consciousness, occur when the cerebrospinal fluid is pressured upwards with specific breathing techniques and a blend of meningeal-osseous spinal adjustments.

According to Yogananda, who is considered one of the preeminent spiritual figures of modern times, the human spine is the "altar and the battlefield of the spiritual warrior."

The Pelvis is the site of human creation where the sperm and ovum meet in the fallopian tubes of the women's uterus. Sexual issues, wounds, and violations are unscripted in the Pelvis and Sacrum. Most Chiropractic techniques place great emphasis and attention on the Sacrum and its positioning and function.

Ironically, unbeknownst to many parents and doctors, the Sacrum is quite frequently traumatized by falls in babyhood during the early walking stages. Later on, in childhood and throughout life, insults to the Pelvis and Sacrum are common through various sports, from snowboarding to football, hockey, ice skating, and gymnastics, amongst others. Prolonged sitting, getting in and out of cars, contorting to lift babies out of their car seats, or carrying luggage one-sided are common causes of Sacrum subluxations.

At the very bottom of the spine, four fused vertebrae form the Coccyx or tailbone. It talks to us loudly when we land on it in the classic mischief of someone pulling a chair away as we are about to sit. The Coccyx, being the site of attachments of small ligaments that connect to the meninges, has a marked impact on the functioning of the nervous system when subluxated.

As an engineering marvel, the 23 shock absorbers or spacing discs, for size and weight, can bear more load per square inch than any metal known to humankind while allowing three-dimensional movements. Astoundingly, the difference in weight ratio of the vertebrae as we move from the last lumbar to the Atlas is identical to the difference in wavelength ratio of the chromatic scale of light, leading every vertebra to have a peculiar and specific tone. Some Chiropractors who are auditory dominant can actually sound each vertebra by placing their fingers on them, attuning and hearing their specific tone.

Others feel the energetic tone of each vertebra kinesthetically, while still others obtain a visual picture of the spine by palpation. In these various ways, they can determine when a vertebra is subluxated. One of the fundamental principles of Chiropractic is that Life is the expression of tone.

A spine that is attuned allows the nerve system to have a healthy tone, like the tuned-up strings of a guitar, not too tight or too slack. Since muscles contract and expand only when receiving nerve impulses, a balanced tone leads to proper muscle tension and appropriate functioning of the body.

The spinal cord, like a train passing through a tunnel, runs the length of the neural canal. It is the pipeline of Life Force and the information highway transmitting data to and from the brain. It is where the opposing and subtle currents of prana and apana flow. As the spine moves, so do the spinal cord and meninges as they are married to one another in an intimate relationship.

The neuro-spinal system is the most sacred, essential, and core system in the human body, it is the first to develop in the embryo and the last to go into decay. When hiking in the majestic San Juan Mountains of Southern Colorado, I often stumbled into the decaying remains of wild animals. All have been removed but the spine. In open pyres burning bodies in India, if the fire is not powerful enough, all will turn to ashes except the spine. It is our core backbone, like the spine of a building.

In short, the neuro-spinal system is the health keyboard and the lifeline of the human body. When one is invested in health and wellbeing, core healing, and spiritual growth, the neuro-spinal system takes center stage. Caring for it regularly becomes essential.

Death and Dying

Death is frequently a word not to be mentioned, especially in America. No one wants to hear about it. Let's put the old people away, hidden from view, in retirement communities and nursing homes. Why? Because just looking at them reminds us of our own mortality. It can be depressing, and who wants to be depressed when there is life to enjoy? By contrast, in most of Europe and many countries I have visited, the elderly gather with their counterparts at sidewalk cafes, around town squares, at games of Petanque or Bocce ball, or just sitting in public parks watching children play. In most cultures, the elders live with their children and grandchildren. The imminence of upcoming mortality is in plain view.

Our American society hides death as much as possible. We make it aseptic, hidden behind curtains, away from sight in a hospital room. According to Stephen Levine, author of *Who Dies?* seventy-five percent of the population dies in institutions where death is considered the enemy. When we consider all the people who die from gunshots, suicides, and accidents, we are left with an even greater percentage of people dying in hospitals. Our society is afraid of death because it is a process hidden from us behind closed doors in institutions for most of our lives. The fear of the unknown has led to a dehumanization of death.

But death is so much part of life that none of us will escape it. We are born to die. Death is, with birth, the one single thing that we are sure to have in common with all other human beings. It is what binds us in an irrevocable manner.

Anyone with an open heart at the bedside of a dying person to the very last breath will experience the bond that joins the dying with the living. It is our common plight. Could the fear of death be lessened, if not eliminated, should we all be exposed to it openly?

As people approach death, they slowly and progressively enter the Divine consciousness. Their energy begins to glow. Their inner spirit shines through. The physical vessel has become so frail there is not much physical matter left. The veil between physical and spiritual becomes thinner. The spirit radiates outward and expands while the body recedes and shrinks.

This is a very precious time for both the dying and the living, especially for close relatives. It is a time when the dying often expresses, silently or by words or gestures, total compassion, acceptance, understanding, wisdom, love, forgiveness, vulnerability, surrender and frequently, fear. To have the opportunity to stare into the eyes of the dying is the chance to see into their Soul, to feel and experience pure love, and to melt with tears into the bliss of that love. Despite the fear that might be present, all armor or defenses have usually melted away. Vulnerability reigns supreme. As expressed so poetically in the lyrics of Jacques Brel's song *My Last Supper*: "I know that I will be fearful, one last time."

There is abundant beauty to be harvested in a vulnerable, wide-open human being. The approach to death often reveals our own shortcomings. Deep existential questions arise: what prevented me from giving more? Why couldn't I have loved more? How can I rearrange my priorities in the short time left? What did I withhold in my relationship? What really matters in life? What will I take with me when I die? The lyrics of the song from Dido, *The Day Before the Day*: "You who love to love, and believed we can never give enough" beckon us to new heights. Being with the dying is often a catalyst for inner growth and transformation.

In countless ways peering into the Soul of the dying is so similar to looking into the eyes of a newborn; we see the pure nature of the Soul. A cycle is about to be completed. What moves us is the reflection of our own Soul. It is an opportunity not to be missed if possible and to reconcile the sorrows, pains, and discordances of life. It is a time of great validation and celebration of one's love for another.

The illuminated state of the dying usually comes when death is not interfered with. The progressive fasting that so often accompanies the winding down of one's life frequently brings the dying into an altered state of consciousness. This state goes through various stages as the fasting prolongs. Tube feedings and most medications may disrupt and disturb that state while robbing the dying of their blissful experience. Our time on earth is already but a speck in the cosmic scheme of all of humanity. Do we really have to prolong our earthly stay by a few hours or weeks with heroic measures?

It is crucial that the closest relatives not be in denial as to what is happening. Avoiding the reality of what is taking place may not allow the living to meet the dying where they are. The issue is not whether that person lives or dies. The issue is to enter into communion with them to allow them to give and receive freely, unencumbered, to choose their own path.

It is not unusual for a dying person to hang on longer to wait for a friend or relative to arrive. On occasion, the dying will hang on longer to give their loved ones time to accept the imminent death. By tuning in early and accepting openly the unavoidable, friends and relatives may prevent the dying person from needing medical support in order to hang on to life a bit longer. A conscious death can take place.

The energy of natural death is very similar to that of natural birth. It is the magnificent experience of the spirit passing through. It is an honor and a great gift to be present at someone's death. Mother Teresa, while afflicted with heart dysfunction, asked the medical personnel in her Calcutta hospital to let her die in peace. This is a message for the modern industrialized world. Indeed, natural death can often be peaceful. Medical personnel still view death as a failure and consequently try with heroic effort, and at tremendous cost, to prolong life. This is not only pricey but sadly has become a financial necessity for many medical institutions, even though this approach might generate unnecessary suffering.

My wife's mother, Helen, lived a good life. The day after her last Thanksgiving with family, she did not feel well. She went to the hospital in Doylestown, PA. The doctors wanted to perform a gastroscopy. She refused. They told her, "Mrs. Sheehy, if we do not do this test and determine what ails you, you will die." To which she replied: "That sounds good to me." Within twenty-four hours, she had passed peacefully at the ripe age of eighty-eight. There is a lot of wisdom here to take in.

How could Universal Intelligence, or God for many, have created all that we know and witnessed — yet screwed up death? We may be the ones who have messed up death. It is amazing and puzzling that most of the world's inhabitants will pray to God on Sundays, if not two or three times daily, yet when it comes time to finally have an appointment with the Maker, nobody wants to go or let the dying go. What a rejection for the Maker!

In the mid-1980s, my wife Jane and I had the privilege of being asked to attend numerous deaths. Most of these people were not close friends or family members. They were people or relatives who had received care in my practice. Somehow they wanted us to be there for them in the hours of their passing. I had read books on the subject. Among them: *On Death and Dying* by Elisabeth Kubler-Ross and *Who Dies?* by Stephen Levine. I then dived into *Dying Well* by Ira Byock, M.D., and *The Tibetan Book of Living and Dying* by Soyal Rimpoche as well as *Death* by Alan Watts.

However, the understanding gained through books is still a departure from knowledge gained through being a witness of death. Experience supersedes intellectual understanding.

None of the readings prepared me for the beauty, gifts, and blessings of being invited to a passing or transition. Most of these books dealt with the fear, loss of dignity, and moral, social, or spiritual issues surrounding dying. It may sound strange, yet at the time, I believe I could have become addicted to being by the side of a dying person. The energy present, the love flowing, and the sacred spiritual space became an elixir I wanted to drink daily. As much as there are doulas and midwives for birth, there are also death doulas who dedicate their time and energy to assist the dying. If it was not for my love of chiropractic, I could easily have become one of these people.

The passing of my close friend Danny Moon impacted Jane and me in profound ways. We met Danny through Barbara Tompkins. She was the vibrant, giving, loving, and bright ex-wife of Carl Tompkins; a Doctor of Chiropractic from Peekskill, New York. Barbara's philosophy was quite different from most people. She strongly believed in Universal Intelligence, which is the Source of everything that is and is not. To her, the part of Universal Intelligence that inhabits a living vessel is our Innate Intelligence, the Intelligence we are born with. It is responsible, through the vehicle of life force, for the entire control and coordination of every single cellular function. It is that intangible part of us that runs, instant by instant, the magical show within our body. Consequently, she adheres to a natural approach to health and healing, and non-interference from the outside-in. She recognized the need for medical intervention, but strictly in emergency first-aid such as accidents, poisoning, and severe injuries, or to palliate intractable pain. She saw death as a natural body function; after all, tissue cells constantly die every moment of our lives.

Danny and Barbara were married, and her philosophy had greatly impacted him. He had been getting adjusted in my office for a number of years. He exercised daily, was a runner, and ate mostly fresh organic food and home cooking. He was a tall, handsome man in his forties. We had become close friends and spent a lot of time together. Following a bite by a bat, he decided to have a series of rabies shots, which is often prescribed following such an incident. Within a few months, he began to have severe migraine headaches. They became so persistent that he went for a CAT scan, which revealed a cancerous tumor in his brain. He was told that brain surgery was possible but that he would lose his eyesight. He and Barbara decided not to intervene and to do everything they knew to support his body in healing if it was possible. He continued to get adjusted regularly, kept exercising and running daily, and switched to a macrobiotic diet specifically prescribed for him by Michio Kushi, the renowned Japanese leader of the Macrobiotic movement.

Danny began to lose some weight, which was to be expected from the new diet. Over a period of a few years, he became increasingly thinner and weaker yet had little pain. Follow-up tests showed that cancer had spread to his liver. One day, sick of eating the same bland food, he binged and ate spaghetti and meatballs. His body reacted violently, and he was doubled over in severe pain for days. He resumed the macrobiotic diet; the pain subsided, then vanished. With time passing, Danny became frail. He had become extremely thin but could still function and go about his day. Toward the end of that summer, he grew quieter and talked little. One week in September, he requested that we rent a house at the Jersey shore for a long weekend. We chose Long Beach Island in New Jersey. Those three days together by the seaside, he spent sitting in a rocker on the deck, looking at the ocean. He did not speak a word. The silence in the house and on the porch was comfortable. The roar of the distant surf was soothing. His silent state clearly projected a field of inner peace; it was palpable.

Barbara, my wife Jane, and I respected his state and his space. We felt totally connected to his being, his mood, and his thoughts. He was in a beautiful, serene state. His energy and inner being were so expanded that we could feel his radiance from many feet away. Pure love and compassion emanated from him. Being in his presence was a blessing and a gift.

The following weekend, I was lecturing at a convention in Levittown, PA, on the birth process. I was near the end of my presentation on natural birth when someone brought a folded note to my lectern. It read: "Barbara wants you home now." I calmly finished my talk, picked up my belongings, and drove to Trenton to pick up Jane. She was coming back from New York by train. As I pulled in front of the train station, here she was, just walking out. Neither she nor I had to wait. It was perfect orchestration and timing. I told Jane about Barbara's request to come to her home, knowing that the end was near for Danny. We calmly drove to his home in New Hope, PA.

We arrived to find him lying on a couch by the large bay window in the living room. The sun pouring through the glass was bathing him. His head was laid back, his mouth was open, and he was making the rattle of death. A woman whom Danny had never met was there by his side. We found out later that she was a childhood friend of Barbara, who happened to be in New Hope that Saturday and had taken the chance to call directory assistance in the hope of contacting Barbara. They had not seen nor spoken with each other in twenty years. Upon hearing of the situation, she came over right away. Jane and I went to support Barbara. She was at the kitchen table sobbing, surrounded by close mutual friends. We hugged her, kissed her, and held her.

After what seemed like a long moment, the woman by Danny's side came over and said: "Arno and Jane, you better go over to him." We kneeled by the coach, held his hand, and touched his forehead gently. Softly we spoke to him: "Danny, we love you, and all those who are your spiritual family are here with you; you can go now." Jane held his hand and whispered, "Danny, we love you; let go now." A tear appeared at the corner of his eye, and he left. It was a beautiful moment, a profound experience, an exquisite gift.

To have the chance to be there with him to the very last breath, to feel his energy, to be in his love, and to share the deep emotional sorrow with Barbara and our close friends was truly a blessing. Danny had orchestrated a perfect death. His true friends and his spiritual earth family were present. Even Barbara's childhood friend, the one person who had not known Danny, and had little emotional connection with him, had appeared with perfect timing. She was now the one who was able to handle and take charge of all the logistics and arrangements that followed a person's passing. What a blessing of hyper-synchronicity. This gave all of us the space and time to grieve. I understood that day that death needs not to be feared. I saw the wisdom and beauty of natural death at home. I also saw how non-intervention allowed Danny to go through his process undisturbed. He passed with virtually no pain, despite the brain cancer metastasizing to his liver. That is quite rare with advanced-stage liver cancer.

What was also amazing was that Danny had been incapable of expressing emotions. He could not let his armor down even when we had cornered him and pressed him to open up. Yet, at the last moment of his life, he was able to shed a tear and feel. To me, this was his great victory. How special, I thought, that he had died the very day that I was giving a lecture on birth. Jane and I experienced Danny's death as having the same energy as a natural home birth. The only difference was the joy of one and the sorrow of the other. However, the energy present in the room was identical. The respect, the awareness not to disturb, the silence and connection, the opening of the heart, the spiritual state, and the love flowing were the same. Natural, at-home death, if at all possible, is a magical process not to be missed, just as natural home birth is a transcendental experience.

Ida Reed's death: Ida was my brother-in-law Russell's mother. She was in her late seventies, I believe, when she lost her husband. The two of them were lifetime companions. Simple, honest, plain, both the salt of the earth, they were very involved with their church. When Ida's husband, Glen, passed away, it broke Ida's heart. Thereafter she went downhill pretty fast. After spending some time in a retirement community with special care, she quickly ended up in a nursing home in Buckingham, PA. This is where Jane and I came to visit her numerous times. The place was spotless, clean, bright, and well-staffed. It was, however, like entering a Federico Fellini movie set. People were parked along the hallways next to their rooms in their wheelchairs and exhibited grotesque tics, repetitive motions, spoke in broken verbal records, or just hung there in total stupor and stillness as if frozen. It was not a pretty sight, yet for me, it was very insightful.

I could really witness the effects of this medicated environment, full of people who, more likely, had lived an entire lifetime within the medical arena, constantly suppressing or cutting out their symptoms with drugs. This was in sharp contrast with the Quaker hospice atmosphere I had experienced when I visited a client named Josephina a few months earlier as she was preparing herself for her transition. Hospice and nursing homes are worlds apart. Ida was an exception to the circus of tortured minds and bodies. She was calm, always smiling, and would welcome any person with: "Beautiful, beautiful people, love you so much. Love, love, love, love you so much. God bless you!" She was radiating love and inner peace.

On the last evening of her life, we gathered by her bedside. Those present were her son Russell with his wife Mary Ellen, their young daughter Autumn, and my wife Jane and me.

We surrounded Ida and held her hands, laying our hands on her heart and face so that all of us would be connected to her by touch. She had ten hands loving her, virtually, to death. We spoke little. There was no need for it. We had turned off the light to eliminate any distractions and create intimacy or into-me-see. The room was full of love and energy. We were all wide open-hearted. It was an oasis of peace. We entered a total time warp. Ida's breathing began to be more labored. Her rib cage would rise and fall at an increasingly slower pace. Then the rhythm of her inhales and exhales changed. She only took a breath or so per minute, and her heart slowed down to a near standstill. She was so at peace. It was very comforting for all of us to see her tranquil, open, and serene. For a while, there was complete stillness, but then a few more breaths came, separated by long intervals. Finally, she took her last breath, and a few drops of blood appeared at the corner of her mouth. She was gone. The light, the life force, her spirit had left her body.

We remained there for hours, incapable of moving, with tears of sorrow running down our cheeks. Ida's granddaughter, Autumn, stayed with us, bathed in this extraordinary moment of love. Autumn was hyperactive and had attention deficit disorder, yet she was glued to the experience of stillness. Ida died that evening around ten o'clock, and it was well after midnight when we left her room and notified the nurses that she had passed away. This must have been a first for the staff because it did not register well with the nurses. They could not comprehend why we had not called them earlier and definitely not why we would stay around a dead body for hours in the dark.

When we stepped out of the nursing home, it was a cold, clear mid-November night. We looked at the sky, and there was a perfect cross over the moon. Ida left all of us with a clear message, which remained encrusted in our consciousness to this day and more likely for our lifetime: "Love, Love, Love." There is nothing else. Since then, her voice resonates in my head as a mantra, I see her peaceful, radiant face, and I hear: "Love, Love, Love." These three words became our family's sign-off message.

This was just another blessing and gift that death brought to all of us. The perfection of the timing was amazing. The fact that we could all be there, in spite of our hectic lives and busy schedules, was magical. The quiet environment of the nursing home late in the evening, the two hours of undisturbed space following her passing, the non-interference by the staff, and the cross over the moon, to remind us to live from above-down and inside-out was a gift well orchestrated by life.

Josephina's passing: Josephina arrived at my office without a referral. I do not know how she found me. She was a short, emaciated, scrawny, yet vivacious woman with a sunken face and disheveled gray hair in her late sixties. It did not take a genius to see she was ill. She revealed during her first visit that she had advanced cancer with a large inoperable tumor in her lower abdomen, which caused her severe back pain. I felt intuitive that not much could be done for her on a physical level. It would take a miracle for her to reverse her condition.

I kept that possibility in my mind, as it is impossible to know what life has in store. But I knew she had come to me for a reason.

I could give her love, support, and understanding and assist her in healing at a deeper core level through the reconnection that touch and adjustments provide.

I made it clear to her that I could not heal her cancer or cure her even if I wanted to. Healing comes from the inside-out. It is an internal process that comes from the Life Force within. Anything was possible, even total remission, yet it was not under my control. I could, however, be the facilitator of that internal innate process yet have little to no control over the outcome. She understood all this and said that she had not come with any expectations. We were on the same page. As she was approaching the end of the road, I strongly suggested to her husband, who was apparently fine, that he begin chiropractic care so as to give himself every chance possible to not end up in the same predicament as his wife. He was adamant that he was perfectly well and that he did not need to receive such care. He had no symptoms, which to him spelled out that he was healthy. I knew better. The fact that we have no symptoms does not necessarily equate to being well and healthy. His overall outward appearance told a very different story. It was clear to me that he was in poor health. Yet I could not influence him to start care and get adjusted.

Josephina began regular care with me and felt great improvement on many levels, including her back pain. She very much looked forward to her visits and always left uplifted mentally and spiritually. I was loving her up to death. My heart was open to her, and I felt a special tenderness for her. Months passed, and Josephina was hanging on. She was still losing weight and could not eat much at all. However, what she ate was good nutritious food. One day she arrived at my office in apparent distress, and the instant I walked into the room, she burst into tears.

Her husband had left that day for his morning walk around the block and dropped dead from a heart attack. I was stunned but not entirely surprised. Most people would have bet a million to one that he would bury his wife. But the fact that we have no outward symptoms or discomfort has really little to do with our internal state of health, function, and wellbeing.

Obviously, this was a terrible blow for Josephina, who, by now, did not weigh more than 73 pounds. In her condition, she managed to fly with her husband's body to Israel to bury him, stay there for months, and return to my office the following summer.

In August, I took a trip to Bermuda with my wife, Jane. Just before we left, Josephina had moved to New York City to stay with her sister. This was to be a temporary emergency accommodation. As it became apparent that she could no longer take care of herself nor be cared for by a family member at home, she pleaded with me to help find a bed in a hospice. I was able to obtain a bed for her at the local Quaker's hospice called Chandler Hall in Newtown, PA, where I had connections, but she was still on the waiting list when we left for Bermuda.

Upon our return, our very first stop, straight from the airport, was the grocery store. As I got out of my car, I ran into a councilman from my town of New Hope, PA. I had not seen him in at least ten years. He was a man of great stature, which you could not ever forget. His physique was so distinctive. The first thing he said to me was that Josephina was at Chandler Hall, the Quaker's hospice. He was a volunteer there. He had talked to her and knew she had been receiving chiropractic adjustments from me. Pure coincidence or perfect synchronicity? I believe it was impeccable universal timing.

In the following weeks, I went to see Josephina nearly every day. She was slowly dying but was in total denial of it. She was a very strong-willed and feisty woman. By now, she was skin and bones with parchment-like paper taut over her facial features, truly a skeleton. After a few visits, I decided to break the news to her and confronted her with the possibility that she may not recover and could possibly die soon. I was being gentle, letting her know that no one could possibly know what the future held but that it did not look favorable toward remission and that she might want to prepare herself.

At first, she became angry with me, thinking I was betraying her by not going along with her denial. After a while, however, she began to talk to me about her life. She started confiding in me, sharing all of her bad deeds and purging herself of long-held secrets. I listened attentively, moved by this confidential outpour. I had just read the *New York Times* best-seller, *The Tibetan Book of Living and Dying,* by Soyal Rimpoche. It had given me insights, and my heart was wide open. I reassured her that God was not a judging God but an all-loving God. She asked about Karma, and I could only tell her that I thought she was a good person, loved by many, that I loved her, and that I was sure she had done her best in life with countless good deeds. In a flash, I had become her priest and spiritual confidante with no previous qualifications.

I returned to see her many times thereafter, and she was more at peace. I would gently ease the pain and discomfort of being bedridden with a loving touch. We would talk and look into each other's eyes for long moments. She was now skin and bones, her face covered with translucent skin. There was nothing left to her, a skeleton of sixty pounds at best.

The hospice staff were wonderful and attuned to the energy of the dying. Quiet in their movements, tender in their touch, loving with their words, gentle, caring, and respectful with their being. They were present and connected to the energy of transition. This was in sharp contrast with the nursing homes or hospitals I had been in around the dying. During the last few days of Josephina's life, candles were burning in her room.

My wife Jane had accompanied me many times to visit Josephina, and so did my secretary Kelly, who happened to be my sister-in-law. Jane and Kelly are replicas out of the same mold sixteen years apart. They both emanate a radiance of clear and loving energy. Kelly was the last one to see Josephina. Jane and I missed her passing by a few hours. The evening she passed, Jane and I returned to see her for the last time. Her family had arrived from Israel, and we broke bread with them. Chandler Hall's staff thought all along that Jane, Kelly, and I were family members. When they found out that I was her Chiropractor, Jane was my wife, and Kelly was my secretary, they were amazed. Yet to us, it was the most normal and natural thing to do. Josephina had asked us to be with her throughout her process. So, of course, we would answer that call. We are here to serve, and we have committed our lives to health and healing. Being a chiropractor is much more than just showing up in the office to adjust people. It encompasses being a key figure, a point of light, in most of our clients' lives. It was only natural to be by Josephine's side while she was winding down on her way to the other side.

We all knew that much healing could take place around death. It was the case with Josephina.

George Andras was the man who could not die. George came to see me in my office in 1986. He was a tall, slender, handsome man. Although he was in his early fifties, he was the type of person whose age was difficult to determine. He had been a superb jazz musician in the sixties, able to play the saxophone perfectly. As with most musicians of that time, he had engaged in heavy drug use. He had had three-quarters of his stomach removed following a gastric ulcer. From that day on, his health had never been the same. A few years after the surgery, he developed cirrhosis of the liver that healed by itself when he began a fresh apple and apple juice fast for three months.

George was involved in Tibetan philosophy and natural healing. He was a private, secluded, and solitary individual.

He lived, like a hermit, in a dark house on the banks of the Delaware River with his wife, Susan. George was frequently grumpy and angry and did not reach out to others. He was strong-minded, determined, committed to his own beliefs, and displayed deep inner strength. During his regular visits, I had occasionally been at the receiving end of his intense, angry outbursts.

In the summer of 1993, he fell ill. All of the lymph nodes and glands in his face and neck became enlarged. His legs and joints were painful. At times his eyelids were swollen shut as if he had just completed a boxing match with Mike Tyson. This was always associated with severe back pain. Over time his eyelid pockets would open up, and pus would pour out of the tear ducts; his back pain would immediately subside. The pus would drain for days; his face would return to normal except for the lumps from the lymph nodes in his neck. Since his stomach operation, George could not eat much, which accounted for his low weight. Now that he was ill, most of the little that he ate would come back up. Finally, he was unable to eat altogether.

Listening to his body, he fasted for twenty days, just sipping on date juice. Every day he became weaker and weaker, spending most of his time sleeping on the living room couch. During his few awakened hours, he would listen to Tibetan healing prayers. The sound and vibrations of which soothed him.

I would come to see him every other day on my way home from the office to check on him, adjust him if needed, and care for him. As the days went by, he became emaciated and so weak that he could no longer move from the coach. Toward the end, he would rally when I came to see him and became open, loving, and talkative. He dispensed great wisdom. He was increasingly spiritual in his interaction with me; it became apparent that his spirit was coming out.

I had been around dying people during my years at the cancer ward of the Amboise Paree Hospital in Paris, France, so I was familiar with its process and energy. It appeared that George was indeed dying.

On a Friday night, I arrived at 9 p.m., and we talked for a long time. He gave me two precious African antique knives that he wanted me to have. He said good-bye to me, and we cried together. It was one in the morning by the time I left to drive home, yet it felt as if the evening had happened in a flash. Time had stood still. We had become very close, and I had grown attached to him. I hugged and kissed his wife, Susan, on my way out and asked her to call us when George had passed away. All weekend I waited anxiously for her call, but nothing came.

Monday morning, I called her. To my surprise, she had gone to work, leaving her husband. Out of nowhere, George had gotten up that Monday morning, made his breakfast, and eaten it. That very week I went with him to help him buy a motorcycle, which he rode home. He weighed less than 100 pounds.

I asked him what had happened. He said: "I went to the other side, and they did not want me yet." I did not ask who *they* were.

He had just gone through a powerful healing crisis. That was a big lesson for me.

George regained considerable momentum and, for two and a half years, lived with minimal pain and discomfort. He weathered a few other healing crises and then plunged back down for two weeks, taking a very deep turn. He nearly died again but then went on a prolonged fast and again came out of it.

Six months later, in July 1996, he re-entered a severe crisis. His wife, Susan, kept quiet for a week and then called me on a Wednesday morning, asking if I could come over. George was dying again, but this time I did not see how he could possibly come out of it. He was ravaged by pain. He was skin and bone, had swollen legs, and sunken eyes; there was not much left of him nor in him. I saw him that morning

319

on my way to the office. I left to practice all day and returned to see him with my wife Jane by early evening. As we entered the house, George was on the floor totally naked. He had lost bowel control four times and was lying in his own excrement. We tried to clean him up, but any attempt proved too painful to him. We just covered him with a sheet and tried to assist him in any way possible.

He asked for painkillers and managed with great difficulty swallowing two with a sip of water. At George's request, I called the local hospice, where I had visited other dying people in the past. He was hoping to be taken in. It was a Quaker-run establishment of the highest dedication, respect, and service to the dying. All the beds were full, but they offered to have a physician call in a prescription for liquid morphine. They asked that we come to pick it up. A nurse would meet us there and follow us back to George's home. This sounded too time-consuming; we needed to assist him right away. So we called a local physician who was a client of mine, and he came over with painkillers. He gave George a powerful medication and left.

George was aware and conscious, able to understand what we were doing, and responding clearly to any questions. He was thrashing on the floor from the pain. Once the painkiller took effect, he calmed down and could lie on his side with his head thrown back in extension. He was now letting out the death rattles with every breath. We left to get the liquid morphine and the nurse. When we returned 45 minutes later, he was still alive. The nurse, an angel of compassion, knelt beside him and told him she was going to place liquid morphine under his tongue. He closed his mouth and signaled "no" by shaking his head.

Now Jane and I were totally attuned to his energy and saw that he was leaving. Susan lay down against him, and we held her and him. As his breath slowed down, his toenails and fingernails turned black. It seemed like an eternity between each breath. Then his limbs trembled, and his stare became empty. Susan broke down in a burst of tears, and George came back for another full minute. In that moment, he was more alive than ever; his face was alive, and his eyes were bright with light. Susan spoke gently to set him free; his face twitched a few times, and he left his body.

Susan was too absorbed to notice, but the nurse, my wife, and I all were distracted by the ruffle of the house-plant leaves in the corner of the living room. It seemed to be a bird. Of course, there was no bird to be seen. I am convinced it was his spirit leaving. The place was closed, and no windows were opened. Later, I found out that while we were gone to retrieve the morphine and the nurse, George had told Susan he had to go now. He had said good-bye to her and blew her a kiss. Then he had asked repeatedly: "Where are they, when are they coming back, are they back yet?" Indeed he had waited for us to return. He had been conscious, aware, and in control of his own death to the very last breath.

It isn't easy to express what a gift it is to be allowed to be present at the very end of the life of a dear friend. We saw nothing but beauty, love, and peace in him. We saw into his Soul and spirit. He left us with a vivid reminder to appreciate and be grateful for every moment, every pain, challenge, and difficulty. In his death, he reminded us not to take anything for granted, to live as fully as possible, and to always seek to see beyond the armor and the mask. To us, this was a triumphant, glorious, and beautiful death, a true success. It proved obvious that Universal Intelligence did not screw up death.

My brother-in-law Russell Reed's journey to transition: Russell Reed, alias Russ or Uncle Rush, as my children called him when they were young, was an extraordinary man. Of course, everyone is in some way extraordinary by the sole fact that they are unique. By this construct, Russell was beyond extraordinary. His presence, charisma, exceptional quick wit, brilliant mind, outrageous humor, and unexpected creative thoughts and behavior have been unmatched in my life by anyone. I have met and known lots of people. Adjusting hundreds of people a day for years, teaching, speaking, and coaching for the past twenty years while in part-time practice, allowed me to meet thousands of people the world over. None have come close to Russell Reed.

Things in life can happen fast, usually faster than we think. In May of 2008, Russ was traveling with his wife, Mary Ellen, to our daughter's engagement party in France. Aside from having painful knees, he seemed fine, happy, engaged, and vital. He had beaten non-Hodgkin's Lymphoma by drinking Essiac tea and was in full remission for three years. Then, in July 2008, he complained of stomach pain. He was treated for colitis with antibiotics, but the pain remained. After three weeks, an MRI showed a growth that appeared to be inoperable due to its close proximity to the abdominal aorta. The diagnosis of colitis had been a misdiagnosis. The pain became severe. He began a course of chemotherapy. After a few trips in and out of the hospital, he was back at home in pretty much the same condition. The pain was extreme and relentless. He lived on a diet of oxycodone, soon to be supplemented by morphine. His white blood cell count had not been checked regularly as it should have been with the type of chemo he was receiving. He had fallen through the cracks of the medical system. Russ's suffering was so severe that he had to sleep standing up, as the reclined position proved to be unbearable.

By October, he collapsed, and his wife took him to Doylestown Hospital in Pennsylvania. By then, Russell's breathing was somewhat labored. Jane and I flew from Colorado to the East Coast to visit him and also attend our niece's wedding. Arriving on a Friday afternoon, we went straight to the hospital. Russ was in bed, yet alert, funny, communicative, with a jovial high on narcotics. His pain was under control from the morphine. He had a nasal cannula to supplement his breathing with oxygen. We came to see him again on Saturday afternoon. The only noticeable change was that he now had an oxygen mask, which he often took on and off, clowning with it by placing it on his forehead in a typical Russell fashion. We talked about football, going again on a motorcycle trip out West together, and the upcoming wedding of our niece. The atmosphere was easy and open, with no indication of what would come next.

We left for our niece's wedding, and that was the last time we saw Russ conscious. Within hours he was on life support. By that night, he had been intubated. For the next ten days, we spent our lives at the hospital. Russ was never left alone from that moment forward. Friends and family took turns around the clock to hold a vigil and supervise his care. We slept on the floor in his room, despite the distress of the hospital staff.

Every shift I attended, I witnessed doctors and nurses coming into his room and looking straight at the life-support monitor and not even glancing at him. Only the numbers on the screen seemed to matter. Prognosis and hope offered to his grief-stricken wife came out of numbers on a monitor.

My wife and I knew he was a goner. Anyone with common sense, tuning in to him, the person, the being, who was there in the bed, would have known that. I watched the hospital staff boost any data that appeared deficient with drugs. Blood pressure was low; let's kick it up with Dopamine. Blood pressure was too high; let's lower it with Lopressor. Swelling was up; let's reduce it with Lasix. Heart rate dropped; let's boost it with Adrenaline. This went on for weeks until his heart finally gave out.

To me, it was the most degrading and inhumane treatment I had yet witnessed. It felt so wrong. The only saving grace was that it gave time for his wife, Mary Ellen, to come to terms with the inevitable reality that her husband was dying. Yet it did not allow any of us to have closure with him, hold him, love him, and support him in his transition.

Russell had a living will, but it was not produced by his wife. She just wanted him alive. She was in denial. I truly believe that he would not have wanted it that way. He was a spiritual man with a strong connection to his Soul.

We all had to accept the perfection of life. The perfection I can see is the extra time given to his wife to come to terms with her husband's passing. It also allowed her to share, at a later date, his hospital saga so that it may help others make different choices.

Death is unavoidable. An extra day or an extra hour does not make any difference in the cosmic scheme of things. However, dignity and emotional connection with loved ones do make a difference. Had Russell been left without life support, his breathing would have become increasingly labored. He and all those present would have known he was leaving. Our interaction with him would have been ever so different. We would have had closure with him while he was conscious. As it turned out, the chemo had destroyed his immune system, and his lung's alveoli were melting from the chemo, making breathing increasingly difficult.

Death is not the enemy. The medical profession will go to any lengths to postpone death because they see it as a failure. Again it is a philosophy and approach of *against*. Some would argue that medicine wants to sustain life at any cost and therefore has a philosophy of *for*. That is a noble cause, yet in this instance, there was no life to sustain. Common sense observation made that clear. If medicine were for health, healing, wellbeing, wellness, and life, the medical profession would be pouring the billions of dollars spent every year on drug advertisements to educate the public about maintaining a proactive, healthy lifestyle. Regrettably, that is not the case. Unfortunately, the chiropractic profession does not yet have the financial resources available for such a campaign as there is little money in pro-active wellness care. At this point, individual practitioners do the necessary wellness education in-house.

Death being such an unavoidable part of life, I believe that to be at peace with dying is the beginning of living fully and freely. As my friend Corey Moody, Men over 50 4 x 400 meters run world record holder, shared with me: "It's not about avoiding death; it is about embracing life and living fully."

I believe death is a necessary introspection and conversation to be had early in life with ourselves and certainly with our spouses, partners, and family. Meditating on death, on our own impermanence, gives spice to life. We have much to learn from native cultures, where conscious death was part of their lives. The stereotype of

American Indians walking out in the cold to die in peace after having had closure with their family and the tribe may not fit the modern worldview of death. It opens a possibility that might appear too extreme for some but enticing for others. Present society may have gone so far in the other direction that balance might be needed.

No one knows when death will show up or how it will orchestrate itself. I believe, like most, I envision a conscious death if at all possible. I desire to have closure with my children, my wife, grandchildren, and extended family and friends. I desire to transition at home, in nature, or as a last resort in hospice, connecting to what feeds my Soul if at all possible. I do not wish to prolong my life with heroic measures. Am I concerned about possible pain and suffering? Yes, as I believe most are. I would like to have no interference or at least minimal ones in the process. Being conscious and connected to the very end is my deepest wish.

The words just written might seem trivial and easy to set down. Unless one has steered death face to face, not much weight might be given to written words. In 2014, however, I experienced seven cerebellar strokes. The first took place in front of my wife Jane and my two grandchildren.

I had just returned from a canoe trip on Lake Dillon in Colorado with my grandson Khy. I was walking up the rocky shore and had just taken three steps onto the grass. With zero warning or ill feeling, I dropped dead weight, completely unconscious in one instant. One split second earlier, I would have cracked my skull wide open on the rocks. When I regained consciousness minutes later, I thought I might have had a sunstroke. So I dismissed the event as just that. For the next 24 hours, I felt extremely weak, as if all life energy had drained out of me.

A week later, I rode my motorcycle from Durango to Silverton and back. It was a 100-mile round trip of turn after turn on unguarded, narrow roads over four stunning mountain passes. The next day I had another mild stroke, dropping unconscious in a fraction of a second. Again, it left me feeling dizzy, weak, and lethargic for a day. A few days later, Jane and I were having breakfast at the College Cafe in downtown Durango. As I sat down and opened the menu, I dropped unconscious under the table in an instant, again without any warning, having lost all muscle control. When I came to, I was surrounded by patrons and paramedics. I declined to be taken to the hospital as we were on our way to Denver to fly to Europe for our son Boo's wedding in Poland.

I had four more strokes-two in Denver and one on the plane flying to Berlin. The last one came the first night in the hotel in Berlin. That time I faced death. After regaining consciousness, I sensed I was leaving my body. I had to harness all my might and willpower to stay in my body. Yet I was at peace with dying. Jane had awakened and was holding me, asking: "Do you want to go to a hospital?" I could only whisper: "No, stay with me; I want you here if I go." By dawn, the crisis had passed.

We made it to our son Boo's wedding in Poland. His new father-in-law was a pediatric heart surgeon. Alarmed by my numerous strokes, he took my blood pressure: 230/160. Astonished, he repeated the procedure two more times; the readings stayed the same. He immediately ordered a prescription to lower my blood pressure and arranged a full medical work-up at his hospital for the next morning, including brain CT scans, MRI, physical exam, blood work, urine analysis, electrocardiogram, and a sonogram of all my arteries, heart, and internal organs. All came back negative, along with a $600 bill that would have probably cost $35,000 or more in the USA. Puzzled, all my results were sent the next day to the best diagnostician they had. After reviewing all the test results, she could not determine any diagnosis or cause for the multiple strokes and extremely high blood pressure.

That night I emailed Dr. John Donofrio, D.C., who I knew was very knowledgeable as he was the leading teacher of national board reviews for our profession. He suggested a high-resolution sonogram of the adrenal medulla because he suspected a tumor of the adrenal medulla gland. The Polish hospital did not have such a high-tech sonogram. Once back in the states, I had the test done at Mercy Hospital in Durango. The results proved negative. Dr. Donofrio told me he thought the only other possibility to explain the strokes and dangerously high blood pressure was a poison that had entered my body somehow. I will never know for sure. Eight years later, I have not had another occurrence, and my blood pressure normalized. What I know is that night in Berlin, I faced death head-on. This, I believe, gives weight and credence to my words on the subject of dying.

Touch Heals

Touch is the universal language of love. Jane Goodall, the famed British primatologist, brought to the world's attention the moving and touching behavior of chimpanzees. Humans, as well as animals, touch their newborns to convey their presence, and provide a sense of security, protection, and nurturing, as well as love. Courting, foreplay, and lovemaking surely encompass touch. The touch of a handshake can convey so much about connection, from distant to warm. Empathy and compassion are often passed on to a friend by the touch of a hand.

Children intuitively will place their hands on their forehead while running to their mother, saying: "Mommy, my head hurts." Most everyone has experienced hitting their thumb with a hammer or getting it caught in a car door and immediately wrapping it into their other hand while breathing deeply and dancing around, all done to soothe the pain. We place our hands over a stomach ache or an aching tooth. This is instinctual. Most of us have experienced the comforting power of touch when confronted with emotional upheaval. Yet, as a society, we have lost touch with the healing power of touch. The fear of sexual harassment has caused many to withdraw the natural impetus to touch.

Chiropractic, Reiki, Massage therapy, Rolfing, and Heller's work have contributed to bringing back the simple awareness of the power of touch to heal in a professional setting. Ashley Montagu wrote a brilliant book called *Touching*. It validates the importance of touch and its effect on growth, neurological development, and immune response. It documents that the skin is the primary sensory organ.

In a square inch of skin, there are 77 feet of nerves, all linked to the brain via the spinal cord. Stimulation of the skin through touch is vital to our health. It engages the nerve system and its life energy flow. Touch is indeed the universal language of love and healing. As we have become increasingly bound to computers and technology, the need for touch is critical. It is said that if you cannot be touched, you cannot be healed. Could the health decline observed in the elderly be partially caused by the lack of human touch? Many times romantic relationships that have become stale, distant, or even bitter lack touch. Lovemaking, in these couples, frequently becomes a rare occurrence, if at all.

A void, an emptiness presides. Touch can restore the connection.

We can all make a difference through the simple act of a gentle, caring, comforting, and loving touch. From an intentional handshake to a furtive laying of a hand on a grocery clerk's shoulder as a gesture of thank you to holding a senior's hand in assistance, touch heals humanity. It magnifies connections. When in practice, I used to send thank you cards to people who had referred others for care. Written on beautiful hand-made paper, the double-folded card had on its front: "We can touch with our hands, with our heart, with our mind, with our deeds; what is important is to touch."

Then a personal note of gratitude from me was the final touch on the card. This simple act of appreciation and recognition emphasized the power of touch to make a difference in life.

Death

Chapter 7: Desserts and Pastries

Universal Intelligence

I live in Colorado, in what is called the four corners of the United States: the borders of Colorado, New Mexico, Utah, and Arizona. It is possibly one of the most magnificent regions of the U.S. My wife and I frequently camp in Canyon Land, an area near Moab, UT, where the desert landscapes are stunning. There is no light pollution at night. The silence is deafening. As often as we can, we watch the sunrises and sunsets. Daily, nature displays remarkable dynamic paintings that dwarf the best artists in the world. At night, we sit in zero-gravity chairs under the canopy of stars; billions of them in our one galaxy alone, and there are billions of galaxies, according to astrophysicists. It is always bewildering to us. It humbles us. We are astonished at the great mystery of life and the universe.

I cannot help but think: "What kind of Intelligence orchestrates all this? Can we control the gyration, elliptical motion, and trajectory of celestial bodies?" No, no more than we can control the inner workings of our body. The macro-universe and the micro-universe within are one and the same, controlled by Universal Intelligence. As Marilyn Fergusson puts it in the chapter on Healing Ourselves in her book titled

The Aquarian Conspiracy: "We can no more manipulate the body into health by external ministrations than we can manage the ebb and flow of the tides by an organized system of mops. The healer inside us is the wisest, most complex, and most integrated entity in the universe. We now know there is always a doctor in the house." What a comforting, reassuring, and empowering realization.

Is it possible that we have it all upside down? Could it be that nature is our teacher and the natural world has a greater intelligence than human intellect can presently express? Universal being omnipresent, plants, animals, insects, rocks, etc., are bathed and permeated by Universal Intelligence. Every year, with the help of remote cameras, we uncover more and more of the amazing intelligence of animals and behaviors we never knew existed.

I have camped at Cedar Mesa in Utah and witnessed nature's incredible power and tenacity: trees growing amidst rocks in the middle of a thousand-foot stone wall, blades of grass, plants, and flowers surviving in arid desert climate under extreme environmental conditions. I have seen the resurgence and rebirth of nature after the devastating Missionary Ridge fire that burned for weeks in front of our house in the Animas Valley of Colorado; indeed, life is all-powerful in its capacity to heal and regenerate.

Human beings have, for millennia, regardless of race, traditions, cultures, or religions, acknowledged an unknown, intangible, and immaterial entity. There is no place to look for it, for there is no place where it is not. It is a circle whose center is everywhere and whose circumference is nowhere. We truly live in a soup of Intelligence, so much so that it becomes extremely difficult to be aware of it because it is all we have ever known and been with.

Like fish in the ocean, we swim in the waters of Universal Intelligence. We are impregnated, infiltrated, immersed, permeated, imbued by, and bathed in this Universal soup. As Richard Gerber stated in his book *Vibrational Medicine*: "Universal Intelligence controls and orchestrates the entire universe from the largest galaxy to the smallest particle of matter."

The reality of Universal Intelligence has now become a scientific fact. Recent scientific discovery reveals that the knowledge for the creation of the entire universe is locked in every cell and part of our being. It exists in every speck of matter, from atoms to quarks to prions. In a holographic manner, every part contains the whole. Physics calls it the unified field, the superstring theory, and the implicate and explicate order.

If we had asked a scientist in the '60s if they believed in God, most would say: "You are crazy; there is no such a thing. I am a scientist!" By the '80s, the majority of them began to state: "Of course, there is a God. I am a scientist." Jean Guitton, one of the most prominent Christian philosophers of our time and a member of the French Academy, wrote in his book *God and Science*: "The universe is a vast thought. In each particle, in each atom, in each molecule, in each cell of matter, lives, and acts, unnoticed, an omnipresence." Grichka Bogdanov, astrophysicist, and theoretical physicist wrote: "There are more and more physicists for whom the universe is but a vast matrix of Intelligence." This statement from Albert Einstein expresses it well: "The scientist's religious feeling takes the form of a rapturous amazement at the harmony of natural law, which reveals an intelligence of such superiority that, in comparison with it, the highest intelligence of human beings is an utterly insignificant reflection." This feeling is the guiding principle of his life and work.

Indeed, as Jean Guitton wrote: "A great hope rises for those who think. The moment of the fatal reconciliation between science and religion, science and faith, is approaching." The merging of science and spirituality has indeed begun. "Energy and matter are dual expressions of the same Universal substance. That Universal substance is a primal energy or vibration from which we are all composed."

I believe that anyone who has gone deep and long enough into any field of study, from chemistry to physics, biology, medicine, or chiropractic, will always arrive at the same conclusion: we cannot know, and we know so little, yet in that recognition, we gain great reverence for the unknown where all things are known. In this act of reverence, there is also an act of volition, of surrendering to the greater wisdom of the universe. We become an instrument of the divine, a vehicle to serve, a hollow bone, a channel. Our intellect takes the back seat. As Einstein wrote: "We should take care not to make the intellect our god."

To me, the recognition and full acceptance of Universal Intelligence deepened my spiritual faith. It allows me to accept life as it is. There comes an acceptance of the uttermost perfection of what is. This does not mean passivity in the face of what the heart calls for to be improved. It just facilitates the process of contributing to change and evolution. There is nothing to push against, only something new to create as we are co-creators.

Rev. Dr. Martin Luther King Jr, through his faith, accepted the perfection of the situation of black people in the Deep South in the '50s and '60s. Yet he knew in his heart that the principle of equal civil rights was speaking loud and clear. He became an instrument of the divine to bring this principle forth to humanity. By accepting what was, he moved forward with the principle of equal rights and made no attempt to push against prejudice and racism. He was *for* equal rights, not *against* racism.

That subtle key is powerful.

In health care, it is time to stop pushing *against* disease or symptoms. In bringing forth the principle of life, we are *for* life, *for* health, *for* healing, *for* wellbeing, and in that, we can make a significant difference in the world.

Innate Intelligence

The knowledge and understanding of Innate Intelligence have been a pivotal point of transformation in my life. I trust it will be in yours as well.

When I share it with audiences, the most frequent comment I receive is: "This new understanding has deepened my faith and trust in the Divine within me."

Innate is the Inborn Intelligence that resides within living things. It is within all of us. It is the know-how, the mind, the architect, and the designer behind all anatomical, physiological, and biological processes. It is the Intelligence we are invented from and born with. It creates, controls, coordinates, organizes, inspires, motivates, heals, and repairs all organs, tissues, and cells in the body.

It is wise to ask ourselves what kind of Intelligence designed cells, mitochondria, ribosomes, vacuoles, nerve synapses, and such complex processes as the Krebs cycle, the double helix of our DNA, or the semi-permeable membrane of cells. What Intelligence has the knowledge, the power, and the know-how to take a single cell, the fertilized ovum, barely visible with the naked eye, and transform it into a ready-to-be-born baby in about nine months? Clearly, an Intelligence of infinite magnitude.

Locked within the microscopic egg is the knowledge of embryology, biology, biochemistry, neurology, osteology, cardiology, gastroenterology, nephrology, myology, bacteriology, splanchnology, immunology, endocrinology, dermatology, and all the other -ologies that health professionals study in Gray's Anatomy, Guyton's Physiology, and William Boyd's Pathology books.

What is remarkable when looking at embryological development is that one cell —the egg— generates billions of cells as different as skin cells, liver cells, kidney cells, or lung cells. To boot, it is not like we have eye cells growing where our nails are or nail cells emerging in our heart. All is orchestrated and controlled during fetal development by an invisible unified Innate field.

Within us resides an Intelligence that can take a peanut-butter-and-jelly sandwich, break it down into its basic molecular structure via digestion and, through absorption in the small intestine, build eye cells, skin cells, muscle cells, and every other kind of cell out of it. What kind of Divine magic is that?

The Innate Intelligence that created us out of one cell did not abandon us the day we were born. It is present, on the job 24-7-365, from conception to transition. It is always perfect and at a hundred percent. Its knowledge is infinite and does not increase with education or time. It cannot be diseased. It never rests or sleeps. It is all-knowing. It directs and guides all the 30 to 40 trillion tissue cells in our being while we run, sleep, make love, or play the piano. Every second, 37 thousand billion billion chemical reactions occur in our body; no, this is not a typo; repeated word. Truly beyond comprehension.

Each cell is 8/1000 of an inch in diameter, contains multiple chemical factories called organelles, and is made up of about 100 million proteins. At the center of an infinitely microscopic cell is located a nucleus that houses six feet of DNA. How is this even possible that six feet of hyper-microscopic DNA could possibly fit inside the nucleus? An astonishing feat and mystery.

The brain alone is a marvel of creation we mostly take for granted. It is 1.5 pounds of water and fat-based analog. Water and fat... and here we go... thinking, remembering, learning, seeing, hearing, feeling, creating, analyzing, correlating, understanding, orchestrating! Neuroscience estimates the brain contains in the vicinity of 86 billion neurons, each of them making 10,000 synapses. In one cubic millimeter of brain tissue alone, there are over one billion synapses. Messages travel at 260 mph. It is truly impossible to comprehend the complexity of such interconnectivity.

Inside each neuron, tens of thousands of molecules are engaged in a magical dance. More than 100,000 chemical reactions take place every second in the human brain, another bewildering tango of chemical cocktails performed at lightning speed. The brain processes about 11 million bits of information per second as it links brain cells to every tissue cell in the body.

How does this inner universe work so amazingly well with all our life functions happening outside our conscious awareness? Can we all wake up to the marvel and magic living within us? When we begin to put things in perspective, we realize we are witnessing Divine Intelligence that lives within us.

A few years ago, I asked a Ph.D. professor of anatomy, physiology, and pathology from the Southern California University of Health Sciences in Los Angeles what he thought we knew about the human body. He replied: "Probably not even the entire alphabet." After millennia of studying the human body, we have not yet come close to the words, the sentences, and the grammar, certainly not to the poetry, of the language of life within our body. Yet within every human being resides an Inborn Innate Intelligence that created, speaks, and mastered this biological language.

In 1950, B. J. Palmer wrote: *"Man has been studying man, dead and alive, sick and well, in an organized manner, for 5,000 years. He has systematized, card-indexed, and cross-filed this mass of alive and dead education into libraries of millions of books on multiple subjects. He has spewed this education through colleges into millions of brains through hundreds of thousands of professors, and hundreds of universities, for thousands of years. He has deduced theories, tried them, discarded them, and tried them again. He has experimented and practiced his education on patients in hospitals on all kinds of cases. "If it was possible to condense all this unreliable intangible not worthwhile information; discard all these false and untrue premises, condense it all into an essence and inject it into the brain of one man, in one laboratory, there wouldn't be one educated man who could manufacture, make, or compile ONE tissue cell, organize its elements, compound its ingredients, cause it to live and function. Yet, within every female, be she white, black, yellow, or red; ignorant or university graduate; savage or civilized; African or American, is an Innate Intelligence that can and does make hundred billion tissue cells in two hundred eighty days. Not only does Innate Intelligence make these cells, it organizes them into respective kinds to do certain kinds of work, properly distributes each into its respective locality, builds them into organs to do various functions; harmonizes each into and with each other, and all into one harmonious whole; causes all to coordinate one tissue with another, one organ with another into systems, chemically, mechanically, functionally; then, at the proper time and place, causes them all to spiritually begin working, each with each other part. In due time, Innate Intelligence builds the structure so it reproduces its kind. If he could, how would an educated man build a baby? After all this expressed inability, education still looks to his theories to compound something outside the human body to cure and heal its sicknesses."*

Health and the power of natural healing depend greatly on the Innate Wisdom of the body expressing itself freely via its nerve communication network. By removing interferences, the Inner Wisdom of the body has the potential to perform miracles.

A clear nerve system leads to a greater expression of life on all levels. Innate is The Law of Life. Knowledge of this natural law is vital. Violation of the Law of Life causes suffering. We cannot get away from breaking a natural law because the law will break us, no matter what. The law is not affected. The law does not care whether we are violating it or not. Yet, in time, we feel the effect of the violation. When Innate has no interference to its expression, the Law of Life is in full application, and the 30 to 40 trillion cell society lives in harmony.

Awakening to the infinite power and knowledge of Innate Intelligence within is a game changer. It has made a significant difference in my life and the lives of countless others who were exposed to this understanding. Confidence, trust, faith, respect, gratitude, and surrender became the vibrant colors of my mind's relationship with my body and Innate.

Triune of Life

What is life? What constitutes life? What are we made of? What elements must come together to have life? These are critical questions I was fortunate to be presented with early in my life while in Chiropractic College. With inquiry, observation, and introspection, answers to these existential questions arise.

Universal Intelligence being omnipresent means that all matter, whether a stone or a human being, has universal life. A rock is not alive. It does not display the five basic signs of life of growth, reproduction, adaptation, assimilation, and excretion that living organisms do. A corpse is in the same predicament as a stone; it cannot perform the essential signs of life. To manifest and express life, a third component must be present: the Life Force, which is the spirit and the light of life in the body. The knowledge of Life Force is nothing new. Hippocrates wrote: "The natural healing force within each one of us is the greatest force in getting well." Over 97 cultures worldwide acknowledge a Vital Force. The terms Prana, Chi, Élan Vital, and Qi are the most common names known in the industrialized world for Life Force. The presence of Chi or Life Force is truly the sole difference between a living human being and a dead one.

If you were to take cyanide, as it was done by many resistance operatives caught by the Gestapo in France during the Nazi occupation, your body would die within a few seconds. Your blood would still be warm; you would have all your organs, systems, tissues, and cells. You would look the same, weigh just about the same, and measure the same. You would have a brain and nerve system; forensic experts would be able to identify you, as your genetic makeup and entire DNA would still be present, yet you would not be alive; you would be dead. Life Force inherent to your existence would have left. Indeed when the light of life exits the body, we are a goner!

The brain generates Life Force by transforming Universal Energy into *Forun* or a quantity of Life Force. A Forun is to Life Force what a unit of power called a Watt is to electricity. Luigi Galvani became the father of electrophysiology when he demonstrated that the human brain generates electricity. Subsequently, B.J. Palmer, D.C. invented the electro-encephalo-neuro-mento-typograph, which was the precursor of the electroencephalogram or EEG. His invention was designed to monitor the amount of Life Force generated by the brain and chart the interference to the flow of Life Force along the neuro-spinal system.

Life is necessarily the merging, the tri-unity, of intelligence, matter, and life force. The invisible, intangible life energy is the great distinction, and frequently the cause of the rift, between mechanistic sciences, medicine, and the emerging sciences and vitalistic health-care disciplines. The old adage: "If you can't see it, it does not exist," seems to be dying hard. To cling to such a belief has become unscientific. New technologies are penetrating what is invisible to our senses. Dr. Karan Raj working in National Health Science reveals that over 99% of reality is not perceived by our senses. Ever more sensitive devices now detect subtle bio-energies and bio-frequencies in ranges previously not perceptible by our senses. Animals have a spectrum of perception way beyond ours. One only needs to know that birds, dogs, cats, and most animals had vanished to the hills ahead of the tsunami that hit the shores of Thailand in 2004. Their level of perception and awareness escaped most humans vacationing on the coast and sunbathing on the beaches.

Nearly every spiritual and religious tradition refers to a Triune of Life. The Holy Trinity of Christianity has the Father-Son-Holy Spirit. The Father being Intelligence, the Son being Matter, and the Holy Spirit being Force.

Below are samples of various trinities from different traditions.

Buddhism: Buddha-Dharma-Sangha

Hinduism: Brahma-Vishnu-Shiva

Philosophy: Thought-Word-Deed

Psychology: Past-Present-Future

Spirituality: Mind-Body-Spirit

Science: Ether-Matter-Energy

Tantra: Sattva-Rajas-Tamas

Reality: Space-Time-Object

Shakti: Para-Parapara-Apara

Tantra: Shiva-Shakti-Nara

Chiropractic: Intelligence-Matter-Force

Universal: Creation-Sustenance-Annihilation

This Trinity or Triune is clearly inherent to Life.

Life Force, or Chi, is so inherent to our existence that we are oblivious to it, yet it is a key element in health and healing. Not only is the sole difference between life and death the presence or absence of Life Force, but also it becomes very clear that neither the brain, nerve system, nor genetic material control life in the body.

Let me explain: The electrical wires coursing through the walls of a home do not run the refrigerator, the oven, the air conditioner, the lamps, and other appliances. It is the electrical energy *flowing* through the wiring that activates them all. By the same token, it is the Life Force *flowing* through the brain and nerve system that activates the strands of DNA and causes the body to function.

Without the flow of Life Force, the DNA, brain, nerve system, and all other organs, tissues, cells, and systems are incapable of expressing life. This subtle difference and distinction are what separates the mechanistic model of life from the vitalistic life model. The Life Force factor is paramount and crucial.

Unless we address all aspects of a human being, by including Life Force, we are addressing a dried-out, desiccated, and truncated version of it. Health, healing, and wellbeing can only be understood if we include Life Force, its flow, and possible interferences. It is Life Force infused, encoded, impregnated, and imbued with Innate intelligence that organizes, controls, coordinates, animates, motivates, inspires, heals, mends, and repairs us. Life Force is what stirs us into life. It is like a puppeteer causing a marionette to dance across the stage. Without someone to pull the string, there is nothing but puppet and wood. Without Life Force pulsating through our bodies, we are merely a pile of inert organs, tissues, cells, molecules, and biochemicals.

Now, this might be simple, yet it is key. The human body can survive about forty days without food, three days without water, four minutes without oxygen, and the world record without sleep is eleven days. However, we can't survive an instant without the Life Force. This insight makes nurturing the flow of Life Force paramount in health, healing, and wellbeing.

There is perfection to the design of life and its Trinity:

- Innate Intelligence is always 100% perfect, omnipresent, and all-knowing in the body.

- Matter is always at 100% within its limitations. Stones, wood, steel, tissues, bodily structures, and organs all have limitations, being limited in their resistance to external forces. All can be flammable, damaged by chemicals, blunt force, excessive pressure, bullets, etc.

- Life Force, light, or spirit is always generated at 100% as long as we are alive. However, the transmission of force through matter can and may be interfered with. These interferences may be caused by chemical, physical, emotional, or mental trauma or stress that were overwhelming to our being. Frequently, at the time of trauma or stress, the system could not adapt in a way that integrated the overbearing experience.

Subluxations, whether physical, mental, emotional, or chemical are one primary form of interference to the transmission of Life Force. Such interference blocks the expression of Innate Intelligence through the body's cells, tissues, organs, and systems.

It can lead to silent malfunction, dis-ease, and, over time, abnormal physiology, pathology, and premature death. Toxic chemicals, stressors, over-the-counter drugs, and most medications interfere with the normal expression of Life Force in the body. Pharmaceuticals such as birth-control pills interfere chemically with the function of the body, blocking ovulation. They contain a small amount of synthetic estrogen and progesterone to inhibit the female body's reproductive cycle to prevent pregnancy.

Fertilization is blocked by a combination of factors. The pill usually stops the body from releasing an egg from the ovary. Birth control pills change the chemical composition of the cervix to make it difficult for the sperm to find an egg. The drugs can also prevent pregnancy by making the lining of the womb inhospitable for implantation. A seemingly harmless pill actually causes much interference with the normal function and expression of the woman's body. The longer the contraceptive use, the greater the risk of cervical and breast cancer. Ten or more years of use is linked to a 60% increase in risk of cervical cancer and a 50% risk in breast cancer.

In the 1950s and the early 1960s, thalidomide was used to treat morning sickness during pregnancy. But it was found to cause severe birth defects. Babies were born with embryonic arms or legs. Morning sickness is a normal, natural symptom during the early stages of pregnancy, a way for the body to eliminate any potentially toxic or harmful substances in the food so as to safeguard the growing embryo. Interference with this process had dire consequences. Emotional traumas or stressors are insidious and not usually accepted by the public as a common cause of interference to Life Force's flow in the body. They may come in one blow or as subtle repeated micro impacts.

Most everyone has witnessed, at one time or another, a child running toward a parent, excited, joyful, and open, being met with a severe scolding because the parent was not available and did not want to be disturbed. The instantaneous reaction of the child is to turn around and fold its arm around the chest while caving in at the rib cage, closing the treasure chest of emotions and leading to a rounded spinal posture. Such trauma, when repeated over time, causes a marked interference with the emotional expression of the child. Soon the child shuts down, becomes numb and insensitive, while storing anger and resentment. A wide array of symptoms and pathologies, like asthma, bronchitis, respiratory illnesses, and lung disease, might develop from such long-standing interference.

Emotional subluxations are as frequent, if not more common, than physical subluxations, yet are often overlooked. Our emotions live in our physical body residing in our body frame, muscles, fasciae, tendons, and ligaments, notwithstanding our guts. The movie *Ray* brings to the screen the life of Ray Charles. When young Ray saw his brother drown, he could not process the emotional pain, guilt, and responsibility he felt. Soon after, he became blind, a vivid demonstration of the effect of an emotional subluxation. The trauma was overwhelming and could not be integrated at such a young age. It locked itself into the nerve system and led to blindness. My father-in-law Bill became legally blind at an early age after accidentally stumbling into his mother having sex with another man than his father. He just would not want to see what he saw.

Physical traumas are not just the blows, tumbles, hits, accidents, and car crashes encountered by many children, athletes, and most adults; they are also sustained by newborns. The birth process, especially as it is being handled in most hospitals with the use of forceps, vacuum extractors, or manual pulling of the infant out of the birth canal, or extraction via C-section incision, is a common cause of spinal subluxations. The traction force being exerted on the delicate neck of the infant is on the order of 140 pounds. The drugs and medications surrounding most hospital births present strong chemical interferences to the nerve system as well.

The traumas of childhood are more obvious, especially when watching a child or babysitting a baby. The countless falls, jolts, and bumps sustained during early childhood are so numerous that Ida Rolf, the mother of Rolfing, Ph.D. in biochemistry from the College of Physicians and Surgeons of Columbia University, stated that most physical insults to our body take place between birth and eight years of age. Thereafter contact sports, like football, among others, are great contributors to subluxations. To this point, the life expectancy of NFL players is very low, merely 53 -59 years. Of course, car crashes, excessive lifting, and repetitive motion stress also cause subluxations.

When the integrity of the triune of life is maintained, life is expressed at 100%, the body functions as efficiently as possible, and health and wellness are at optimum, all within the limitations of the deck of cards we are born with.

The general public may not know that Chi-ropractic and Chiro-practic combine the words *Chi* and *Chiro*. The first means Life Force, and the second means hand. Chiropractic care means releasing Life Force by hand. When regular chiropractic check-ups, to clear interferences to Life Force flows in the neuro-spinal system, become part of a family's proactive lifestyle, the experience of health becomes a wide departure from the typical sample population. Clinically, it makes a night- and- day difference.

The use of drugs and medications is minimal, if not absent, visits to medical doctors are mostly related to injuries or broken limbs, and surgeries, in general, are limited to repairs. The cost to society for such a family's positive health care is minimal.

Richard Sarnat, M.D., wrote about true healthcare reforms: "Regular utilization of chiropractors reduces the need for hospitalization by 60.2%, hospital days by 59%, pharmaceutical usage by 85%, outpatient surgeries and procedures by 62% and overall global health care costs by more than 50%."

This speaks volumes about the positive effect of restoring and keeping the integrity of the Triune of Life by removing interferences caused by overwhelming stressors.

The Metaphysical and Esoteric

Christ, Stefano Battaglia, Arigo, the surgeon with the rusty knife, and countless others over the millennia were the catalysts for healings labeled as miracles. Miracles, in quotes, because once we understand the bioenergetic-physiological process of such events, they are explainable and can no longer be labeled miracles. None of these people— some high spiritual beings, some ordinary— ever attended a medical or chiropractic curriculum. They were devoid of any added intellectual information about physiology, anatomy, biology, biochemistry, or any other -ologies.

Some claim to channel an entity, a surgeon, or a healer from the great beyond. In the end, beyond their healing modalities, it is their state of being, their state of union with the Divine, that creates a love field so powerful that it entrains dis-eased or diseased biology and physiology back into harmony and wholeness with the consequent healing. This is the metaphysical part of healing that surfaces sporadically within healthcare professions. Imagine the difference it would make in the world once taught as part of the curriculum within the healing art professions. Learning to enter the *empty space*, learning to dwell in the inner chamber of the heart, learning the most important and difficult discipline of silence, learning to become an empty vessel, or as B.J. Palmer wrote, *a hollow bone* is key and critical. It is an offering to all who seek to facilitate health, healing, and wellbeing.

Conventional education has added plenty to the intellect through the ever-expanding data and information hubs. The left brain is saturated, while the right brain is starving. The heart is closed down while the head is full to the brim. We are far out of balance in our educational process. Becoming an instrument of healing is about shedding layers, not adding more. Of course, education is important but ask any seasoned practitioner with years of experience, and they will tell you that only a fraction of their education comes into play in actual practice. In the end, armed with the knowledge and tools given, it is about standing naked in our humanity with a wide-open heart that differentiates a technician from a healer.

Actually, the entire current journey through medical, osteopathic, or chiropractic curriculum is antithetical to its premise of life and health: the journey is downright unhealthy, abusive, stressful, sleep-depriving, blatantly off, and incongruent. It leaves the new graduates exhausted, drained, and in sympathetic dominant fight-flight mode, notwithstanding large financial debts. How is that a suitable state of being for health and healing? What kind of examples are the schools setting? What kind of six, seven, or more year's unhealthy pattern is established? How depleted are the new doctors? No wonder the success rate is low and the dropout high.

The schools that would correct the present course of education and engage in re-balancing their curriculum may see themselves expand greatly by attracting a latent, already present, already hungry, already waiting student constituency. Men and women who are caring and humanitarians wanting to serve in the healing arts, yet who are repelled by the nature of the current education. As a young adult, I had a burning desire to help, soothe, heal the sick and suffering, and give of myself. My years within the medical world did not quench that thirst. It was only when I found a vitalistic alternative that it was satiated.

There is a hunger out there for such personal development and esoteric training, especially within the vitalistic health and healing field. I was very fortunate and feel blessed to have attended a Chiropractic College that had a healthy balance between curriculum and student life.

Consequently, I graduated energized, full of life and passion with a burning desire to serve humanity, and eager to start practicing. Why not teach and practice a healthy lifestyle? What prevents health-oriented institutions from offering the esoteric and metaphysical dimension of healing: presence, inner connection, vulnerability, sensitivity, heightened perception, deep listening, openness, heart-centered, love, core healing of wounds, removal of baggage, extrasensory perception or ESP, and capacity to move the chi or life energy?

Loaded and empowered with these esoteric skills, health practitioners would soar and blossom while harvesting a profound inner fulfillment. Health professions would take their rightful place as an influential healing force in society.

Just imagine what would take place if such a curriculum were to be taught as early as in high schools, colleges, and universities. What kind of humanity would arise as a result? I know it is idealistic and may not yet be based on present reality, but why not? Could planting the seed already prime a potential future? Could the emergence of artificial intelligence lessen the need for left-brain learning, and open up yet untapped dimensions of our being? Today's dream – Tomorrow's reality!

Power of Love

Chapter 8: After-Dinner Drinks

Law of Interconnectedness

All things in life are interrelated and interconnected. All things are one. Everything is made of the same stuff. A table is made of wood that is made of cells, made of molecules, made of atoms, made of subatomic particles, made of energy in motion. Separation is an illusion. Quantum physics shows that everything is made of energy. Matter is just *energy pregnant with information* in vibration.

Under psilocybin's influence during shamanistic journeys, one can experience and observe that everything is made of the same stuff, linked together by an underlying matrix. I remember reading a text from a living Buddhist monk who shared that he saw the Universe, God, in a grain of rice. For years I did not get that. Then as my consciousness rose, I totally got it. Within a grain of rice, one can see rice paddies, green plants, water, rain, sky, sun, soil, earth, insects, microorganisms, nutrients, chemicals, gravity, humans, water buffalo, rice bags, straw hats, corn fields, clothes, cotton fields, dyes and stains, laborers, paper labels, trucks, diesel, rubber, steel, refineries, factories, showrooms, computers, electronics, silicon chips, plastics, inventors, money, printing machines, ink, bank tellers, etc., ad infinitum. The entire Universe, from cosmic creation, through human evolution, to the present moment, exists in a grain of rice.

In complex open, dynamic systems, such as a human being, everything affects everything else because it is all interrelated. One input into a dynamic, open biological system generates a cascade of effects that alters the entire system. The Butterfly Effect was coined after the fact that a butterfly flapping its wings in Peking can be the cause of a hurricane over Florida. Native Americans were very much in touch with the law of interconnectedness. They intuitively knew that polluting water in a nearby river meant polluting all the earth's water, including the water in their own body. They had a Seven Generations Principle and philosophy of life. They contemplated how their present actions would propagate to impact future generations. This understanding appears to still elude many in modern civilization.

In the human body, which is a dynamic, open complex system, everything interacts with everything else, and every cell is interconnected to every other cell by the infinitely complex and extensive nerve network laden with neurotransmitters. One single input or force introduced anywhere within the system can cause enormous transformations. Any interference within the nerve network affects the function of all other systems, organs, tissues, and cells. The simple law of interconnectedness presents a clear explanation of the clinical results obtained by holistic health practitioners, which at times are short of a miracle or appear to be miracles. B. J. Palmer, D.C., developed an approach called upper cervical. It consisted in adjusting only the Atlas or Axis, the first and second vertebrae in the neck. He labeled the adjustment: "Hole In One." It is also "whole in one." Astonishing results were obtained using this approach with all kinds of conditions and disorders, from cancer to mental illness.

Alex Gray has exceptional artistic renderings of the interconnectedness between all beings and their surroundings in his book titled *The Sacred Mirrors*. Biologist Rupert Sheldrake called the Spiritual Law of Interconnection the morphic field. He describes it as: "A field within and around a morphic unit, which organizes its characteristics, structure, and pattern of activity." The term morphic field includes morphogenetic, behavioral, social, cultural, and mental fields. As humans, we are engulfed in an invisible field of energy information. It is commonly observed that within a family unit, one may exhibit symptoms or even pathology, yet the cause is actually located in another member of the family who may be completely asymptomatic. This is especially well documented in psychology. Many health practitioners are adamant about having the entire family receiving proactive Salutogenic care. It makes sense. The family unit can now benefit as a whole, with no one left behind. In the light of the Law of Interconnectedness, family care becomes every true health professional's responsibility.

I recalled that when I first took care of Amy Schreiber. The moment I laid my hands on her shoulder, Amy's mother, Mary, broke into tears and full-body convulsions. Amy had been anorexic for years. The cause of her condition was held within the mother's emotional pattern and her daughter's response to it. In my view and experience, it is essential for health practitioners to hold a world vision of health and healing. If not that, at least have a vision for their community, state, and country.

Health is not individualistic; it is a community endeavor that is contagious. We are all cells in the body of humanity. Six degrees of separation has been a recent common theme amongst people. The farthest we can be from any other human being is our 50th cousin. Regardless of race, color, or location, humanity is one big interconnected family. It is not uncommon for a mother to feel chest pain at the same time that, unbeknown to her, her daughter's thorax, thousands of miles away, is being crushed by the steering wheel during a car crash. The recent CNN interview with Tyre Nichols' mother, reinforces that we can feel the pain and distress of another being at a distance because we are all interconnected. While five police officers were beating her son to death, kicking him in the abdomen, she experienced stomach pain, not knowing what was happening to her son.

The experience of oneness occurs when our heart opens fully. Suddenly the illusion of separation melts away. The Law of Interconnectedness comes into reality. We begin to see clearly. During the intensive training sessions I was leading, we always came to a point when the morphic field became cohesive and coherent. The entire group became one unit. We had created a safe, sacred, and sealed container. We shared numerous intense, challenging experiences. It became clear to everyone that we were one, united in our humanity and being, yet individuals by our uniqueness. We were all in a state of love with one another. We experienced our communality more than ever before and felt the love and spirit that united us all. This experience is readily available in groups working for the highest good of the whole.

In the end, we are one, interrelated and interconnected. It is a Law of Life. By reminding ourselves of our connectivity, we can monitor our thoughts, emotions, and actions as they affect all of us, especially those closest to us. Each and every one of us has the power to make a significant difference in the health of the body of humanity through heightened awareness.

Quality of Life Indicators

As one becomes healthier and more vibrant, factors like quality of life indicators rise. This requires inner reflection and observation. Am I more aware, expressive, open, inner-directed, creative, alive, vital, loving, caring, compassionate, understanding, and joyful? Do I gravitate toward things that are positive for myself — or destructive? Am I accumulating positive survival values or negative ones? Am I growing and evolving or stagnating in life? Do I have an increased desire to exercise, meditate, eat healthy food, connect spiritually, and contribute to the whole of humanity? Do I live a life of purpose? Am I in touch with my Soul's calling? Am I inner-directed or outer-affected? Do I stay centered in the midst of the outer turmoil of society? Does the voice inside speak louder than the voices outside? The list goes on and on.

Those are quality-of-life indicators vitalistic health practitioners are interested in. They seek to improve the quality of life, regardless of the presence or absence of symptoms or illness, by removing interference to the expression of Life Force flow. Healthy living from above-down and inside-out means being connected to our deeper self, expressing our Soul's calling and purpose as fully as possible.

Each one of us has that choice. One needs not be a vitalistic doctor to be their own health practitioner. By empowering ourselves through healthy choices, thoughts, and actions, we make a positive contribution and a difference in the world.

The Birthing Process

We are all born, an inescapable necessity of life. Our commonality is possibly one of the most important, determining, and decisive processes of a human being's life. It is the very first imprint our nerve system has outside the womb. Possibly it could mark us for life. Some believe that societies live by the way they birth their young. Violent birthing may mean a more violent society overall. Could gentle and loving births lead us to a more loving world? This possibility is well worth investigating. What's there to lose? Yet, a lot to potentially gain. Could shifting our view and approach to birth make a significant difference in society?

A fact that is often overlooked is that the Dutch national healthcare system encourages home birth and birth with midwives over hospital birth with obstetricians. Consequently, Holland has one of the lowest infant and maternal mortality rates, along with the lowest rate of interventions and procedures of any industrialized country. Home births, without or with doulas and midwives, are focused on a gentle approach to childbirth. It seeks to respect and honor women's bodies and their natural rhythms. As a result the progress and timing of the birthing process are allowed to unfold naturally.

My amazing wife Jane has been a doula at many births. Her patience, perception, encouragement, support, and connection to the birthing women have led many pregnant women to deliver naturally at home and/or in a birthing center. We live at 6500 feet, so even high-altitude home births are indeed possible. The relationship, trust, and friendship established early on during pregnancy have proven to be a critical component of successful births.

In approaching birth from a new perspective, frequently overlooked subtle and insidious interferences need to be addressed:

- The due date is seldom recognized as one, yet it can have dire consequences on the birth process. To tell a pregnant woman that she is due on May 10 may create undue anxiety as the date approaches or passes. To put it in perspective, it would be like telling a virgin girl that she will have her first sexual experience on May 10. Apprehension, anxiety, and fear will mount as the due date nears. Her body physiology will tense up, her mental-emotional state will fuel her bloodstream with fear chemicals, and her stress hormone levels will go up by the minute. To give a birthing woman the best chance for a smooth labor and delivery, she has to feel at peace, comfortable, in trust, and free of anxiety. Again, the chemistry and physiology of fear have a different outcome than the one of trust, a fact that can no longer be ignored. Native culture will speak of the baby arriving around the harvest moon. This gives a flexible, fluid, open window of time. The reality of pregnancy is that every one of them is different, and every baby has its own timing. In other words, when the cookies are ready, that is when they will come out of the oven!

• Prenatal vitamins, which became in vogue in the 1970s, might sound great if you live in a country where malnutrition is rampant. Yet, in the western world, it might not be the best idea. Vitamins are not just nutrients; some are hormones. They can lead to weight gain in babies, potentially making them oversize to fit within the birth canal. This may contribute to the sharp rise in the C-section rate.

• Leaving home for a trip to a hospital is another subtle interference with potentially severe consequences. We know today that mammals release hormones that stop labor when they have to move from one location to another to birth their young. This is a survival mechanism in case predators are nearby, endangering the vulnerable birthing mother. When women in labor leave their homes to enter a hospital or birthing center, labor is frequently halted and will not resume quickly. Consequently, labor might have to be induced. Imagine what it would be like to ask a couple in the throes of lovemaking to stop, get in a car, go to a hospital, fill in the appropriate forms, go to a room, undress, and resume under the watchful eyes of cheering obstetrical staff. The team encouraged them to stop, breathe, push, slow down, or speed up. We all know that flaccidity would befall the man and inhibition would overtake the woman!

• Gravity is a powerful force to be used as an ally in birth. It is interesting to me that many French obstetricians have been instrumental in shifting the consciousness of humanity in regard to birth. Maybe it is karmic restitutions for the damage inflicted by Louis XIV, who had the physicians of the royal court design a delivery table with stirrups, so he could satisfy his sexual perversion by watching the private parts of women giving birth. This proved to be tragic for birthing women. They now had to deliver against gravity, a strong force we are mostly oblivious to until we stumble and fall. Now the babies have to ascend rather than descend through the birth canal. In a home setting, freedom of movement and positions in labor are readily available in order to use the G force advantageously.

- Breech presentation can make home birth a challenge. My friend Autumn Gore, D.C., from Dallas, Texas, is an amazing chiropractor and a birth doula. She is invited regularly by Baylor Medical Center to adjust laboring women in the delivery room. The obstetrical team has recognized that clearing the neuro-spinal system of subluxation frees and facilitates the birth process. They also let her handle the newborns right out of the womb to check them for subluxations and adjust them if needed. When a rare breech presentation occurs, she applies the Webster turning technique, a gentle adjustment of the pelvis, that has an 80-plus percent success rate in facilitating the baby turning into a head-first position. Today countless Chiropractors worldwide are certified in the Webster Technique providing a safe and effective way of solving breech presentations. Having put the above subtle interferences aside, birthing can be approached with new eyes. Except for rare instances, due to various medical conditions that could endanger pregnant women and/or their babies, the home is the safest environment for most birthing women. It is their nesting environment where they have all the freedom needed for successful deliveries.

Birth is, without a doubt, a natural, normal, innate body function like digestion, respiration, or elimination. The female body's physiology, biology, chemistry, and psyche are architecture for pregnancy and birth. By recognizing birth as a body function, women can move into full surrender and trust. They can embrace and welcome the process openly. They can become powerful participants in this extraordinary experience.

What is to follow came from inspiration flowing through me while preparing a talk on natural birth. It was Innately downloaded. When it happened, I found no support to validate the insight that birth and lovemaking are identical processes, with birth being magnified in intensity by nine months of gestation.

Over the years, Marilyn Moran and her book *Birth and The Dialogue of Love* provided sustenance for my perspective. Since then, many women have shared their birth experiences as being joyful, pleasurable, or even orgasmic. *Orgasmic Birth* by Elizabeth Davis offers a guide to a safe, satisfying, and pleasurable birth. Birth erotica shares stories of women having sensual, sexual births. They provided me with needed validation in the face of incredulous crowds whenever I shared my view and insights on birth.

If such births are possible for some, they might be possible for many, if not most. It might take time to evolve toward a sensual-sexual loving psyche around birth. Could adopting a novel mindset already create unexpected birthing experiences? There is nothing to lose and everything to gain by opening up to a new possibility.

Birth as Lovemaking from the Inside Out

This is a radical claim. Before anyone shuts down, puts the book away, or claims sexual perversion, keep an open mind. Become curious. Can you question, inquire, investigate, and think for yourself as to the possible truth of such a statement? Skepticism is wise and healthy. Attempts to refute what will be laid down next need to be respected. So go for it. In doing so, make sure to attune fully to what follows.

Is it possible that birth could be a pleasurable and even orgasmic process? Could it be that the old adage: "You shall give birth in pain," has become a self-fulfilling prophecy? What if women were designed to give birth with ease and even pleasure? What if the screaming and moaning of labor were conveying a completely different message rather than pain? Aren't women moaning and screaming in the throes of lovemaking?

I am aware that this proposition of birthing with joy and pleasure may seem extreme. Could birthing in fear and pain be just as extreme? We have embraced one model for centuries; what about giving another approach a few centuries before the jury is out? What if changing the beliefs that women, men, society, and the medical establishment hold around birth could create a completely different experience?

In my view, it is worth going for it with the same blindness that met the pain-fear model. My inner truth oscillator does not allow me to negate the pure common sense of the understanding that birth is indeed lovemaking from the inside out. Birth is one with the act of lovemaking. The two processes are intimately connected and interrelated. They are inseparable.

Lovemaking starts with heart connection, caresses, kisses, and foreplay. It mostly takes place in privacy with soft, dim surroundings. It is laden with passion. It leads to arousal, pleasure, and lubrication. The same fire is burning bright into a full-term woman after nine months of a baby growing in the womb. In early labor, such loving foreplays can bring comfort, support, relaxation, and arousal to the woman. Lubrication is undeniable as the water breaks. Actual nipple stimulation and suckling cause a release of Oxytocin, the natural love hormone of birth. It induces and/or strengthens contractions.

During arousal in lovemaking, the pace and rhythm of respiration quicken. It is well matched by the increased breathing of early labor. As a result, oxygen levels in the blood rise as well as the heart rate. Nutrient-rich blood is pumped to engorge the sexual organs as well as saturate the baby's blood levels with oxygen. In birthing, it provides increased blood flow to the uterus, pelvic muscles, umbilical cord, placenta, and fetus, all designed to prepare the mother and baby for the labor at hand.

At some point during lovemaking, the urge for penetration arises. When well attuned, the urge is mutual, coming from both partners. Penetration of the penis into the vagina is from the outside-in. In birth, the penetration is from the inside-out as the baby enters the birth canal. The urge is mutual, coming from the baby and birthing mother in unison. Penetration can be teasing, slow and progressive playing, and sensuous sexual dance.

At this stage of lovemaking, breathing accelerates to become uncontrollable while the heart rate skyrockets, further flooding the sexual organs with blood and warmth.

We are in the heat of passion. In birthing, the breathing, if left uncontrolled, will speed up to border hyperventilation. Rapid respiration is built into the function of birth in order to anesthetize the woman. The breath can transcend pain into a numbing pain of the nature of the white light, a mixture of pain and pleasure as built-in physiological anesthesia takes place.

Just prior to orgasm in lovemaking, clinching, clasping, and grabbing are common. The entire body goes into contraction prior to the extension that will follow. During birth, the so-called carpopedal reflex occurs. Anyone not forewarned may end up hurting should fingers be caught inside a birthing woman's hand. Facial flushes appear in women, in the acts of lovemaking and birthing.

During orgasm, there is emoting, moaning, and screaming. In birth, the moaning comes long and slow during the early stages of labor to crescendo into a primal scream at the climax of birth. Crowning, the height of the birth's orgasm, occurs as the head of the baby has fully dilated the birth canal. Stillness, as if frozen in time, emerges the instant that crowning and orgasm are reached. It is that intense moment of deep merging, communion, and oneness common to lovers. The breathing shifts, amplitude, pace, and rhythm decelerate, heartbeats slow down, and awareness expands.

After a lag, the male penis shrinks and withdraws. In birth, the rest of the newborn body is expelled or slips out. After lovemaking, there is a discharge of semen. In birth, this is mirrored by the discharge of the placenta.

Following lovemaking, lovers lie together in embrace, binding, joining in the love and deep relaxation of their mutual experience. In birth, the woman reaches between her legs and brings the baby onto her wet, warm abdomen, duplicating the curve of the baby's spine, bringing comfort, support, and security. The baby's head buries itself between the breasts, and the rooting reflex, the need to suckle, is triggered.

In time lovers gaze into each other's eyes to deepen the connection and express love silently. The gazing of a mother into the eyes of her newborn is the most precious and moving experience of unconditional love. It is like looking into the eyes of the Divine. It seals a built-in biological maternal bond as two Souls merge.

How we cannot see that birth is indeed lovemaking from the inside--out is beyond comprehension. Common sense is often the last thing we see, say, or do. It is undeniable that birth is a physical, emotional, sexual, and spiritual experience. Yet is this how most births are experienced? The physical part has been acknowledged for centuries, while the sexual, emotional, and spiritual aspects have been mostly denied. When approached and perceived from a place of connection with spirit, the deepest part of us, from a place of trust, joy, and love, from a heart-centered space, sensuality, and sexual pleasure, a new experience is possible.

The prospect of birthing babies with joy and pleasure in the depth of the most intense lovemaking experience available to a woman is a promise of a new humanity.

True lovemaking is giving and receiving love and pleasure. During intercourse, the man gives off his sperm; the woman receives it. During birth, the woman gives birth to the baby, and the man receives it. When this happens, the cycle is completed, and there is a union.

Just as lovemaking is a rite of passage that evolves a girl into a woman, birth transforms a woman into a mother. The first sexual experience may have been preempted with apprehension and anxiety, just as the first birth experience may also be. Presence, reassurance, emotional, and physical support from a partner, spouse, or lover is warranted. Young women being a witness and exposed to other birthing women early in life can build ease and trust in the process for the next generation.

Imagine what could be created if we were to manifest the very best possible environment around lovemaking and birth. What would a couple in love seek? A hospital room with bright circular lights and a cheering team? No, what they would seek is the security, the soothing, supportive settings of their love pad, a setting where they are in control, in charge, and where privacy is king. The world-renowned obstetrician Michel Odent, M.D., wrote, "Home is the only place where a woman has the degree of privacy needed for maximum efficiency of the physiological and hormonal response." After attending one of his seminars, where he did a paralleled timeline slide presentation of hospital birth and home birth, including water birth, I was inspired to become an advocate for gentle home birth.

Couples in love seek romantic settings with dim lights or, even better, candle lights. They desire silence or soft background music to tune into the rhythm of their breath, the rustlings of the friction of their skin, and the sensuous sound of their moaning. They enjoy being naked and certainly would not want the freezing temperatures of most hospital delivery rooms. Couples in the midst of intercourse want freedom of movement to be able to change sexual positions whenever it's called for. Certainly, lovers do not like to have a timeline for lovemaking; the slower and longer it can last, the better.

So in birthing, the optimal setting is home, with candle lights or even complete darkness to foster a total attunement within. Animals seek an isolated, safe, dark cave to birth their young. We must learn to mimic nature. Nature needs no help, just no interference.

We live in an instant society where we have instant banking, meals, coffee, and even drive-by-viewing at funerals. When we reconnect with the timing of life by watching sunrises and sunsets, something awakens inside; a new awareness emerges. I frequently would ask people in my practice to sit in front of a burgeoning bud in the spring or in front of a green leaf in the fall and not move until they see it change form or color. The movement is so slow that it cannot be perceived with the eye, only with time-delayed photography. This simple exercise reconnected them to the timing of life, healing, and birthing. Just as we cannot see our hair or nails grow, the timing of birth can be very slow. We need to relearn respect for the pace of nature. The funny thing is that, in this fast-paced society, the one process we would love to slow down is lovemaking. So why rush birth?

Once we have brought back into the birthing process all that surrounds lovemaking and move from fear to trust, from control to surrender, from educated intellect to Innate attunement, birth can be a beautiful, intense, joyful, fulfilling experience. The possibility for a sexually pleasurable birth opens. In the process, we can honor life, nature, and creation and minimize or eliminate the incidences of trauma and neurological and physiological damage.

There is clearly a night-and-day difference between infants born via typical hospital birth and home-birthed babies. The radiance, the peacefulness, the color, the tone of their skin, and the eye connection is the difference. These babies emanate light. When I went to Sherman College of Chiropractic in 1973, many couples gave birth at home, by themselves, or with a doula or midwife. When going into the West Gate Mall in Spartanburg, S.C., one could quickly differentiate home-birthed babies from hospital ones. The alertness, capacity to connect, the color of the skin, overall vitality, and the light in their eyes was the distinction.

Except for rare instances, the home is the ideal place for women to give birth. Today in America, unless one lives in a remote area, there are no emergencies around birth. Any complications can be handled with a 911 call, and the birthing woman will be in a hospital in little time. Homebirth is the best option to minimize the incidence of interferences and interventions, as the Dutch National Health Care reminds us. Could the home be the premium setting for a safe, joyful, pleasurable, and possibly even orgasmic birth? Only by presenting an alternate path can we give back true freedom of choice to all expectant women. This perspective alone can make a significant difference in countless lives as it already has transformed many who opened up to it.

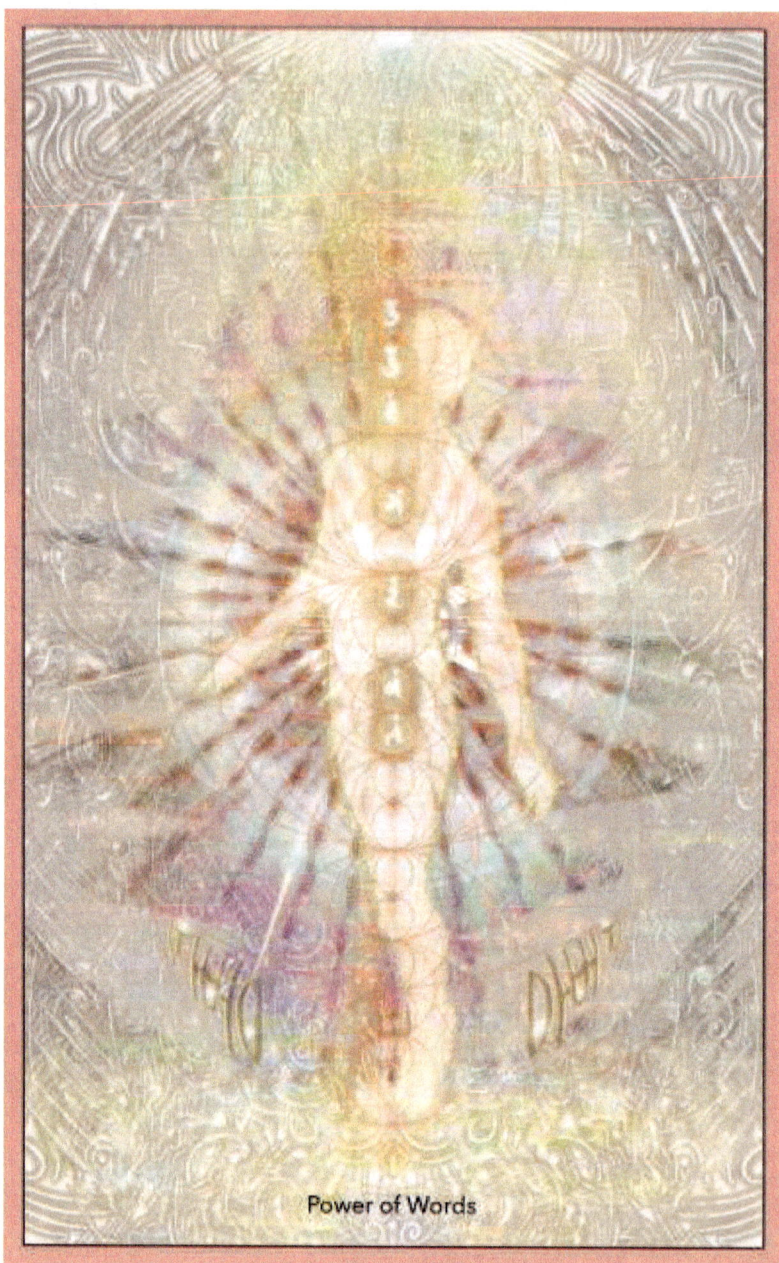

Power of Words

Postscript

What Love is

My journey into love began out of a lack of it. The wound of an absent father and a mother who had a closed heart turned out to be a gift. Early on, I began to crave love. As a child, I did not know how to satisfy this hunger. I adopted the common child strategy of being like my parents in the hope they would love me more. If they could see themselves in me, love was sure to follow. Of course, this was not a conscious decision for a young boy. I developed an ironclad control of my emotions, my actions, and myself; to match the control I felt bearing down on me. As a teenager, this approach continued with my peers. The more I could be like them, the more connected to them and loved I felt as a feeling of belonging. The cost was losing myself to become an amorphous mix of everyone else. In time, this path to seek love led to the downfall of sapping my life force and personal integrity. Who am I if I have to be like others to receive love? Twisting myself into a pretzel to feel loved can't be the way.

My very first experience of love was with Arianne, a radiant, vivacious, luminous, stunningly beautiful, and joyful young five-year-old blonde with blue eyes as deep as the sea; a little princess. At least this is how I saw her back then, and I still retrieve her in my memory decades later as if it were yesterday. This was pure love. No hormones raging at that age, just the luminous wonder of marveling at the perception of another pure being.

My second purest love experience was my first teenage relationship with Cecile. A totally platonic love, spending hours in mutual communion, staring into each other's Soul in deep silence. It lasted a few years. It was divine and so pure. The thought of any physical contact would only lead to staining the purity of what was between us. It was indeed virgin love.

Thereafter what I experienced and thought of as love was nearly all hormonal rage, strong sexual chemistry, and powerful physical attractions, all laden with a need for companionship or, more honestly, avoiding loneliness. Like most, I fell in love many times. Falling in love is really nothing more than meeting the catalyst that another person provides to open us up to reconnect with the love we already are. It is a brief peering into what is possible, soon to be overridden by the reality of the next phase of the relationship. So many fall in love only to break up or divorce down the line. Was it love, then? I think not. Certainly, in retrospect, that has been my experience and observation.

Unbeknownst to me, I was being fooled by what I thought was love: an emotional feeling laden with pheromones.

For years, I yearned to be loved. I desire to be loved with pure love, just as I am. I long to be accepted just the way I am. Accepted with my deficiencies, my quirks, my special gifts and talents, my ups, my downs, my losses, my wins, my victories, and my defeats. I have known for quite some time that whatever is happening for me is also happening for most, if not all, other human beings. In the end, we are all the same; we are not so unique, so special, paradoxically, as much as we are unique and special in our personalities. We all seek to be loved for who we are and just the way we are. We want pure love embracing all of what and who we are.

I know I wanted that for years. Where can we find that today? Who will give us that today? Where can we be met as a whole person, no matter how we view ourselves? Where can we be safe, feel safe, feel embraced, and be seen fully in our humanity? That special place is within and within only. We are the only ones who can give this to ourselves. In our solitude (or Soul-I-tune), we are whole, complete, at peace, and in bliss. We are not broken there; we are complete. What a gift. There is nothing to fix, nothing to cure, nothing to heal, for in that space, in that moment, we are whole; we feel whole. In the end, we are alone in this world, no matter how it appears. The sooner we realize this, the quicker we can start to love ourselves.

With years passing, I began to realize that if I wanted love from others, I needed to give it to myself first and, of course, to them second. That is when it occurred to me that love was more a decision than a feeling. As I decided to love, love was retrieved from within. The hormones of my teenage years, a mixture of love and lust, had fooled me. Love does not come from the outside; it comes from the inside as a decision to love. With age and maturity, this definition of love as a decision began to fall apart. Sure, it was a concerted choice to love. But love is more than a decision; in the end, it is a state of being.

Through my journey in life, I had the fortune to stumble into a spiritual guru. The very brief interaction, shorter than a minute, connected me with a heightened state of being. It became a touchstone, a point of reference, a target to aim. Years passed before I could self-generate that state through calm introspection and meditation. It became clear to me that in that state of being, love is who I truly am. The inner and outer blend, as my physical vehicle, my body, is no longer perceived as a thin veil separating me from the outer. Innate and universal have merged. That is love, a pure state of being. It wants nothing, seeks nothing, and yearns for nothing; just Being is pure bliss. I wish I had received the guidance and roadmap as a young man to guide me on this journey to true love. I hope that what I just shared might make a difference to whoever reads these words.

Words Heal, Words are Powerful

Each word has a vibration, a force that travels through the ether to enter all beings; their brains, and nerve systems. Words are powerful at creating reality.

Emile Coue, a French physician from the early 1900s, was a pioneer in healing with words. He would ask his patient to repeat daily: "Every day, in every way, I am getting better and better." Autosuggestion, maybe, yet we cannot deny the power of words. In the Bible, it is written in John 1:1: *"In the beginning was the Word, and the Word was with God, and the Word was God..."* In Genesis 1.1, one can read: *"God said let there be light and there was light."* The power of manifestation through words. The word also refers to tone and sound, energy infused with a specific vibration. The Sanskrit word *Om* is thought to be the primal tone of the universe. Om is the most often chanted sound among all the sacred sounds on earth. This sound is considered the sound of existence.

Swami Chidvilasananda, known as Gurumayi, a spiritual teacher with whom my wife Jane and I had a very brief encounter, asks the question: "What is the best and worst thing in the world?" Answer: "The spoken word. With our word, we can send humanity to hell or to heaven." The power of her presence and words still affect my wife and me profoundly on a daily basis. Loving words of hope, positivism, trust in life, and in the wisdom of the body arising out of an understanding of Innate Intelligence, the power of Life Force, and the inborn capacity of the body to heal itself are golden nuggets for people. As Pasquale Cerasoli, D.C., frequently stated in his public speaking: "Words are things."

Speaking healing words is central to healing professionals, yet not their sole domain. Everyone can choose to heal with words. Canceling the fear-based message propagated by the media and adopted by the general mass consciousness is essential to holding a centering, loving, and healing presence within. Having awareness around the power of words is transformative for us all.

In the end we are the central nucleus of our world. We create the world we live in. By focusing moment by moment on our health, and becoming aware of our thoughts, actions, emotions, words, and inner state, we metamorphose. We become an enzyme of transformation contributing to a healthier, more aware and conscious humanity.

Epilogue

What are the gems to mine from this book?

- A commitment to walk through life in total trust making a difference by your presence, your words, deeds, your being, and your integrity.
- An engagement to dedicate your life to your own health and healing.
- A new awareness and elevated consciousness about the multifaceted aspects of true health and healing.
- Knowledge, wisdom, and living principles as a GPS for your life.
- Cherishing the key that surrender and allowing lead to effortless manifestation from the Universe when holding a clear vision in your mind.
- A reminder that LOVE is Key, epitomized by the lyrics of the *Love Song* by Elton John:

The words I have to say

May well be simple but they're true

Until you give your love

There's nothing more that we can do

Love is the opening door

Love is what we came here for

No one could offer you more

Do you know what I mean?

Have your eyes really seen?

You say it's very hard

To leave behind the life we knew

But there's no other way

And now it's really up to you

Love is the key we must turn

Truth is the flame we must burn

Freedom the lesson we must learn

You know what I mean

Have your eyes really seen?

Love is the opening door

Love is what we came here for

No one could offer you more

Do you know what I mean?

Have your eyes really seen?

Like the underground root system of one of the largest living organisms on earth, the aspen tree, our contribution as loving, healthy, and healed beings joins a growing network of awakened humans. Wherever we are, humanity will be touched by the glow and radiance of our presence. Like a mosquito, we might become a disruptor, yet one for the greater good of humankind.

Printed in Great Britain
by Amazon

24209712R00225